1994

Literature and Feminism

Literature and Feminism

An Introduction

PAM MORRIS

BLACKWELL
Oxford UK & Cambridge USA

Copyright © Pam Morris, 1993

The right of Pam Morris to be identified as author of this work has been asserted in accordance with the Copyright, Designs and Patents Act 1988.

First published 1993

Blackwell Publishers
108 Cowley Road
Oxford OX4 1JF
UK

238 Main Street, Suite 501
Cambridge, Massachusetts 02142
USA

British Library Cataloguing in Publication Data

A CIP catalogue record for this book is available from the British Library.

Library of Congress Cataloging-in-Publication Data

Morris, Pam, 1940–
    Literature and Feminism: An Introduction/Pam Morris.
        p.   cm.
    Includes bibliographical references and index.
    ISBN 0-631-18419-8. – ISBN 0-631-18421-X (pbk.)
        1.   Feminist liberary criticism.   2.   Feminism and literature.
    I. Title.
    PN98.W64M67   1993
    801'.95'082 – dc20   92-41839
                                                                              CIP

Typeset in 11 on 13 pt Garamond by Best-set Typesetter Ltd., Hong Kong

Printed and bound in Great Britain by Biddles Ltd, Guildford and Kings Lynn

This book is printed on acid-free paper

In memory of Alke

Contents

Preface and Acknowledgements

The idea for this book comes from the students I have taught: Open University students, postgraduate research and women's studies course students, and university undergraduates. A great many have been excited by the prospect of a feminist approach to literature, eager to find out what it means and even more eager to do it for themselves. It has been difficult to find a text to recommend which would introduce most aspects of what is now an extremely complex variety of practices so that they could make an informed choice of approach and find ways of initiating it in their own work.

Having grown used to reading feminist discourse we easily forget how much of the background and terminology we take for granted. I have, therefore, tried to begin from scratch, assuming no previous knowledge, but developing a framework of ideas with which to move into more complicated areas of theory and debate. Throughout, my emphasis is on feminist literary criticism as an empowering practice of reading. My main aim has been to make that process available to readers. I have attempted to foreground here what seem to me the most positive aspects of the various forms of feminist criticism and theory outlined. I have used and referred to the most widely available critical works and anthologies so that follow-up reading is reasonably easy. I have also tried to use the work of as many women writers as possible as a means of introducing to readers poems and stories that have, in the last few years, enriched my own reading.

My main thanks go to students in Edinburgh, Glasgow and Dundee whose enthusiasm, questions and determination to find out have kept me going. I am especially grateful to Claire Houghton for providing a detailed reader's response to early drafts of chapters. I am also indebted to colleagues in the Open University and at Dundee University for their encouragement and continuous supply of new ideas. Special thanks are due to Graham Allen who shared his expertise on Harold Bloom, and to Mark Curry for discussions on deconstruction and postmodernism. Many thanks also to Vicky and Val for providing me with books. As always, Jeannette King and Liz Allen gave unsparingly of their time and support. Without Colin this book would not have been completed.

I would like to thank the following for permission to reprint poems and extracts from copyright material: Bloodaxe Books for Marina Tsvetayeva, *Selected Poems* (Copyright © David McDuff, 1987); Cornell University Press for Luce Irigaray, *This Sex which is not One* (Copyright © Cornell University Press, 1985); Faber & Faber for Sylvia Plath, *Collected Poems* (Copyright © Estate of Sylvia Plath, 1981); Harvester Wheatsheaf for Hélène Cixous. 'The Laugh of the Medusa', in Elaine Marks and Isabelle de Courtivron (eds), *New French Feminisms*; New Direction Books for *H.D.: Collected Poems 1912–1944* (Copyright © Estate of Hilda Doolittle, 1982); Routledge for *The Hugh MacDiarmid Anthology* (Copyright © C. M. Grieve, 1972) and for Gayatri Chakravorty Spivak, *In Other Worlds* (Copyright © Methuen, 1987); Triad Grafton for Toni Morrison, *Song of Solomon* (Copyright © Toni Morrison, 1977); Virago Press for Maya Angelou, *And Still I Rise* (Copyright © Maya Angelou, 1986), for Grace Nichols, *Lazy Thoughts of a Lazy Woman* (Copyright © Grace Nichols, 1989) and for Agnes Smedley, *Daughter of Earth* (Copyright © The Agnes Smedley Estate, 1950).

Introduction: Why 'Literature' and 'Feminism'?

Let's start with some obvious questions. What is feminism? What does it mean to be a feminist? What is the purpose of feminist literary criticism? How can it affect the way we read? The words and phrases and the questions have become familiar, yet they can imply quite different things to different people. It may, therefore be helpful to pause before reading on and consider how *you* would answer these questions. What do the words mean to you?

Feminism

I shall begin with 'feminism' and then move on to 'literature'. My definition of feminism, which will inform the rest of the book, is that it is a political perception based on two fundamental premises: (1) that gender difference is the foundation of a structural inequality between women and men, by which women suffer systematic social injustice, and (2) that the inequality between the sexes is not the result of biological necessity but is produced by the cultural construction of gender differences. This perception provides feminism with its double agenda: to understand the social and psychic mechanisms that construct and perpetuate gender inequality and then to change them.

A feminist understanding starts from a clear definition of the terms 'female' and 'male' to denote biological categories of sex. Women have suffered from a long tradition of what is generally called 'biological essentialism', that is the belief that a woman's 'nature' is an inevitable consequence of her reproductive role. What is natural or essential cannot be changed in the way that social attributes of character can, hence if biology were actually to render women more submissive and less adventurous than men there would be little that anyone could do about it. This kind of essentialistic or deterministic argument has been used throughout history and across societies to justify women's subordination, even though what are considered to be essentially 'feminine' characteristics vary from culture to culture. For this reason feminists use the terms 'femininity' and 'masculinity' to refer to acquired cultural gender identity, even though for most of us this social and subjective sense of self is constructed so early in our lives as to seem naturally coterminous with our sex. Nevertheless, we are all familiar with the idea that a male writer may at times show what are culturally designated 'feminine' characteristics in his work, and likewise female writers are sometimes said to have 'masculine' traits. That such recognitions often invoke a negative judgement as well is just one indication of how carefully societies defend gender boundaries and their associated values.

So, we cannot assume that all writing by women will be necessarily or essentially 'feminine' in its perspectives and values. Even less can we assume that anything and everything written by women will be – somehow – feminist, that it will share the political assumptions and agenda outlined above. An intriguing question arises from this line of thought: can a man who *does* share and express this perspective be termed a feminist? I think the logical answer is yes, while at the same time it has to be recognized that a feminist man will always be positioned quite differently from a feminist woman in relation to gender-based social injustice. He can recognize and deplore the structures of gender inequality, but he cannot experience them as a woman. However, this has become an issue of debate among feminist critics and not all feminists would agree with me on this.[1] Later, and especially in Part II, we shall look more closely at the complex interrelationahip between the three terms 'female', 'feminine' and 'feminist'. For the moment I want simply to distinguish between 'female' as designating biological sex, 'feminine' as referring to cultural conceptions of gender and 'feminist' as involving political perceptions and aims.[2]

The idea of gender as culturally constructed invites the objection that recent improvements in the social position of women have rendered feminism irrelevant and outdated. It has been argued that women are no longer denied entry to any career, and educational opportunities are equally available to both sexes, while advances in contraception and child-care provision have ensured that even pregnancy and mothering need no longer disadvantage women. Equality has been achieved, it has been said, so why go on making a fuss? But is this true? Has equality of opportunity really been achieved?

Recent comparative statistics for men and women in economic, employment and education spheres indicate that women are much more likely to be in part-time work than men: one in ten men is a part-time worker compared to four in ten women. Among those leaving school without qualifications 50 per cent of women work in semi-skilled or unskilled manual occupations compared to 29 per cent of men. Twice as many men as women earn over £200 a week, and the average weekly wage for manual workers in 1989 was £159 for men and £97 for women. All the reliable statistical accounts point out that the single most important factor determining a woman's work pattern and earning capacity is whether or not she has children. Having a family has no statistical effect at all on the shape of men's careers.[3]

Educational figures indicate similar continuing disparities. Although women are more likely than men to continue in some form of full-time education after leaving school, and gain equally good results in university entrance examinations, twice as many men as women attend university. Among those who obtain degrees, three times as many men as women go on to professional occupations. Attitudes are more difficult to quantify, but the continued institutionalization of stereotyped gender assumptions is indicated by the definition of 'head of household' still used by the Office of Population Census, which states that 'when two members of a different sex have equal claim, the male is taken as head of household'.[4] The assumption also underlies governmental thinking on pensions, welfare provision and benefits.

The latest report of the Organization for Economic Co-operation and Development (OECD) committee on *The Integration of Women into the Economy* does not make heartening reading. It states: 'The persistence of inequality in the labour market, in education and training and in social security and taxation systems, along with the uneven division of domestic work, has helped to maintain women in a position of economic disadvantage, rendering them vulnerable to poverty and dependence.'[5] Experience of discrimination and sex role stereotyping, the report concludes, cause 'women themselves [to] be discouraged from investing in marketable skills [and therefore] this circularity of cause and effect, the pattern of discrimination and disadvantage is difficult to break'.[6] It is sobering to remember that the signatory nations of OECD, including the United States, the UK, Canada, Denmark, Germany and France, are among the most economically developed in the world. Sadly, in many other parts of the world the position of women is much worse.

What these details demonstrate is not just the existence of gender-based inequality, but its pervasive systematic form. It is important to recognize that the focus of feminist studies is this institutionalized male dominance, operating through social structures like the law, education, employment, religion, the family and cultural practices. None of these is to be explained simplistically in terms of conscious intent, of ill-will or of conspiracy of individual men or even groups of men. These self-sustaining structures of power, by means of which women's interests are always ultimately subordinated to male interests, constitute the social order known as 'patriarchy', a designation which applies to almost all human societies, past and present. Nevertheless, we need to be careful in our use of the term so that it does not become an over-simplifying totalizing concept, that is a term that masks the many specific forms and degrees of women's inequality in different societies, and the strategies and resistances with which they challenge those injustices. Such over-simplification constructs a myth of women as everywhere and always the passive victims of a universal, unalterable male oppression. It would be to accept a sense of cultural essentialism every bit as hopeless and depressing for women as the traditional insistence on biological deter-minism, the insistence that a woman's fate is governed by her womb.

Another related term that it is helpful to clarify here is 'ideology'. The word has come to be used in a number of ways, and this can cause confusion. It can refer to a consciously held system of beliefs which people knowingly choose or reject, such as competitive individualism, communism or Christianity. In some societies patriarchal beliefs are part of the culture's conscious ideology. 'Ideology' is also used to refer to the way we perceive 'reality'. It is in this sense that I shall be using the word in this book. This understanding of 'ideology' rests on the assumption that as we enter the cultural life of our society – as we acquire language and interact with others – we absorb and assume its ways of seeing. We are drawn imperceptibly into a complex network of values, assumptions and expectations which are always already there prior to us and so seem natural, just the way things are. Feminism is a consciously held ideology (in the first sense of the term) which opposes consciously held ideologies that maintain the primacy of masculine authority and power. However, a great deal of feminist study is concerned with patriarchal ideology in the second sense, that is with ways in which women's subordination is naturalized, made to seem just the way things are. It also has to be recognized that feminism itself is not a unified, coherent ideology. While just about all feminists would accept my initial definition, there have always been passionate debates within the women's movement. The multiple lines of approach, the diversity of theoretical investigation and the imaginative energy generated by this open polemicism constitute the great strength of feminism.

One important debate among feminists concerns the degree of radicalism with which they interpret the double agenda of understanding patriarchal structures of power so as to change them. All feminists are angered by the forms of economic, educational, professional and legal inequalities referred to above and by the disappointments, deprivation and suffering that they inflict disproportionately on women. Almost all feminists pragmatically urge the immediate need for more maternity and women's health care, more nursery and child-centred provision and legislation to promote equal civic rights in all fields of activity. However, many feminists also argue that these must never be the ultimate goals of the women's movement. The aim should not be simply to claim more space in the sun for women within the existing social structures. They want to deconstruct the prevailing status quo completely, so as to transform the existing order of reality. Since, as French feminist Julia Kristeva says, women are 'one half of the sky',[7] changing the existing power relations between the sexes would mean a social revolution; the present world order would necessarily be transfigured.

Feminists following this more radical, or revolutionary, logic argue that we should be aiming not so much for equality between men and women as for a transcendence or transformation of the present over-rigid definition of gender as difference. The construction of gender identity on oppositional terms – to be masculine is to be *not* feminine and vice versa – is too limiting. It dangerously and damagingly regiments and restricts the full range of potential human experience. Human sexuality is too amorphous and complex to be contained within simplistically oppositional categories. Individual identity cannot be fixed and pinned down to any static unitary definition; identity is always a flux, always in process, never finished. Feminists argue that we should no longer accept this narrowing down of individual energies and possibilities, that our mutual adventure as a species on this small planet cannot afford such accumulative loss of creative and productive power.

More radically still perhaps, feminists claim that the defining of gender identity by opposition and difference lies at the heart of our whole system of meanings and values, and thereby sustains a sense of reality based on difference and separation rather than identification and community. This in turn encourages the impulses in both sexes for hierarchy, competitiveness, aggression and domination rather than for empathy, co-operation and compassion. In 1938, just before the outbreak of the Second World War, Virginia Woolf wrote despairingly that for centuries men had been 'childishly intent upon scoring the floor of the earth with chalk marks, within whose mustic boundaries human beings are penned, rigidly, separately, artificially, [for] . . . the dubious pleasures of power and dominion'.[8] Feminist aims of undermining and replacing the present rigid division of gender identity therefore have as their ultimate goal a new way of knowing ourselves and our world, a new ethical order of meanings and values.

Literature

What does the study of literature have to do with these political and ethical debates? How can an understanding of literature promote understanding of the nature and causes of women's inequality in the non-fictional world and help to change it? Perhaps we should begin by defining what is meant by 'literature'. Again, you may like to pause for a moment to consider what the term means to you. 'Literature' is normally used to refer to a body of texts that are perceived to have certain aesthetic qualities; this body of writing is often also called the 'literary canon'. Secondly, 'literature' is also an institution which is embodied primarily in education and publishing. And, finally, 'literature' is a cultural practice involving the writing, reading, evaluation, teaching and so on of the literary canon.

If we begin with the first sense of literature as a body of respected writing we might start to answer the above questions in terms of the relationship between literature and life. It has traditionally been believed that creative forms of writing can offer special insight into human experience and sharpen our perception of social reality. Literary texts may, therefore, provide a more powerful understanding of the ways in which society works to the disadvantage of women. In addition, the strong emotional impact of imaginative writing may be brought into play to increase indignation at gender discrimination and hence help to end it. Positive images of female experience and qualities can be used to raise women's self-esteem and lend authority to their political demands. Utopian literature may figure a new ethical order projected on 'feminine' qualities. As we shall see, feminist critics have looked at literary texts, especially those written by women, with all these possibilities in mind.

However, a more compex issue is involved here. Although we may turn to literature for insights into real life, and often commend pieces of writing in terms of their truth to life, we rarely feel in danger of confusing the two. 'Life', we feel, is just lived, is naturally given and is therefore, in that sense, always prior to literature. Literature constructs a representation of that already existing reality by means of words. Considered more carefully, though, it soon becomes clear that our sense of life or experience is far from 'natural' or given. It is from the first mediated through cultural froms − images and words − which allow us to differentiate and so impose a sense of order on what would otherwise be only an unboundaried, continuous flow of sensory stimuli. We can know our world only because we can represent it to ourselves. Representation is perhaps the most fundamental of all human activities, structuring our consciousness of ourselves and of external reality. For example, how could a child acquire any sense of self if it could not represent itself in words, if it could not say or think 'me' as opposed to 'you', 'I am a girl, not a boy', 'I am small, not big', 'I am good, not bad', and so on?

As we gain the ability to represent ourselves, our experience and our world by means of language, so we inevitably come to perceive our world through the system of values inherent in the words we use. To name or know myself as a 'girl' and not a 'boy' is to assume, or to internalize, all the cultural implications contained in that word. Because the process of learning to use language takes place so early in our social development, and is indeed the necessary basis for social development, the values seem to us to be 'naturally' inherent in the thing we name. To be a woman can seem 'naturally' to involve being gentle and nurturing, in other words being 'feminine'. To be a man normally involves some sense of being strong and active – of being 'masculine'. Thus language is the main means by which cultural values are recycled and sustained from generation to generation.

Once we recognize that our perception of reality is shaped largely by our representational systems, the predominant one being language, it becomes clear that the distinction between literature as a body of texts and life is more complex than it seemed, and that the boundaries between the two may well be permeable, allowing interaction and influence. What we consider to be 'manly' may derive as much from the way in which masculinity is imaged for us in stories, pictures and the media as from some pre-existing norm of masculinity 'out there' in reality, which we then copy in literature and visual art. Moreover, in many cultures the literary canon is esteemed as the most prestigious form of representation; in literature, it is claimed, we find the expression of the highest ideals and aspirations of humankind, the noblest examples of human thought and action to emulate and aspire to.

This is why feminists are interested in literature as an influential cultural practice embodied in powerful institutions. They are concerned to discover how literature as a cultural practice may be involved in producing the meanings and values that lock women into inequality, rather than simply reflecting the already existing reality of women's lives in literary texts. What perception of reality do the great books of our language offer us? Whose perception is offered? Who evaluates and selects the texts that form the literary canon? Why is it that when we think of 'great' books the names that come most automatically to mind are those of male writers? What sort of images of womanhood are constructed for us in their work? Whose values and ideals are represented in the highly acclaimed literary *master*pieces of our culture? Are there really so few 'great' women writers? Can we hope to find in writing by women indications or directions for a new ethical order, which transforms the present perception of reality based on difference and repressive separation? Or is to ask this question specifically of women's writing to perpetuate the very divisions of gender we wish to transcend? Indeed, is there any essential difference between men's writing and women's writing?

Feminist literary criticism has developed out of the need to explore and answer questions like these.

The chapters that follow aim to describe and illustrate the main topics and methods of approach that together comprise feminist literary studies, and give some sense also of their historical development. The argument is constructed around three central thematic concerns: the question of a woman's identity, the formation of canons and the politics of aesthetic evaluation. To my mind these issues have generated the driving energy of feminist literary criticism and are still its most important challenges. I hope that readers will engage with this debate. However, it is not a central issue of any one chapter, each of which deals with a separate area of feminist criticism and can be read independently of other chapters. The first part of the book brings a feminist interrogation to bear on literature as the canon (an existing body of respected texts), and on literature as an institution and a practice. It closes with a look at a possible alternative canon – at writing by women. In Part II, I use 'literature' defined as the production of writing to question what feminists mean when they use the term 'woman'. The emphasis in Part I is essentially practical: it aims to develop the skills of sensitive, discriminating, gender-aware reading. Part II articulates the theory underlying that practice. In this sense, it's quite possible that some readers may find all they need in Part I. It is my belief, though, that awareness of the ideas outlined in Part II, which are exciting and challenging in themselves, will lead to yet more complex ways of reading.

Finally, let me say something about the practical ways in which this book may be used. Feminist criticism is primarily something you *do*, and my fundamental aim has been to facilitate a feminist reading practice. My main concern throughout has been to empower readers, to develop confidence in an ability to read prose, poetry and passages of criticism. In a sense, then, it is intended as a kind of do-it-yourself manual, allowing opportunities and space for readers to work out their own response to textual passages and issues. I have therefore included in each chapter practical questions about particular approaches or ideas. I envisage two ways these might be used. Readers might like to pause and think out their response before reading on to see what I have to say, or alternately they can proceed straight on to my discussion. I have attempted to structure the demands of the passages to encourage increasingly complex ways of reading. I have included quite a lot of poetry since it comes in a usefully compact form. At the end of each chapter there is a summary of its main points; alternatively these can be read before beginning the chapter as an introduction or signpost to the issues which will be developed. At the end of each chapter there is also a brief list of further introductory reading on the topics discussed. More specific follow-up reading is suggested in the chapter notes. Throughout, I have aimed to introduce readers to as wide a range as possible of the most significant and interesting feminist criticism and to the immense variety of creative writing produced by women, some of it perhaps not so well known. Sadly it has been possible to include only a relatively small sample of all that is now available. Hopefully, readers will feel encouraged to discover much more for themselves.

Notes

1 For a complex personal exploration of the debate see Stephen Heath, 'Male Feminism' in Eagleton (ed.), *Feminist Literary Criticism*, pp. 193–225. Heath refers to several theorists and topics that will be discussed in later chapters; however, the first pages of his essay provide a clear setting-out of the problems.

2 For a fuller discussion of the terms see Toril Moi, 'Feminist, Female, Feminine', in Belsey and Moore (eds), *The Feminist Reader*, pp. 117–32.

3 Figures in this and the next paragraph are taken from the *Annual Abstract of Statistics* (1991) and *Social Trends 21* (1991 edn).

4 Malcolm Smyth and Fiona Browne, *General Household Survey 1990: An Inter-departmental Survey carried out by the Office of Population Censuses and Surveys between April 1990 and March 1991* (HMSO, 1992), p. 219.

5 Organization for Economic Co-operation and Development, *The Integration of Women into the Economy* (1985), p. 176.

6 Ibid., p. 177.

7 Kristeva, 'Women's Time', in *The Kristeva Reader*, ed. Moi, p. 202.

8 Woolf, *Three Guineas*, p. 121.

Part I

Literature?

1

Re-vision: Reading as a Woman

'If men could see us as we really are, they would be a little amazed; but the cleverest, the acutest men are often under an illusion about women: they do not read them in a true light: they misapprehend them, both for good and evil: their good woman is a queer thing, half doll, half angel; their bad woman almost always a fiend.'

Charlotte Brontë, *Shirley*

The current phase of feminism is usually seen as originating in the 1960s, in the intense political agitation for civil rights in the United States, and in France where the revolutionary fervour among students, intellectuals and workers culminated in strikes, sit-ins and the manifestos of May 1968, bringing down the government of President de Gaulle.[1] Many of the women active in the various political movements of the time were dismayed to discover that their male comrades, while articulating a rhetoric of freedom and equality, continued to construct their images of women on stereotypical sexist assumptions. It was men who wrote the manifestos; women, too often, were perceived as those who made the tea. Revolutionary men spoke of organizing sit-ins, and – without any sense of contradiction – of 'laying' women.[2] Post-sixties feminism grew from the recognition that women must represent themselves, literally in political practice, and equally by contesting negative verbal and visual images of themselves. Of course, the 1960s were not the beginning of the history of women's struggle. The above quotation from Charlotte Brontë's novel *Shirley* reminds us that, probably since the beginning of cultural organization, many women have been astutely conscious of the inequality of their position and of the male misrepresentation by which it is maintained. Indeed, one of the most fruitful areas of feminist study has been the rediscovery of a lost or unrecognized continuous tradition of women's protest, work and creativity. Her-story as well as history is being re-established.[3]

The quotation from *Shirley* pin-points two important facts. First, the misrepresentation of women by men – their not seeing 'us as we really are' – has been, through the centuries, one of the main means of sustaining and justifying women's subordinate position. If women are 'read' as essentially inferior to, or even innately different from, men, their different treatment can be deemed reasonable. However, the quotation also implies that this view of women is not the result of malicious conspiracy or deliberate falsification by men; even those who are recognized as 'great' writers consistently misapprehend women. Why are women so persistently misread by men? The earliest sustained attempt to answer the question was made by Simone de Beauvoir in *The Second Sex* (1949). Her classic feminist study considers the near-universal inequality between the sexes, across cultures and throughout history, to find an explanation of why women are invariably 'the second sex'. Her answer is contained in the title. The terms 'man' and 'woman', 'masculine' and 'feminine', are not used symmetrically: the term 'man' is always positive, standing for the norm, for humanity in general; 'woman' is the secondary term, what is 'other' to the norm, and so 'woman' does not have a positive meaning in its own right, but is defined in relation to 'man' – as what man is not. For this reason there can be no feminine equivalent for the verb 'emasculate'.

De Beauvoir points out that a concept of 'otherness' is necessary for organizing human thought. We can acquire a sense of self – of 'me' – only in opposition to what is 'not me' – what is other. Racial and social groups gain their sense of group identity by defining themselves against 'others' who are perceived as different. In the same way, 'woman' functions as the other which allows men to construct a positive self-identity as masculine. And because what is other does not have identity in its own right, it often acts as an empty space to be ascribed whatever meanings the dominant group chooses. Thus women are frail not strong, emotional not rational, yielding not virile, so that masculinity can be defined as those positive qualities. In other words, by seeing women as other to themselves, as not-men, men can read into 'femininity' whatever qualities are needed to construct their sense of the masculine. So, a mythicized 'Woman' becomes the imaginary location of male dreams, idealizations and fears: throughout different cultures 'femininity' is found to represent nature, beauty, purity and goodness, but also evil, enchantment, corruption and death. Because men persistently see women as other, de Beauvoir argues, 'Woman' as represented by men 'has a double and deceptive image . . . She incarnates all moral virtues from good to evil, and their opposites . . . He projects upon her what he desires and what he fears, what he loves and what he hates.'[4]

Several unfortunate consequences flow from this persistent mythicizing of 'Woman'. It gets in the way of men seeing 'us as we really are', creating fears and expectations which can only hinder understanding between women and men. More seriously, because men's cultural dominance is the norm – the views of men are taken as the universal human view of things. This perpetuates and authorizes male versions of femininity, male illusions about women, as 'human' truth, as the 'reality'. Thus women, too, come to read women as men read them, accepting men's visions of the feminine as their own: Women, writes de Beauvoir, 'still dream through the dreams of men'.[5] For all these reasons there is an urgent need to start rereading men's readings of women (and not just those in 'literature') so as to learn how to begin reading as a woman.

Two books published in the late 1960s brought the project of rereading male texts back to the attention of women as critics and readers: Mary Ellmann's *Thinking about Women* (1968) and Kate Millett's *Sexual Politics* (1969). Ellmann's book is enjoyable and witty; in it she discusses a wide range of literary and critical writing to demonstrate a pervasive sexism operating within the respected house of 'literature'. She shows how the 'thinking about women' of major male writers and critics is characterized by stereotyped assumptions which misrepresent women and their writing as formless, emotional and lacking control and intellectual range. In short, women and their work are imaged in 'literature' as everything that men, especially male writers, are not.

Kate Millett's *Sexual Politics* caused a greater stir and quickly became a best-seller. Its tone is more contentious and the literature discussed more sensational. It shocked readers by its iconoclastic attack on some highly esteemed and powerful male writers – D. H. Lawrence, Henry Miller, Norman Mailer, for example – and by focusing primarily on the obsessive representation of sexual relations in their work. Millett's thesis is that patriarchal power is maintained and exercised by means of men's control over the sexual relationship. This need to retain sexual dominance explains the recurrent misogynistic images of women in literary texts, as whores or virgins, frigid or nymphomaniac, chaste or licentious. Millett suggests that such images function to justify male sexual authority and the coercion and violence used to sustain it.

Millett has been criticized for producing reductive and over-negative readings of some of the writers she denounces. Some simplification was perhaps understandable as part of the polemical zest of her pioneering enterprise. Certainly, many women found (and still find) the book invigorating, and women critics, inspired by her example, began to reread male texts to reveal the extent of the misrepresentation of women throughout the whole canon of literature. This first phase of feminist criticism resulted in a widespread rereading of writing by men. However, doubts arose as to the continued usefulness of this practice. It was suggested that yet more documentation of literary misogyny could only add more examples to the depressing accumulation of negative portrayals of women by men.[6] The effect could be to sustain the sense of women as always victims rather than as makers of their own images and history, and of the male grip on representation as total and all-powerful.

However, de Beauvoir's earlier analysis of 'woman' as the space (as otherness) on to which men project their fears and anxieties suggests that, rather than confirming male power, men's representations of women may well demonstrate the inconsistencies and contradictions inherent in any ideological fantasy. To reveal this is to begin to unravel the claims to 'human' truth which have authorized male illusions about women as universal wisdom. Writing is rarely under the full conscious control of the writer, and often contains a subtext of what cannot or dare not be said, of which the writer may not be aware. Thus images of women in male-authored texts may offer evidence of a failure of power and of areas of insecurity in men's control of representation. The textual questions and discussions in this chapter aim to encourage this form of critical reading (a term currently used for it is 'symptomatic'[7]), to develop the skill of reading as a woman. The assumption throughout is that men have as much to gain as women from the understanding that a practice of reading as a woman makes available.

Rereading Male Images of Women

De Beauvoir inspired later generations of women readers by her implicit assumption of her right as a woman critically to question the work of prestigious male writers. The canonical 'classics' of literature can be intimidating. The scale of their achievement, their mastery of form, the aesthetic and intellectual pleasure they offer seem to demand our unreserved respect. Yet the reader of Edmund Spenser's *Faerie Queene*, for example, encounters in the text either women who are so helplessly virtuous as to be instantly forgettable or monstrous women as vividly represented forms of evil and destruction.[8] There is no difficulty in recognizing where Spenser's poetic imagination is most stirred. For the questing male heroes of this romance danger and treachery invariably assume female form. In Book II, for instance, Sir Guyon, representing temperance, undertakes a hazardous voyage to the Bower of Bliss to seek out the wicked Acrasia, whose name signifies excess and impotence. Throughout his journey he is tempted towards various dangers and destruction by a succession of sirens, mermaids and enchantresses, and arrives safely at the Bower of Bliss only by dint of manly fortitude. In the following stanzas describing Acrasia, can we recognize stereotypical features in Spenser's representation of woman as seductress? What is suggested about male attitudes by the imagery and language?

[72]

There, whence that Musick seemed heard to bee,
    Was the faire Witch her selfe now solacing,
    With a new Louer, whom through sorceree
    And witchcraft, she from farre did thither bring:
    There she had him now layd a slombering,
    In secret shade, after long wanton ioyes:
    Whilst round about them pleasauntly did sing
    Many faire Ladies, and lasciuious boyes,
That euer mixt their song with light licentious toyes.

[73]

And all that while, right ouer him she hong,
    With her false eyes fast fixed in his sight,
    As seeking medicine, whence she was stong,
    Or greedily depasturing delight: [feeding on]
    And oft inclining downe with kisses light,
    For feare of waking him, his lips bedewd,
    And through his humid eyes did sucke his spright,
    Quite molten into lust and pleasure lewd;
Wherewith she sighed soft, as if his case she rewd.   [pitied]

[77]

Vpon a bed of Roses she was layd,
  As faint through heat, or dight to pleasant sin.
  And was arayd, or rather disarayd.
  All in a vele of silke and siluer thin,
  That hid no whit her alablaster skin,
  But rather shewd more white, if more might bee:
  More subtile web *Arachne* cannot spin,   [spider]
  Nor the fine nets, which oft we wouen see
Of scorched deaw, do not in th'aire more lightly flee.   [float]

[78]

Her snowy brest was bare to readie spoyle
  Of hungry eies, which n'ote therewith be fild,   [could not]
  And yet through languour of her late sweet toyle,
  Few drops, more cleare then Nectar, forth distild,
  That like pure Orient perles adowne it trild,   [trickled]
  And her faire eyes sweet smyling in delight,
  Moystened their fierie beames, with which she thrild
  Fraile harts, yet quenched not; like starry light
Which sparkling on the silent waues, does seeme more bright.

[83]

But all those pleasant bowres and Pallace braue,
  Guyon broke downe, with rigour pittilesse;
  Ne ought their goodly workmanship might saue
  Them from the tempest of his wrathfulnesse,
  But that their blisse he turn'd to balefulnesse:
  Their groues he feld, their gardins did deface,
  Their arbers spoyle, their Cabinets suppresse,   [summerhouses]
  Their banket houses burne, their buildings race,   [raze]
And of the fairest late, now made the fowlest place.[9]

Stanzas 72 and 73 suggest the excessive feminine sexuality that haunts men's fears, undermining their sense of virility and control. Acrasia is 'solacing' herself with a new lover (presumably previous ones have been used and discarded), and although he is utterly exhausted from lovemaking she hangs over him, still insatiable, 'greedily depasturing delight'. Furthermore, she takes advantage of his temporary loss of manly strength to emasculate him further, sucking out his spirit, 'Quite molten into lust' through his 'humid eyes'. The excess and impotence signified by the female form of Acrasia seem in effect to be a projection of male anxiety about sexuality. The fear that sexual attraction towards women emasculates male potency is articulated also in the association of Acrasia's seductive powers with magic and witchcraft: men are portrayed as the victims of women's unfair methods of disarming them. This reverses and masks the actual relations of sexual victimization and power between men and women. Moreover, the sensual delight conveyed in the lingering description of Acrasia's physical loveliness in stanzas 77 and 78 surely belies the need for any magic! However, the imagery of the description moves ambivalently between fear and desire, nature and art. Spenser's language seems to assimilate Acrasia's unblemished beauty to an idealized natural purity: her breast is 'snowy', her perspiration 'more cleare then Nectar', and her eyes 'sweet smyling' are 'like starry light . . . sparkling on the silent waves'. Waves can drown, however, and the natural charm is made more seductive by a transparent covering of silk and silver, which is also a cunningly contrived web. Art disguised as innocence, or nature corrupted into artfulness, pose greater threats to unwary male desire than the painted harlot.

How should we read stanza 83? Does it assert the male right to curb and punish any expression of female sexual power, or does it convey a sense of unease and contradiction? I would say that it does both. Explicitly, male moral authority is reaffirmed and Acrasia is disempowered, herself caught in a cunning net. However, if we attend carefully to the language, contradictions become apparent. The emotion expressed is itself excessive and intemperate. Guyon's 'tempest of . . . wrathfulnesse' is enacted in an accumulative force of destructive verbs: 'feld', 'deface', 'spoyle', 'suppresse', 'burne', 'race'. Such frenzied activity suggests fear and hatred rather than a securely based moral authority. All this violence is turned against the 'goodly workmanship' that created the Bower of Bliss, as if the poem is implicitly turning on its own goodly art for constructing the magical charm of Acrasia which so beguiles the reader – and, we feel, the poet. In this revulsion of feeling what has seemed 'the fairest late, [is] now made the foulest place'. Woman as other is the location of all that is desired and feared, all that is mysterious, magical, unrestricted and all that must be controlled and mastered. She is the entrance to fairest bliss and to the foulness of sin and the tomb.

The power of women's sexuality, since it is the direct measure of men's disempowerment by desire, calls for vigilant control. A further potential source of female power is women's more immediate and dominant role in creation. Since men are born to women and not vice versa, it might have been expected that men should occupy a less authoritative position. In addition, paternity can never be guaranteed. Unless sexual activity is regulated very strictly, men can never rest secure that their offspring are theirs, as women can; male procreation is always open to doubt. Hence creativity and access to knowledge are areas of anxiety for men. Many feminists have pointed out the rather amazing way in which the creation myth reverses the order of things so that a male god creates man first, and then, almost as an afterthought, woman is made from Adam's rib.[10] Hence she is subordinate to and dependent on him for her very being. What is more, painful childbirth is designated Eve's punishment for sin so that woman's creative capacity becomes an index of her guilt and submission. Creation as spontaneous generation remains godlike and male.

Milton's epic poem *Paradise Lost* rearticulates the myth, adding the authority of a majestic artistic form to religious tradition.[11] The following lines introduce Adam and Eve into the poem. How does Milton stress Eve's dependence and subordination? Are there ambiguities or contradictions within this description?

> Not equal, as their sex not equal seemed;
> For contemplation he and valor formed,
> For softness she and sweet attractive grace;
> He for God only, she for God in him.
> His fair large front and eye sublime declared
> Absolute rule; and hyacinthine locks
> Round from his parted forelock manly hung
> Clust'ring, but not beneath his shoulders broad:
> She as a veil down to the slender waist
> Her unadornèd golden tresses wore
> Disheveled, but in wanton ringlets waved
> As the vine curls her tendrils, which implied
> Subjection, but required with gentle sway,
> And by her yielded, by him best received,
> Yielded with coy submission, modest pride,
> And sweet reluctant amorous delay.[12]

In de Beauvoir's terms, Adam is clearly represented as the positive identity here; he is formed for thought and action ('contemplation' and 'valour'). Eve, in contrast, is presented wholly as the passive object fitted to his male needs; she is all 'softness' and 'attractive grace'. The emphasis on Adam's 'large front' (forehead) and 'eye sublime' indicates spiritual and intellectual capacity. The description of Eve is entirely physical; spirituality and intellect are not suggested – for these godlike qualities Eve must look 'for God in him'. Masculine superiority, inherent in their different origins, necessitates Eve's 'yielding' (a word used twice in two lines) in subjection to Adam. Eve's fecundity as mother of the race is indicated in the association of her 'wanton ringlets' with the vine, an image of fruitfulness. But the vine, of course, needs a firm prop and stay to which to cling, and its excessive growth must be kept in strict check.

It is here that we can notice a sense of contradiction. Even in Paradise, straight from the hand of God, Eve's innocent sexuality is strangely allied to seduction and excess. 'Disheveled', 'wanton' hair and 'reluctant amorous delay' suggest the experienced sexuality of a post-Edenic world. These early lines already suggest that Eve's seductive beauty will fatally unman Adam so that their 'proper', divinely ordained, roles are reversed, he 'yielding' to her temptation. Moreover, the image of Eve's hair twining like the curling tendril of the vine subtly associates her with the coiling insinuation of the serpent. Whereas Adam's sin is that of weakness before woman, Eve's, like Lucifer's, is that of pride and usurpation of a godlike knowledge.

Explicitly, *Paradise Lost* continues throughout to insist on Eve's feminine frailty and less-godlike capacities, thereby justifying the need for her subordination to Adam's better judgement. Gabriel is sent by God to explain that all of human woe 'From man's effeminate slackness it begins' (XI. 634). However, what Milton's poem and the biblical myth, read carefully, also suggest is that it is not women's weakness that men fear and wish to control. It is a perception of female sexual fecundity which allies women to a dark mysterious otherness of creative force as perhaps a secret and withheld source of knowledge.

Women's desirability is threatening, for men 'molten into lust' lack firmness of control. But women who are not physically attractive to men are also the focus of anxiety and hostility. Perhaps their uncharming presence hints that women may not be divinely designed just to meet male needs. Graceless women who also refuse submissiveness are therefore the most fearful. They have been pilloried constantly in literature as monstrous shrews and viragos, and were in times past liable to be tortured and burnt as witches.[13] The common assumption behind the caricature of women perceived as insubordinate is that they are sex-starved, that their independent spirit only masks their need of a man. In the case of women suspected of witchcraft the belief was translated into the accusation that they were copulating with the devil.

The novels of Charles Dickens, following the notoriously misogynistic tradition of much eighteenth-century fiction, contain several caricatures of 'shrewish' women. Two of the more ambiguous and interesting examples are found in *Great Expectations*: Mrs Joe and Miss Havisham, the married and the unmarried monster. The presentation of Mrs Joe conforms closely to the stereotype of the virago, and Dickens's representation makes brutally frank the tenor of male thinking about women perceived as bossy or domineering. True to her unwomanly name, she is sharp-featured, rough-handed and angular, and keeps her breasts well covered by a coarse apron, stuck full of pins for good measure. Her husband, Joe, and her young orphaned brother, Pip, are lashed alike by her tongue, her hand and her stick 'Tickler', and live under a state of continual 'rampage'. Women like Mrs Joe are said to be asking for it, and she duly gets it. Orlick, a brutish man working for her husband, comes up behind her and beats her about the head with an iron manacle, 'dropping' her 'like a bullock', as he says.[14] The implication of rape in the language is striking. Thereafter, Mrs Joe is rendered dumb literally, able only to make eager conciliatory gestures towards Joe and especially towards Orlick, the man who finally brings her under control.

Miss Havisham is one of Dickens's most intensely symbolic characters, so much so that the term 'stereotype' is inadequate for the imaginative force of her representation. She is presented as having been jilted on her wedding day; in reaction, she arrests her life at that moment, withering into a skeleton-like form with her wedding clothes still on her. 'Corpse-like' in a yellowed dress and shroudlike veil, resembling 'grave-clothes' on a 'collapsed form', the character seems to come from nightmare or the unconscious, a female figure of death, suggestive of the inner decay of the tomb/womb.[15] De Beauvoir observes how virginity becomes repugnant and disturbing to men when it is allied with aged rather than with youthful flesh, citing a coarse male joke that an unmarried woman 'must be full of cobwebs inside'.[16] At the centre of Miss Havisham's room is the ruin of her bridal cake, 'a black fungus' 'overhung with cobwebs', out of which scuttle 'speckled-legged spiders with blotchy bodies'.[17] Dickens's macabre imagery irresistibly evokes a sense of repugnance and horror for stale virginity as the decay and putrefaction of enclosure. Miss Havisham is intent on revenging herself on all men, for which she is severely punished. Her tattered clothing catches fire and she is burnt like a witch. She survives the purgatorial flames only long enough to beg forgiveness from Pip, the man she wronged.

Such a summary does not do justice to the power and complexity of Dickens's writing. A more sympathetic perception coexists with the hostility to these female characters who refuse a womanly role. His representation of them articulates a sense of the wasted energies and internalized anger of women who are perceived only in stereotyped terms and thereby denied access to the wider opportunities and experiences of life. Miss Havisham represents a male nightmare of woman as confinement and decaying tomb, but she is also a powerful and fitting symbol of the stultifying repressions imposed on women in Victorian England.

What about the heroines of male-authored texts, the female characters who are offered for our positive approval and admiration? Is Brontë correct in claiming that a man's 'good woman is a queer thing, half doll, half angel'? Shakespeare's plays, especially his comedies, offer us many adventurous cross-dressing heroines who certainly cannot dismissed as 'dolls' or 'angels'. He also provides several examples of a 'good' woman, one of the most praised of whom is Imogen in *Cymbeline*. Imogen's virtue lies in her unswerving marital fidelity and chastity and her loving submissiveness to husband and father, despite the arbitrary cruelty of their behaviour towards her. Her father, King Cymbeline, punishes her for marrying against his wishes by exiling her husband, Posthumus, to Italy. There his extravagant praise of Imogen's virtue provokes the Italian Iachimo to declare that any woman's honour is but 'frail' and 'casual'.[18] In the quarrel between the men which follows Imogen's chastity is repeatedly identified with the costly diamond ring she gave Posthumus: both are perceived as his possessions. He stakes both wife and diamond on her virtue, giving Iachimo permission to test her. Imogen spurns Iachimo's advances, but the latter manages to persuade Posthumus that Imogen has been unfaithful. As she is now perceived as debased and worthless, Posthumus writes instructing his servant to kill her, an order which Imogen herself insists he fulfil. When the complications of the plot are unravelled in the final scene, Imogen offers no rebuke to her husband and demands no explanation of his conduct. She kneels to her father for his blessing and embraces Posthumus. His response, 'Hang there like fruit, my soul, / Till the tree die', reaffirms and emphasizes her submissive clinging to him.[19]

Thus Imogen is apparently constructed as a paragon of stereotypical feminine virtue, but the play can also be read as subverting what it explicitly affirms. When women are perceived solely as objects of possession, and their virtue equated with male honour, they are never known for themselves. Posthumus's most lavish praise of Imogen is impersonal and is often couched in the language of commerce: 'I prais'd her as I rated her: so do I my stone.'[20] Confused by their own stereotyped thinking about women, men, as Brontë's heroine says, 'do not read them in a true light'. These words find an echo in the play. Cymbeline discovers that he has been continually deceived by his queen. 'Who is't can read a woman?' he asks; 'Mine eyes / were not in fault, for she was beautiful: / Mine ears that heard her flattery, nor my heart / That thought her like her seeming.'[21] Constructions of stereotyped virtue are likely to prove as fictitious as Iachimo's stereotyped report of women's monstrous sexual appetite. Misled by the projections of their own fantasies on an unknowable female otherness, men lose all contact with women as they really are. Ironically, it is men who create the masks by which women can deceive if they wish, so that even the security of male self-identity is thrown into doubt:

> Is there no way for men to be, but women
> Must be half-workers? We are all bastards,
> And that most venerable man, which I
> Did call my father, was I know not where
> When I was stamp'd. Some coiner with his tools
> Made me a counterfeit: yet my mother seem'd
> The Dian of that time.[22]

The most celebrated and continuous literary form for praising women is, undoubtedly, the love poem. Traditionally, the woman praised was high-born and admired for her refined beauty. Wordsworth can be seen to have democratized the tradition by writing of a woman who lived in ordinary, even humble, circumstances.

In this well-known lyric by Wordsworth how much detail does the language and imagery convey about the qualities of Lucy as woman and person. How fully is she known by the poet who praises her?

> She dwelt among th' untrodden ways
>   Beside the springs of Dove,
> A Maid whom there were none to praise
>   And very few to love.
>
> A violet by a mossy stone
>   Half-hidden from the Eye!
>   – Fair as a star, when only one
>   Is shining in the sky!
>
> She *lived* unknown, and few could know
>   When Lucy ceased to be;
> But she is in her Grave, and Oh!
>   The difference to me.[23]

The image of a single violet and the name of the river contribute to the poem's evocation of Lucy's gentle purity – of a 'Maid' whose life, too, is an 'untrodden way', unsullied by experience of the world. The image of the lonely star reinforces the idea of chaste purity. The movement from nearness to untouchable distance, from softness to coldness, enacted in the shift of image from flower to star implies a similar effortless transition for Lucy from secluded life to death. Lucy simply 'ceased to be'. It is this that might make us uneasy about the poem. It conveys no sense of Lucy as a living sentient woman. That her life ends before it seems to have begun is not lamented by the poet. On the contrary, that she has 'lived unknown' where 'there were none to praise / And very few to love' is central to the poet's own praise and love.

Why should this be? I would suggest that what the poem implicitly praises as well as Lucy is the imaginative and emotional sensitivity of the poet who is able to recognize Lucy's goodness and beauty in its humble setting. The assimilation of Lucy to flower and star renders her a passive object of romantic contemplation; all the living feeling belongs to the poet. The underlying narcissism of the poem surfaces explicitly in the climactic emotion of the two final lines: 'But she is in her Grave, and Oh! / The difference to me.' One might have thought, rather, the difference to poor Lucy! Even in love poems women tend to be constructed to meet male needs; typically, they are assimilated to passive images of nature or of death, an otherness against which the poet may experience the fullness of his own emotional humanity. In another of the Lucy poems Wordsworth writes, 'She seemed a *thing* that could not feel / The touch of earthly years' (my emphasis).[24] The feminine constructed as 'a thing' functions like a narcissistic mirror to reflect the fullness and feeling of a subjective masculine humanity. To be male is to be human, to be female is to be other – 'a thing that could not feel'.

Lest I seem unfair in my catalogue of misrepresentation by some of the most celebrated male writers in our language, let me say that women writers, too, are sometimes involved in recycling stereotyped ways of thinking about women. For example, *Middlemarch* by George Eliot, which is respected as a great novel of psychological realism, has, nevertheless, both a heroine and a 'bad' woman who conform to some of the stereotypes we have discussed. Despite the complex psychological understanding Eliot brings to the presentation of her heroine, Dorothea, what we are asked to admire in the end is her noble resignation of self to her husband's narrow egoism. Dorothea, like Imogen, conforms perfectly to the ideal of submissive self-sacrificing womanhood beloved of men, especially during the nineteenth century.[25]

In contrast to Dorothea, Rosamond refuses to subdue her desires to those of her husband, and brings about the ruin of his aspirations and career. While the text claims to offer an equally sympathetic understanding to all its characters, the imagery associate with Rosamond is persistently sinister. She is likened to a mermaid and implicitly assimilated to a spider, spinning the web that traps Lydgate and looking seductively soft and clinging in delicately drifting drapery (recalling Acrasia's cunning artfulness disguised as innocence). Like many male writers, Eliot seems blind to the contradictions inherent in this representation. Rosamond is depicted as a shrewd, determined woman who easily outmanoeuvres her husband (as Eve's logic overcomes Adam's arguments in *Paradise Lost*), but to admit this explicitly might require some recognition of the legitimacy of her claims as well as those of Lydgate's career. Thus the text continues paradoxically to speak of her weakness triumphing over his noble strength. Echoes of Milton's poem recur throughout the novel as in this final image of Rosamond and Lydgate:

Poor Rosamond's vagrant fancy had come back terribly scourged – meek enough to nestle under the old despised shelter. And the shelter was still there: Lydgate had accepted his narrowed lot with sad resignation. He had chosen this fragile creature, and had taken the burthen of her life upon his arms. He must walk as he could, carrying that burthen pitifully.[26]

Resisting Narrative Point of View

Why have women readers and women writers, not resisted the 'virile myths' that justify a patriarchal, godlike right to judge and regulate women's sexuality? Why have they allowed the heroic proportions of male identity to be constructed on an image of female frailty and yielding passivity? Why have women been content to dream through the dreams of men when they often work against women's interests? 'In such fictions', writes the feminist critic Judith Fetterley, 'the female reader is co-opted into participation in an experience from which she is explicitly excluded . . . she is required to identify against herself.'[27] Yet I had read *Great Expectations* many times before I began to feel anything other than that Mrs Joe's brutal punishment was her rightful come-uppance. From my experience of teaching *Middlemarch* I know that many first-time women readers feel the same unquestioned antipathy that I felt towards Rosamond Vincy for thwarting her husband's career. Like me, they shed no tear for this fictional representation of a young woman's shattered dreams of social mobility through marriage, which is exactly what her expensive education has taught her to expect.

Our unresisting response is partly conditioned by the respect with which we approach these texts. We come to them expecting to be enlightened by great thoughts, to find in them the truth of 'genius'. However, the main reason why we are unresisting readers is that this is how we are positioned to read by the narrative strategies employed. The text itself functions to draw us into compliance with its judgements and system of values. For example, *Great Expectations* is written in the first person from the point of view of its male hero Pip, and through our identification with him we share the fear and humiliation he experiences as a child at Mrs Joe's hands and his resulting hostility towards her. A wider narrative perspective might have been offered which gave access also to the 'I' of Mrs Joe, enabling us to perceive her humiliation as a woman rejected as ugly, expected to devote herself to an orphaned younger brother and only reluctantly married for his sake. Such a female narrative space is never opened up, and as readers we remain within the male point of view.

This is hardly surprising when the story is told by its main male character. But it is not just where the story-teller is a man that a male point of view is constructed for the reader to assume. *Middlemarch* is written by a woman and its omniscient narrator constantly insists that we seek to understand our fellow beings unblinded by common assumptions and prejudices. In the passage I quoted on p. 27 is reader sympathy directed impartially towards both Rosamond and Lydgate? Whose feelings are more closely entered into so that readers gain an identifying access to their view of things?

The epithet 'poor Rosamond' seems at first to invite compassion for her, but immediately the unflattering connotations of a 'vagrant fancy' function to qualify that feeling, and the negative judgement is extended with the implication that only trouble has turned Rosamond back to the protection of the husband she had despised. The implication of shallow selfishness encourages a positive reflex of sympathy in the reader towards Lydgate, which is consolidated by the greater access offered to his feelings. Whereas we have an external account of the effect of trouble on Rosamond, we are shown how Lydgate himself perceives his situation. The emotive language and point of view draws us into his sense of the lost possibilities of his life and we view Rosamond as he sees her, as weak, pitiful and burdensome. The passage subtly draws us into the male perspective to identify with his feelings against those of the woman. The narrative opens up no comparable position from which the reader can experience the situation as Rosamond perceives it.

The construction of narrative point of view is one of the most powerful means by which readers are imperceptibly brought to share the values of the text. The term 'interpellation' is sometimes used to designate the process by which texts, as it were, hollow out a linguistic space for the reader to occupy. By assuming that place we assume also the viewpoint and attitudes that go with it. Not surprisingly, in male-authored texts the attitudes and values are predominantly male-orientated. The effect of this, Fetterley observes, is that 'as readers and teachers and scholars, women are taught to think as men, to identify with a male point of view, and to accept as normal and legitimate a male system of values, one of whose central principles is misogyny'.[28] In *Paradise Lost* Eve, having resisted Adam's arguments that she stay within reach of his protective care, sets out into the garden alone promising to return by noon. At this point in the poem there is an unusual interjection of personal comment from the narrator/poet: 'O much deceived, much failing, hapless Eve / . . . Thou never from that hour in Paradise / Found'st either sweet repast or sound repose.'[29]

These lines construct a lofty omniscient overview of the impending situation. The tone is one of sorrow rather than anger, but as we read we are structured into a position of moral superiority in which we feel that we understand Eve and judge her wilful optimism and folly with a compassionate intelligence which her impulsive mind clearly cannot match. By constructing such narrative vantage-points texts offer to readers of both sexes a vicarious and flattering experience of godlike knowledge and authority. However, women readers gain access to the seductive taste of power only at the cost of identifying against their own interests as women. The active, judging consciousness within most texts, as we have seen, is male; the female is almost always the passive object of the narrative gaze, to be judged or praised or punished. Not infrequently, as in the above stanzas from *The Faerie Queen*, the female figure is first enjoyed as an object of erotic titillation and then punished for precisely that exercise of dangerous seductive charm. By co-operating with the interpellative strategies of the narrative method we become complicit with the patriarchal will to control women.

For this reason there has been a strong emphasis in feminist literary criticism on the need to become resisting readers, to learn to read against the grain of emotive language and imagery and to construct oppositional narrative positions within the text from which to challenge its dominant values and gender assumptions. Some texts use narrative technique to teach us how to do this. The Merchant's Tale in Chaucer's *Canterbury Tales* is explicitly misogynistic, a cautionary satire of an old man, January, who marries 'fresshe' young May.[30] It is intended by its narrator, the merchant, as a warning to men against marriage, for women are cunning and deceiving. The narrative dwells on January's excited feelings on his wedding night, giving us his view of things directly in his own words:

                                                    'Allas! I moot trespace
       To yow, my spouse . . .
       But natheless, considereth this,' quod he,
       Ther nys no werkman, whatsoevere he be,
       That may bothe werke wel and hastily;
       This wol be doon at leyser parfitly.'[31]

Having 'thus laboureth' all night, January sits in bed at dawn crowing
with triumph, the slack skin of his neck shaking. Only then does the
narrative point of view suddenly shift, opening up a speculative space for
the woman's perception: 'But God woot what that May thoughte in hir
herte.'[32] This is the kind of reversal of narrative viewpoint and subversive
questioning we need to develop as a practice of reading, against the
grain of patriarchal texts. As the example from Chaucer suggests, it is a
strategy open to men as readers as well as to women.

Structure: Replotting Female Destiny

Characters are the most obvious form of literary representation, but what
about the story? The shaping of the plot is an unobtrusive but pervasive
form of representation. For example, by the nineteenth century the
natural sciences were established as offering the most authoritative account
of the physical world. The scientific method of deducing the underlying
working of the system by observing the external details of phenomena
became the most respected model of knowledge, and it is no coincidence
that the detective novel developed in the same century. The stories of
Sherlock Holmes offer brilliant demonstrations of the triumph of the
scientific method. For most of the nineteenth century, even 'serious'
novelists shaped their plots in accordance with the general sense of an
ordered universe operating according to divine and natural laws. Novels
that refused the desired happy endings still constructed plots in which
mysteries and conflicts are resolved, complications untangled and reward
and punishment allotted according to a determined system of justice.
The confidence in rational progress, an ordered universe and divine
justice were eroded as the nineteenth century moved towards the twentieth, when irrational forces came to seem at least as powerful as
deductive reasoning, history erupted in the violence of the First World

War, and human life seemed arbitrary and ultimately without purpose. Correspondingly, literary structures have come to highlight lack of meaning; logical progress with a beginning, middle and end are eschewed, along with any final enlightenment. Even in our detective fictions the good cop often turns out to have been twisted all along.

In other words, the shapes of our narratives confirm our perception of existence, of the shape of how things – inevitably – are. What, then, do the narrative structures of literary texts reveal about the perceived shape of women's lives? What are represented as the natural plots of female destiny? One persistent plot pattern is that suffering and death are the inevitable fate of sexually transgressive heroines. This pattern assumes that women are inherently (that is decreed by God and nature to be) pure, and therefore any sexual misdemeanour is a violation of their deepest 'feminine' self. Hence the notorious double-standard: a man is naturally promiscuous and therefore must be forgiven, whereas a woman who 'falls' destroys her very self. Even when such female characters are presented sympathetically as the victims of an unfeeling social world, once their sexual innocence is lost their path leads inevitably towards death.

This is the story of Maggie Tulliver in *The Mill on the Floss*, and of the heroines of *Tess of the d'Urbervilles, Anna Karenina* and *Madame Bovary*. Each twist and juncture of the plot is structured to impress readers with a sense of the inevitability of its ending. Anna Karenina, for example, is presented as suffering a stultifying life as the result of an arranged marriage to a rigidly conventional man who is physically repulsive to her. Not unnaturally, we might think, she seizes at the chance of happiness with a man to whom she is passionately attracted. However, the unfolding of the plot from the moment of her 'fall' develops according to a very different logic. Anna's adultery is perceived as so deeply unnatural to her being as a woman that her mental and emotional stability is unbalanced; she becomes increasingly irrational, self-deceiving and unhappy. Not for a moment does the relentless movement of the plot suggest that there is a way back for the heroine. Like the train under which she eventually throws herself, Anna is propelled relentlessly along the tracks of her tragic female fate. Eve's sin, with its symbolic hint of sexual transgression, is traditionally presented as bringing death into the world. The fates of the transgressive heroines of literature bears this out.

In a literary text where the main character is male the plot is often structured as a quest which traces the hero's active engagement with the world, whether the adventure ends in success or in failure and death. This is the pattern in texts ranging from the tragic story of Othello, to Wordsworth's discovery of his poetic vocation in *The Prelude*, to Leopold Bloom's day-long encounter with Dublin, his marriage and his desire for a son in James Joyce's *Ulysses*. By contrast, central female characters are invariably constructed in a passive relationship to events. Things happen to heroines: Richardson's Clarissa, Hardy's Tess and Dickens's Little Dorrit achieve status by enduring, not by acting. In his preface to *What Maisie Knew* Henry James explains that he chose a girl rather than a boy as protagonist because he wanted 'a vessel of consciousness, swaying in such a draught' and that 'couldn't be with verisimilitude a rude little boy'.[33] In his preface to *The Portrait of a Lady* he singles out as 'the best thing' in it the heroine Isobel Archer's silent night of vigil facing the extinction of her hopes. The representation 'of her motionless *seeing*', is to him as 'interesting as the surprise of a caravan or the identification of a pirate'.[34] Predictably, the novel, which seems to set out as a young woman's quest for life, becomes the story of her renunciation of it, and it is this that makes her a heroine. It is not surprising that James was an admirer of George Eliot. The structure of *Middlemarch* enacts a similar plot in which its main character, Dorothea, achieves heroic status through a pattern of noble resignation. To be heroic, plots tell us, men must embrace action, seeking to shape circumstances to their will, whereas for women heroism consists of accepting restrictions and disappointments with stoicism.

Another persistent structural form has become known in feminist criticism as the two-suitor convention.[35] Whereas the questing male hero has all the world to win – as well as any number of women – the choice for a heroine is usually between one of two men. Sometimes this takes the form of a forbidden true lover threatened by a suitor insisted on by tyrannous male authority, as in *Romeo and Juliet* and *Cymbeline*, for example. In a variation of the theme the woman herself is sometimes unsure of which suitor to pick, and often makes an initial disastrous choice which leaves her imprisoned in a deadening relationship. This is what happens to Clara Middleton in *The Egoist*, to the heroine of *Daniel Deronda*, to Ursula Branwen in *The Rainbow* and to heroines in countless popular films and romances. Meredith's novel *The Egoist* is a telling example of this convention, since the novel is remarkable for its sympathetic insight into the heroine's feelings and its ironic revelation of male egoism. Clara's struggle to free herself from the self-absorbed arrogance of her future husband produces some fine satire against Victorian men. However, in our relief at her eventual escape we can easily fail to register that Clara is freed simply to marry the more suitable man. This is the ultimate conclusion of all the variations on the two-suitor convention: freedom for a woman is simply the right man. Male freedom is a drama that embraces the whole of social, political and moral action; for women freedom is no wider than choosing the best husband.

The practice of reading as a woman, then, needs to oppose the ideological implications of classic plot structures, prising open alternative spaces of freedom for women within the text against the often relentless logic of the story. We need, too, to resist the interpellative power of narrative point of view drawing us into compliance with the text's dominant values, and seek instead the moments or sites of resistance where the writing subverts or questions itself. Our analysis of language and imagery must be responsive to contradiction and ambivalence so that we can rearticulate not just the authority of patriarchal texts, but the fear and anxiety they implicitly express in response to the counter-power of women. Such reading is never reductive or purely negative; the effect is almost always to heighten our sense of the complex interaction of language and literature with our experience.

Summary of Main Points

1   The misrepresentation of women by men is one of the traditional means by which men have justified their subordination of women. A negative identity as 'what men are not' allows men to read any quality into the 'feminine'. They project on to the image of 'woman' their dreams and fears.
2   As the dominant gender, the norm, men's representations are authorized as 'truth', as the universal human view. Thus we need to reread men's reading and writing of women to construct ways of reading *as* women. This will reveal men's fears and anxieties rather than be simply a list of stereotypes.
3   The Temptress: negative represenations of women as sexual seductresses requiring moral censure and punishment (as in Spenser's *Faerie Queene*) reflect men's fear of losing power and control in the sexual act.

4 The Weaker Vessel: women's dominant and secure role in reproduction in contrast to men's is another source of male anxiety. Hence the representation of creativity and knowledge as male and godlike (Milton's *Paradise Lost*) and the insistence on women's dependence on men.

5 The Perfect Woman: virture in women, married or 'maids' is always chastity and submissiveness (Imogen in *Cymbeline*). But because they see women only in stereotypical terms men never actually know them, hence their continual insecurity.

6 The Virago: women perceived as unattractive and unsubmissive are doubly threatening: thus they must be perceived as *really* wanting a man and as deserving punishment.

7 The narrative point of view is usually masculine: it draws ('interpellates') the reader into compliance with the values and assumptions of the text. To read as a woman means learning to read against the grain.

8 Plot structure represents a perception of reality. Traditional structures show female destiny to be the passive acceptance of restricted choice, stoicism in suffering and punishment for transgression.

Suggestions for Further Reading

Jenni Calder, *Women and Marriage in Victorian Fiction* An early 'rereading' approach, but full of interesting facts and examples.

Kate Millett, *Sexual Politics*, and Cora Kaplan, 'Radical Feminism and Literature: Rethinking Millett's *Sexual Politics*', in Eagleton (ed.), *Feminist Literary Criticism*, pp. 135–70. This provides a good example of Millett's criticism on D. H. Lawrence paired with a later critic's reservations about her work.

Adrienne Munich, 'Notorious Signs, Feminist Criticism, and Literary Tradition', in Greene and Kahn (eds), *Making a Difference*, pp. 238–59. An illustration of the insights to be gained from rereading male texts.

Notes

1 Marks and de Courtivron (eds), *New French Feminisms*, contains a useful brief introduction to the history of feminism in France, touching on its relations with American feminism (pp. 10–38). Firestone, *The Dialectics of Sex*, has a chapter 'On American Feminism' (pp. 23–45).

2 For an example of this sort of chauvinism see Marks and de Courtivron (eds), *New French Feminisms*, pp. 30–1.

3 See e.g. Hobby, *Virtue of Necessity*; Strachey, *The Cause*, (probably still the

best account of the women's movement in Britain); Barbara Taylor, *Eve and the New Jerusalem.*

4 De Beauvoir *The Second Sex*, p. 229. For a more recent and quite rare example of French rereading see Herrmann, *The Tongue Snatchers*, which is brief and very readable.

5 De Beauvoir, *The Second Sex*, p. 174.

6 Showalter, 'Towards a Feminist Poetics', in Showalter (ed.), *The New Feminist Criticism*, pp. 129–31.

7 The term will be discussed more fully in its appropriate context in ch. 7.

8 Gilbert and Gubar, *The Madwoman in the Attic*, briefly discuss some of the female monsters in *The Faerie Queene* (p. 30).

9 Spenser, *The Faerie Queene*, II. xii.

10 See Daly, *Beyond God the Father*, pp. 44–68.

11 Gilbert and Gubar, *The Madwoman in the Attic*, discuss *Paradise Lost* and the intimidating effect of Milton's reputation on women writers (pp. 187–212).

12 Milton, *Poetical Works*, IV. 296–311 (p. 282).

13 See Larner, *Witchcraft and Religion*.

14 Dickens, *Great Expectations*, p. 439.

15 Ibid., p. 90.

16 De Beauvoir, *The Second Sex*, p. 187. Appositely, de Beauvoir also says that for men there is an 'alliance between Woman and Death . . . as the dreadful bride whose skeleton is revealed under her sweet mendacious flesh' (p. 197).

17 Dickens, *Great Expectations*, p. 113.

18 *Cymbeline*, I. v. 88.

19 Ibid., v. v. 263–4. It was presumably this loving docility that led the Victorian poet Swinburne to rhapsodize Imogen as 'the immortal godhead of womanhood'. Perhaps not surprisingly, given their idealization of woman as chaste and devoted, the Victorians particularly admired this play and an Imogen cult developed. The quotation from Swinburne is given in introduction to the Arden edition of *Cymbeline*, ed. J. M. Nosworthy (1955).

20 Ibid., I. v. 74.

21 Ibid., v. v. 48, 62–5.

22 Ibid., II. iv. 153–9.

23 *William Wordsworth*, p. 147.

24 'A Slumber did my Spirit Steal', *William Wordsworth*, p. 147.

25 The best-known, not to say notorious, example of Victorian idealization of womanhood is John Ruskin's, *Of Queen's Gardens* (1865). Coventry Patmore's long poem *The Angel in the House* (1849) was also very influential at the time. For a more realistic view of the position of women in Victorian England see John Stuart Mill, *The Subjection of Women* (1869).

26 George Eliot, *Middlemarch*, p. 858.
27 Fetterley, *The Resisting Reader*, p. xii.
28 Ibid., p. xx.
29 Milton, *Paradise Lost*, IX. 404–6 (p. 380).
30 Chaucer, *Complete Works*, ll. 1828–9, 1831–4 (p. 121).
31 Ibid.
32 Ibid.
33 James, *What Maisie Knew*, p. 8.
34 James, *The Portrait of a Lady*, p. xvii.
35 For more extensive discussions of the shaping of female destiny by literary conventions see Kennard, *Victims of Convention*; Abel, Hirsch and Langland (eds), *The Voyage In*.

2

Challenging the Canon and the Literary Establishment

'Mrs Leo Hunter . . . doats on poetry, sir. She adores it; I may say her whole soul and mind are wound up and entwined with it. She has produced some delightful pieces . . . You may have met with her "Ode to an Expiring Frog", sir.'
Charles Dickens, *Pickwick Papers*

Feminist literary criticism as a recognizable practice begins at the end of the 1960s with the project of rereading the traditional canon of 'great' literary texts, challenging their claims to disinterestedness and questioning their authority as always the best of *human* thought and expression. Inevitably, this critical appraisal soon extended to all other areas of the literary institution: literary criticism, literary reviewing, literary publishing and the teaching of literature in institutions of higher education and schools. Indeed, it can come as something of a surprise to recognize just how many people and just how much employment, status, prestige and money are involved in this complicated enterprise termed 'literature'. What has become clear is the interlocking, self-perpetuating functioning of these various areas. They are the means by which the prestige and authority of the canon of literature are constituted and sustained, and, in turn, this prestigious canon justifies and underwrites the existence of the literary enterprise – an enterprise, you will not be too surprised to discover, predominantly controlled by men.

Rereading Male Literary Criticism

Once women started to re-examine the works of canonical writers, it was not long before they began to reconsider the critical commentaries on them. What became immediately apparent was the gender blindness of a great many male critics, who usually assume that their perception of a text will be shared by all readers, even when the interpretation offered is restrictively masculine or even misogynistic. The universal reader, like the writer, is assumed to be male. This kind of criticism was dubbed 'phallic' by Mary Ellmann.[1] Moreover, the phallic critic frequently ignores ambiguities and qualifications in a literary text, so as to impose a unitary, closed meaning on its complexity or polyvalency – its multiplicity of meanings. In this way, phallic criticism works to police and recontain any challenge or danger a literary text may hold for a masculine or patriarchal system of values and dominance.

Probably the best-known example of phallic criticism is cited by Elaine Showalter from Irving Howe's praise for the opening scene of Thomas Hardy's *The Mayor of Casterbridge*. The hero, Michael Henchard, sells his wife and baby daughter at a country fair:

> To shake loose from one's wife; to discard that drooping rag of a woman, with her mute complaints and maddening passivity; to escape not by a slinking abandonment but through the public sale of her body to a stranger, as horses are sold at a fair; and thus to wrest, through sheer amoral willfulness, a second chance out of life – it is with this stroke, so insidiously attractive to male fantasy, that *The Mayor of Casterbridge* begins.[2]

As Showalter points out, 'It is obvious that a woman unless she has been indoctrinated into being very deeply identified indeed with male culture, will have a different experience of this scene.'[3] However, not only has Howe completely ignored the likely response of women readers, he has also, as Showalter goes on to say, distorted Hardy's text, imposing on it his stereotyped image of the wife as wholly hampering and constricting. His commentary slides away from Hardy's text to articulate a recurring male myth that women trap men into an enclosing and suffocating domesticity, which in effect 'castrates' their masculine energies and freedom.

However, phallic criticism is not always characterized by a desire to escape from women as guardians of a constricting domestic order. In *The Resisting Reader* Judith Fetterley analyses a wide range of male critical commentary on Henry James's *The Bostonians*. In the story an attachment between two female characters, Olive, an active campaigner for women's equality, and Verona, a younger more conventionally 'feminine' woman, is challenged and eventually vanquished by Ransome, Verona's male suitor. On reading male-authored criticism of this novel 'one is struck by its relentless sameness', writes Fetterley; Lionel Trilling's description of the atmosphere of the novel as 'suffused with a primitive fear', Fetterley says, could be applied with greater accuracy to the criticism of it.[4] What the male critics fear much more than Olive's campaigning for the women's cause is her relationship with Verona. Strong attachments between women, disinclining them to heterosexual marriage, are recognized as far more dangerous to the patriarchal foundations of society than any amount of political campaigning against specific inequalities.

Although the text itself offers no evidence of a sexual relationship between the two women, the male critics surveyed by Fetterley have no hesitation in assuming that Olive is a lesbian and once this assumption is made it seems the next obvious step for the phallic critic to define her feelings for Verona as unnatural, abnormal and perverted. This leads the phallic critics to their final melodramatic distortion of James's text: the projection of Ransome as a 'knight in shining armour, the repository of all that is healthy, sane, and good'.[5] Fetterley points out that what evidence there is of James's view of the relationship between Olive and Verona provides no support for this almost uniformly imposed interpretation of the novel.[6] His presentation may well have been influenced, she suggests, by his perception of his sister Alice's deep friendship with Katherine Loring whose feelings he characterized as 'a devotion so perfect and generous' as to be 'a gift of Providence'.[7] That male criticism consistently ignores the actual context of *The Bostonians* is, Fetterley argues, 'one more proof of the subjectivity of that criticism and of its inherently political nature'.[8] Male criticism operates a double-standard: it permits the indulgence of male fantasies of freedom and irresponsibility from a domestic order, while firmly outlawing the real threat to a patriarchal society posed by women's refusal of a heterosexual union as unnatural, immoral and perverted.

D. H. Lawrence's short novel *The Fox* also centres on a triangular relationship between two women and a man.[9] The young Canadian hero, Henry Grenfel, conquers his rival, Banford, a querulous woman who is dependent on the greater energies of her beloved friend March, by the simple expedience of killing her: he literally crushes her claims by felling a dead tree on her. The critic Julian Moynahan observes that the narrative is 'unusually successful in bringing the reader's response into line with Lawrence's own visionary perspective . . . When Henry Grenfel drops a dead tree on Jill Banford the reader reflects that the boy has merely employed one dead thing to sweep another dead thing out of life's way.'[10] Moynahan claims that the murder must be read as a triumph of life over death. Henry, 'a man with a gun rather than a man with a hoe',[11] is to be associated with the vitality of wild nature, as opposed to the domestic life of the two women on the farm: 'Henry Grenfel – "a piece of the out-of-doors" – penetrates the stuffy little world the women have made for themselves and hunts one down for life, the other for death.'[12] What assumption is Moynahan making about 'the reader' here? Is he articulating the male fantasy of escape from a domestic world which men fear as enclosing and restrictive of freedom, or is he imposing heterosexual order as natural, moral and healthy against the dangerous challenge of woman-to-woman attachment?

It's only fair to state that Lawrence's presentation of Banford is undoubtedly more negative than James's depiction of Olive in *The Bostonians*. Nevertheless, it is unlikely that many women readers of *The Fox* will react with Moynahan's nonchalance to the murder of Banford as simply the sweeping away of a 'dead *thing*'. It's inconceivable, I think, that a male critic would write in such complacent terms of the murder of a male character by a woman to facilitate her marriage to his best friend. What is even more striking about Moynahan's commentary is the way in which it manages to impose a unitary moral inter-pretation on Lawrence's more open-ended story, simultaneously indulging male fantasies of escape while reaffirming the rightful 'natural' order of heterosexuality. Henry liberates March from a 'stuffy', entrapping domesticity presumably only to replace her in a more subordinated but 'healthy' domesticity as his wife. Moynahan simplifies the ambiguities of Lawrence's presentation of the characters into a melodramatic conflict between life and death, apparently unaware of the grimly comic irony of his glorification of the man with the gun as a life-giving force. The women characters in Moynahan's interpretation are equally passive, simply objects to be hunted down and penetrated by the man with the gun. It does not occur to this critic that women readers of the novel or of his commentary may be less than willing to comply with this order of meaning. It is an order of that excludes the possibility of any alternative women's perspective or interpretation.

Even sympathetic male critics often stop short of, or swerve away from, any implications of an opposing order of meaning which their reading of a text might have led them towards. The character of Sue Bridehead in Thomas Hardy's novel *Jude the Obscure* has been the focus of much critical commentary. Hardy represents her personality as perplexing and resistant to easy interpretation. She is intellectually radical and iconoclastic, verbally scornful of repressive religious and moral codes, and disdainful of outdated modes of thinking. However, she is also fearful of emotional commitment, over-sensitive to criticism, and sexually repressed and repressing; she needs constant sympathy and affection from Jude but is unwilling to give freely in return. Her demand to live beyond moral conventions eventually collapses into a masochistic submission to the physical claims of her legal husband for whom she feels only revulsion. One way of perceiving her tragedy would be to understand it as a destructive inner conflict. Sue's internalization of a repressive moral code forbids, as shameful, any self-awareness of her own sexuality; she displaces that outlawed desire into an ardent intellectualism which, unable to recognize itself, inevitably folds back into rigid conformity at the threat of censure or punishment. That such blighting of life by internalized moral repressions is a constant theme in Hardy's work would lend support for such an interpretation of Sue's character.

Robert B. Heilman's sensitive reading of the novel leads him towards this perception. He regards Hardy's presentation of Sue as a 'remarkable feat of the historical imagination' in that the characterization suggests a conflict between idealism or spirituality and moral conventionality.[13] 'She is made a figure of Shelleyan idealism . . . with a strong infusion of . . . Victorianism'.[14] However, Heilman cannot follow up this insight by exploring what it would mean in terms of Sue's tortured sexuality even though the problem is at the centre of Hardy's novel. To do so, to Heilman's thinking, would be to deny the novel its tragic status. To consider Sue as a woman, he claims, would be to narrow her significance and thus restrict the meaning of the work. Hardy envisages Sue, Heilman concludes, as a bright but ordinary person who aspires to live beyond the bounds of community and convention but whose emotional strength is not up to her intellectual ambition: 'Sue does not have that vision', Heilman writes, 'she is everyman. She is everyman entirely familiar to us.'[15] By this swerve in critical logic Heilman forecloses the dangerous issue of female sexuality which the text clearly opens up, and reaffirms meaning as male. For him the text becomes fully significant only if we can interpret Sue as a kind of man. As Carolyn Heilbrun observes, 'There is no room for a feminist viewpoint . . . There is no male or female viewpoint; there is only the human viewpoint, which happens always to have been male.'[16]

We saw in chapter 1 that much writing by men implicitly expresses male anxiety about the power of women's sexuality and the need for men to retain control of this dangerous, unknowable force. Male criticism articulates a similar unease. The feminist critic Jacqueline Rose has pointed to a tradition of male criticism which functions prescriptively to insist that texts be valued in terms of their aesthetic coherence, censuring the texts in which excess of feeling, uncontrolled by the artistic form, produces an uncertainty or indecipherability of meaning. What is striking about such criticism is how frequently discussion of a work's aesthetic incoherence is displaced into a concern with the deviant or problematic sexuality of a central female character. Rose sees this prescriptive and moralizing tradition of criticism as originating in T. S. Eliot's influential essay on *Hamlet* (1919) in which he criticizes the play as containing an uncontrolled excess of emotion.[17] He claims that *Hamlet* fails to achieve aesthetic unity because the queen, Gertrude, is an insufficient cause for the intensity of emotion expressed by the hero. Just as Gertrude's sexual misconduct destabilizes the social and moral order *within* the play, so too her aesthetic incoherence produces a disorder of meaning *for* the play. Rose concludes that, for the ethical form of masculine criticism initiated by Eliot, the force of female sexuality inevitably produces a problem of interpretation: by its nature it exceeds the limits of male morality and knowledge.[18] Male critical readings frequently seem to attempt to control or to close off any threatening excess of meaning within literary texts, and to reimpose restricted masculine interpretations on potentially disruptive intimations of alternative possibilities. Their singleness of vision necessarily excludes women's sexuality as a knowable presence, which thus persistently returns as indecipherability of meaning or aesthetic incoherence. However it is perceived, it inevitably falls under the censure or censorship of the vigilant male critic. The perception of feminine sexuality as a subversive excess in texts has become an important idea for some French feminists, and this will be more fully dealt with in chapter 5.

If interpreted in terms of being a woman, the character of Sue

Bridehead cannot attain artistic significance for the male critic; she remains only a special case – even a pathological one. Sue can assume full meaning only as every*man*: only man can represent the human norm. In considering the work of female writers male critics use the same logic to deny, ignore or marginalize women's artistic achievement. Women writers are always regarded as special cases: writing is male, and women are always primarily women and only secondly writers. Ellmann has wittily summed up the predominant attitude of male critics: 'There must always be two literatures like two public toilets, one for Men and one for Women.'[19] Male critics, she says, always treat books by women as if the texts themselves were women, and thus they impose on them the same kinds of stereotypes that generally characterize thinking about women. Writing by women is accused of being formless, restricted, irrational, over-emotional and lacking in discipline. Ellmann concludes: 'In the criticism of women's writing, not even the word *hysterical* recurs as regularly as *shrill*. The working rule: blame something written by a woman as *shrill*, praise something as not *shrill*.'[20]

Arnold Bennett managed to find an even more unpleasant epithet to express his distaste for women's writing: George Eliot's style is *rank*.

Her style, though not without shrewdness, is too rank to have any enduring vitality. People call it 'masculine'. Quite wrong! It is downright, aggressive, sometimes rude, but genuinely masculine never. On the contrary it is transparently feminine – feminine in its lack of restraint, its wordiness, and the utter absence of feeling for form that characterises it.[21]

Joanna Russ, herself a creative writer, has also written amusingly, if more impressionistically than Ellmann, on *How to Suppress Women's Writing* (1984). If a work is undeniably good, she says, male critics attempt to attribute its excellence to the improving influence of a male figure close to the writer, like a father or husband. For example, serious claims were made for *Wuthering Heights* being the work of Emily Brontë's brother, Branwell. More generally, male criticism functions to exclude or to marginalize women's writing by censoring its permitted subject-matter ('no nice woman would write about such things'!) or by deeming its subject-matter to be insignificant, unrepresentative, unimportant and lacking general interest. As Virginia Woolf remarks, 'It is the masculine values that prevail . . . This is an important book, the critic assumes, because it deals with war. This is an insignificant book because it deals with the feelings of women in a drawing-room.'[22]

In *A Literature of their Own* Elaine Showalter provides scholarly documentation of the operation of a critical double-standard during the nineteenth century, which severely restricted the subject-matter that was open to women writers and then castigated their work for its restricted range. Showalter echoes Ellmann's claim that 'To their contemporaries, nineteenth-century women writers were women first, artists second.'[23] Negative male criticism of women writers, Showalter argues, justified assertions that writing by women was and always would be inherently inferior to or weaker than men's writing by associating it with essentialist views on female biology: 'When the Victorians thought of the woman writer, they immediately thought of the female body and its presumed afflictions and liabilities.'[24] Women's 'natural' creativity was seen as centred around child-bearing and child-rearing and their 'proper sphere' of action was held to be domesticity. There were constant insinuations by male critics that only those unhappy women denied family fulfilment needed to write and there were many solemn warnings that the mental excitement would seriously damage a women's always precarious physical and mental health. As recently as 1892 it was asserted that 'Happy women, whose hearts are satisfied and full, have little need of utterance. Their lives are rounded and complete, they require nothing but the calm recurrence of those peaceful home duties in which domestic women rightly feel that their true vocation lies.'[25]

We would like to think that such attitudes no longer prevail, that the work of women is now judged entirely on its merits without any regard to the body of its writer. However, consider this extract from fellow poet Robert Lowell's enthusiastic foreword to Sylvia Plath's final collection of poems, *Ariel*:

> In these poems written in the last months of her life . . . Sylvia Plath becomes herself, becomes something imaginary, newly, wildly and subtly created – hardly a person at all, or a woman, certainly not another 'poetess', but one of those super-real, hypnotic, great classical heroines. The character is feminine rather than female, though everything we customarily think of as feminine is turned on its head. The voice is now coolly amused, witty, now sour, now fanciful, girlish, charming, now sinking to the strident rasp of the vampire.[26]

There can be no doubting Lowell's genuine appreciation of Plath as an extraordinary talent. (The way he more 'customarily' thinks of women poets is revealed in the dismissive tone of 'certainly not another "poetess" '.) However, his comments continually blur Plath's person with her poetry and this [con]fused identity is persistently described in gender stereotypes even though it is 'hardly . . . a woman'. What does he mean by saying that this super-real, heroinic character is 'feminine rather than female'? Is he suggesting that the conjoined person/poetry has escaped the weakening attributes of the ordinary female body? For Lowell the poetry seems to be the spontaneous utterance of the mysteriously transformed actual woman, Sylvia Plath, into a mythic femininity, wild and imaginary.

What Lowell tells us nothing about is the merit of Plath's poetry as poetry − material words on a page − of her disciplined attention to formal arrangement, the hard-won precision of her language, the deliberate ambition and perfectionism with which she pursued her craft. The mythicizing and confusion of Plath's person with her poetry has continued in much critical commentary on her work.[27] Her remarkable poetic achievement is presented as a spontaneous, almost demonic articulation of a special, wild and non-rational feminine psyche. This mystifies Plath's hard-working commitment to making herself a good poet, while the mythicizing of her femininity makes her a special case, so that admiring her achievement in no way entails modifying the general assumptions about women's poetic capacity − their inherent status as 'poetesses'. A similar process of mythicizing, of fusing person and work, has been applied to Emily Brontë.

Not all women writers are fortunate enough to be regarded as special cases of *disembodied* femininity by the male critic. In an ambitious and influential study of literary criticism Geoffrey Hartman discusses only one woman writer among a galaxy of 'great' male authors (more on this below). He needs an example to illustrate what he sees as a puritannical refusal or 'fear of excess' in language. What better for this purpose than the poetry of Emily Dickinson whom all his readers know lived a secluded life and died unmarried. The aspect of Dickinson's poetic style that Hartman focuses on as sign of her denial of excess, her espousal of death, is her persistent use of the hyphen: 'Perhaps because it both joins and divides like a hymen . . . That hyphen-hymen persephonates

Emily.'[28] Hartman has no shame in this verbal violation; women's writing, as an extension of the female body, is an object to be grasped and mastered by the strong male critic.

There is, however, in Hartman's vulgar commentary on Dickinson an unwitting comicality which nicely reveals the gender blindness of many male critics. For them, writing by women is always 'women's writing', to be understood and evaluated in terms of the special case of their gender. Writing by men is just writing. Here, then, is a typical example of Hartman's style: 'What I am saying then – pedantically enough, and reducing a significant matter to its formal effect – is that literary commentary may cross the line and become as demanding as literature.'[29] What are we to make of Hartman's own stylistic addiction to the hyphen-hymen, his need to 'cross the line'? Following his own critical example cannot this be read as the mark of his castrated confinement within the sterile unwildness of male criticism, unable but desiring to cross the line into an imaginative realm of feminine creativity?

If writers of reputation like Plath and Dickinson cannot escape the perspective of gender in male commentary on their work, new or unknown writers face even greater difficulties. Margaret Atwood writes: 'A man who reviewed my *Procedures for Underground* . . . talked about the "domestic" imagery, completely ignoring the fact that seven-eights of the poems take place outdoors . . . In his case, the theories of what women ought to be writing about, had intruded very solidly between reader and poems, rendering the poems themselves invisible to him.'[30] Many women writers believe that their work is less likely to be reviewed than that of men, and that when it is, it is treated with less respect. They also complain that reviews frequently lump together work by women writers as if the common gender were the most significant thing about it, or that reviews of women's writing are placed on women's pages rather than on the general arts pages of journals and newspapers.

Reviewing Reviews (1987) by the Women in Publishing group provides a systematic statistical survey of the treatment of women writers by journals and reviews. Their findings, which are based on the monitoring of twenty-eight British publications – weeklies, monthlies, newspapers, general magazines and literary reviews – for the year 1985, substantiate many of these suspicions. An analysis of the length of reviews shows that in all publications except women's magazines men's books are accorded significantly more space. In the *Listener*, for example, the average ratio is

27 to 15 square inches in favour of men. The more important status accorded to books by men is underlined by more prominent positioning at the top of the page. In the *London Review of Books*, for example, men received top billing 100 per cent of the time; during the survey-year books by women were never placed first on a page. The relegation of women writers to a secondary position may be explained by the fact that most literary editors and reviewers are male. In all publications apart from women's magazines women reviewers make up under 30 per cent of all reviewers and share a parallel fate with the woman writer: reviews written by women are accorded a lower status in terms of length and position on the page.

This state of affairs produces a double bind for women writers. If they are reviewed by a male critic, which is statistically more likely, they may well suffer the kind of gender stereotying described by Margaret Atwood. A woman critic may bring greater sympathy and insight to the work, but a review by a woman may signal a lower status for the writer, as of limited interest and restricted appeal.

Recognizing a Male Literary Canon

Recently, the feminist critics Sandra Gilbert and Susan Gubar have suggested that despite serious discriminations against women writers, a perceived increase in the number of professional women writers since the late nineteenth century has provoked a crisis of anxiety among literary men, both writers and critics. One way in which they have attempted to defend themselves from the imagined threat 'involves the construction of a literary history that denies the reality of women writers . . . the emergence of modern male literary discourse, exemplified by theoretical and canon-forming works . . . can be seen as an attempt to construct *his* story of a literary history in which women play no part'.[31] In other words, the reverse side of the coin to regarding all women writers as special cases is a perception of a heroic tradition of literature composed entirely of a succession of great fathers and great sons. There are no mothers or daughters within the dynasty of the literary canon as constructed by male critics – the crown of greatness passes solely through a male line.

One canon-forming work that has become rather notorious in feminist literary criticism is Harold Bloom's *The Anxiety of Influence* (1973). This short but highly influential book claims to offer a new history of literature and a new critical practice based on it. Bloom argues that literary history must be seen as the struggle of each successive poet or writer against the influence of a strong precursor, of the need to appropriate or misread the work of the earlier writer so as to create the self as poet. He employs an epic language to describe the struggle: it is a 'battle between strong equals, father and son as mighty opposites'.[32] Throughout the book artistic creation is figured as a scene of warfare: Tennyson engaged in a 'long hidden contest with Keats', and Stevens in 'civil war' with the major English and American Romantic poets.[33] It is therefore hardly surprising (and, perhaps, we may feel, not even desirable) that none of Bloom's great warrior-poets are women. 'Poems are written by men', he affirms.[34] The only female presence admitted within his construction of literary *his*tory is the male poet's muse. It is here perhaps that we get the clearest glimpse of Bloom's implicit contempt for women: the strong poet's anxiety is that 'his word is not his word only, [that] his Muse has whored with many before him'.[35] Bloom's ultimate aim is to construct himself as heroic warrior in the contest of creation. Since poets make themselves by means of misprision (misreading), the difference between poetic and critical writing is only one of degree: 'There are no interpretations but only misinterpretation and so all criticism is prose poetry.'[36] Thus Bloom is able to enter the lists as a death-dealing hero of creativity. Needless to say, no women critics are recognized by Bloom as present on the battlefield of 'prose poetry'.

Another major canon-forming work is Geoffrey Hartman's *Criticism in the Wilderness: A Study of Literature Today* (1980). With the single exception of Emily Dickinson, Hartman constructs a literary and critical history of heroic male writers: Coleridge, Carlyle, Nietzsche, Yeats, Benjamin, Harold Bloom and Derrida form a male dynasty of writers driven by a sense of demonic excess in language. Hartman's ostensible aim is to rescue literary criticism from the academic wilderness; 'Unless we can find some doors . . . that lead from the humanities into society . . . the humanities are bound to become service departments to other divisions of the academy.'[37] His solution, which may seem paradoxical, is implied by the list of names in his pantheon (see above). Criticism must shake off its stylistic decorum and espouse the religious excess of literary language. The critic must become poet: 'Literary commentary may cross the line and become as demanding as literature.'[38] Whatever doors Hartman envisages this 'excessive' form of criticism opening, it is obviously not the door to the other half of the species. For Hartman women represent constraint as exemplified by Dickinson. The muse of the critical decorum that he deplores is 'more a governess than a Muse'.[39] It seems that, like many male critics, he is blind to the limitations of his own vision. 'The inspiring teacher of the humanities', he says, 'will always be pointing to something neglected by the dominant point of view, or something blunted by familiarity or despised by fashion and social pressure.'[40] But what kind of inspiration does Hartman offer to women students, women readers and women writers with his canon of creative excess which neglects and despises their very existence?

A greater questioning of the exclusivity of male literary histories seems to be promised by the title of *English Literature: Opening Up the Canon* (1979), edited by Leslie A. Fiedler and Houston A. Baker Jr. The introduction declares the aim of the text to be 'an attempt to escape parochialism', but it suffers from the same gender blindness. The range of social activity of human beings is conceptualized as 'economic man . . . and man at play'.[41] While the writer is no longer perceived as necessarily white, he is still presumed to be male: for the Yoruba writer '*his* knowledge of English includes the rules and relationships, signs and codes, that make the language suitable for *his* expressive designs' (my emphasis).[42] Tom LeClair's *The Art of Excess: Mastery in Contemporary American Fiction* (1989) continues the tradition of male canon-forming, as the title suggests, in the macho language of epic struggle and conquest. Writing in the late 1980s, however, LeClair cannot shrug off an uneasy awareness of feminist objections to such works, and rebukes those who in an effort 'to open up the historical canon [have] substitute[d] works of little reputation for former masterpieces . . . these canon revisers have created suspicion of contemporary male writers whose ambition is to master and attack'.[43] He includes a novel by Ursula Le Guin in his canon of masterworks, but not surprisingly, given his valorization of aggression and power, all the other masterworks he selects are by men. LeClair reveals his blindness to the gender assumptions governing his critical values with disarming ingenuity: 'I once asked Alice Walker . . . why women novelists didn't write like

Thomas Pynchon. Walker replied, "Why should they want to?" '[44] Indeed!

Is 'literature' something created by writers of ability and imaginative distinction or is it the product of literary criticism? The discussion so far suggests that it is at least partly the construction of the latter. It would seem that '*master*works' are selected and canons assembled not on genuine criteria of excellence, but on unquestioned gender assumptions and blindnesses of powerful male critics. Literary publishing and literary departments in institutions of higher education collude with the construction of literature as predominantly male. Major anthologies and course syllabuses feature a massive disproportion of writing by men compared to women. In a survey of 223 undergraduate literature courses in the United States, conducted between 1970 and 1976, the writer Tillie Olsen found the ratio of women writers to men to be 6 per cent to 94 per cent.[45] In a recent book *Canon and Contexts* (1991) Paul Lauter describes his similar survey during the 1980s of introductory American literature courses. Not only did women remain largely excluded from the syllabuses, but he also noted that a renewed resistance to change had emerged during the course of the decade.[46]

Tillie Olsen also revealed the absence of women writers in major anthologies used for undergraduate teaching and bought by the general public. Perhaps more than any other source, such anthologies construct the most generalized public sense of what constitutes 'literature'. Olsen found in her survey of anthologies a disproportion of 9 per cent of women's writing compared to 91 per cent of writing by men.[47] This figure agrees with the 8 per cent representation of women poets in anthologies given by Joanna Russ, who comments, 'What is so striking about these examples is that although the percentage of women included remains somewhere between five and eight per cent the personnel change rather strikingly . . . Elizabeth Barrett Browning and Emily Brontë bob up and down like corks, Edith Wharton is part of English Literature in 1968 and banished into outer darkness in 1977 – and yet there are always enough women for that five per cent and never quite enough to get much past eight per cent.'[48]

In Britain the situation is very similar. A detailed statistical survey of the main poetry anthologies from 1920 to 1980 reveals that women poets make up only 9 per cent of the entries.[49] The prestigious *Oxford Anthology of English Poetry* (1986) claims in its introduction 'to provide a representative sample of the main course of English poetry'.[50] Volume 1 (Spenser to Crabbe) contains four women poets out of the ninety-five poets represented; in volume 2 (Blake to Heaney) there are ten women poets out of a total of 112.

Challenging the Canon

Male control of the canon across every field of literary activity – criticism, reviewing, publishing and teaching – has been challenged in two major ways by feminist critics. As we saw in chapter 1 and at the beginning of this chapter, there has been and continues to be a large-scale programme of rereading male-authored canonical texts, male literary criticism of both women's and men's writing, and male constructions of literary history. The feminist poet and critic Adrienne Rich writes of this essential task in positive terms: it is 'Re-vision – the act of looking back, of seeing with fresh eyes, of entering an old text from a new critical direction – it is for women more than a chapter of cultural history: it is an act of survival. Until we can understand the assumptions in which we have been drenched we cannot know ourselves.'[51]

Alongside this work of re-vision, an enterprise of scholarly research aims to establish a women's tradition of writing which can be set beside the male-dominated canon of 'masterworks'. The forgotten and neglected writing of women throughout history is being rediscovered, reassessed and made available, to a wide readership, often for the first time. The work has been assisted by the development of women's publishing groups, which have also offered much support and encouragement to new women writers. In colleges, polytechnics and universities, largely due to student demand, courses are being offered in women's writing and women's studies departments have been established. The increased market for books by and on women has in turn stimulated the large publishing houses to produce women's texts and anthologies.

The vibrant concern with women's writing is the subject of the next chapter. Here, I shall simply outline some of the issues and problems raised by this second way of challenging male dominance within the literary institution. In our enthusiasm as readers, students and teachers for courses on women's writing and for separate departments of women's studies, we would be foolish, I think, to ignore the danger of tokenism and of the further ghettoizing of work by women. The perception of literature at its most significant, universal and aesthetically prestigious as a predominantly male preserve is not really challenged at all, while most writing by women retains its special-case status, relegated to specialist women's courses and departments. What is more, a 'women's studies' approach tends to detract from the specific literary qualities of a writer's work – of the writer as a Modernist, say, or a lyricist. This in turn limits and distorts our sense of Modernism and of lyric poetry, and promotes the prevailing construction of such genres as male. (See chapter 3 for a discussion of women writers and Modernism.)

It is only by insisting that women writers be included as part of the significant mainstream canon that we can begin to oppose the construction of literary history as an all-male dynasty. There has already been pressure in this direction. Most courses on Modernism, for example, now include a novel or two by Virginia Woolf and possibly even some poetry by H.D. (Hilda Doolittle). However, the method of increasing the number of women's texts within the canon by arguing for them on a case-by-case basis can actually function to strengthen male dominance. The few women who are included by this means are so outnumbered by male writers that they inevitably seem to be special cases – different or even odd. Moreover, their acceptance has to be argued for in terms of criteria of excellence that have been established for male writers. As Tom LeClair put it succinctly, it, 'why [can't] women novelists . . . write like Thomas Pynchon'? As we have seen, so-called criteria of excellence and aesthetic judgements are often no more than the gender blindness and prejudice of male critics. This is, potentially, one of the most controvertial issues in feminist literary criticism.

The token inclusion of one or two more women in the traditional canon simply underwrites a male aesthetic. This can be challenged only by insisting that many more texts by women be introduced. Since the canon in its practical manifestation as course syllabuses and anthologies is not infinite, this entails a head-on conflict with the existing literary establishment. As Lillian Robinson writes in 'Treason our Text: Feminist Challenges to the Literary Canon', 'There comes a point when the proponent of making the canon recognize the achievement of both sexes has to put up or shut up; either a given woman writer is good enough to replace some male writer on the prescribed reading list or she is not.'[52] But what is 'good enough'? Should the case for many more women writers be centred on equality of representation rather than on so-called excellence? There is a strong argument to be made that any literary or cultural history that ignores or excludes half of human experience is hopelessly impoverished. Although this line of reasoning has undeniable force, it would seem to lead in the direction of cultural rather than literary studies. This is not a direction that all feminist critics wish to take, for they want to remain literary as well as feminist critics.

However, the alternative line of approach, of establishing genuinely gender-free aesthetic criteria, is also fraught with difficulty. As we shall see in the next chapter, many feminist critics have argued that women writers encode their experiences differently from men, that their imaginative world is articulated by means of a different range of symbolism and imagery, and that their structures have been developed from different sources and traditions to those of male writers. How, then, can we compare unlike with unlike and do justice to the achievements of both sexes? Moreover, for much of history and in many cultures women have been denied a public voice, closed off within the private sphere. Should we not, therefore, include personal writing like letters and diaries as legitimate genres within the canonical tradition, and how, if we do so, shall we evaluate them alongside a work like Milton's *Paradise Lost*?

There is a further problem for establishing objective evaluations in that different readers respond differently to the same texts. How far do aesthetic criteria inhere in the texts themselves, and how far is excellence constituted by the cultural values and expectations that each reader brings to her or his act of interpretation?[53] Paul Lauter in *Canons and Contexts* claims that there exists a good deal of anecdotal evidence to suggest that students from diverse class and racial backgrounds respond quite differently to books such as *Daughter of Earth* written by a white working-class woman, and *Their Eyes were Watching God*, by a black woman.[54] The playwright John McGrath makes a similar point in relation to theatre in Britain. He insists that art is not universal, that so-called 'traditional' values of English literature are only an indirect cultural expression of the dominant class: 'I *do* believe that there is a working-class audience . . . which makes demands and has values . . . no less "valid" – whatever that means – no less rich . . . no thinner in "traditions" and subtleties than the current dominant theatre culture.'[55] Clearly, we could translate such comments into gender terms: women readers no less than women writers may encode and evaluate experience from within a tradition that is different but no less valid, rich or subtle than that of male readers. Their sense of what is a good book has a validity that must be registered as part of any adequate aesthetic value system.

However, Lauter's and McGrath's focus on class and race reminds us of a further problem for artistic evaluation. Women are not a homogeneous group; they, too, are divided by differences of class, race and sexual orientation. In 'Treason our Text' Lillian Robinson expresses disquiet that much of the research to establish a separate women's canon has drawn on 'a body of work whose authors are all white and comparatively privileged'.[56] Clearly, it would be a travesty of feminist aims if the writing of black, lesbian or working-class women were accorded only token or special-case status within a women's history of literature.

Is it a realistic project to attempt to find aesthetic criteria that encompass the merits not just of writers of both genders, but of many cultural experiences, values and traditions? And if we cannot, how are we to argue for the inclusion of some writers rather than others on our literature courses, in our published anthologies and our constructions of literary history? These are difficult, urgent and controversial question to which feminist criticism has as yet been unable to offer fully satisfactory answers. It is, however, largely due to feminist critics that the issues have been raised. I shall return to some of them in chapters 3 and 7.

Summary of Main Points

1 The rereading of male critics on canonical male-authored texts reveals a persistent construction of man-centred, reductive meanings.

2 Male critics marginalize women's writing by treating it as a 'special case'. They regard male writing as the norm, and women's writing as linked to their 'femaleness'.

3 Reviews of new writing by women reproduce this special-case marginalization of their work.

4 Male critics have constructed literary canons that exclude women writers from the history of literature.

5 The construction of literature as male by male canon-forming is reproduced in anthologies and syllabuses which massively over-represent male writing.

6 Establishing an alternative women's canon: there is a danger the special-case

status and marginalization of women's writing would be perpetuated if it were taught only within women's writing or women's studies courses.

7   Women's writing as part of mainstream literary studies: this brings the risk of tokenism and hence emphasizes the need to establish gender-free aesthetic criteria. How fully representative is a woman's canon?

Suggestions for Further Reading

Carolyn G. Heilbrun, 'The Politics of Mind: Women, Tradition and the University', in *Hamlet's Mother and Other Women*, pp. 213–26. The whole of the section in which the essay appears, 'Feminism and the Profession of Literature', contains interesting discussions in relation to topics covered in this chapter.

Lillian Robinson, 'Treason our Text: Feminist Challenges to the Literary Canon', in Showalter (ed.), *The New Feminist Criticism*, pp. 105–21. Probably the most useful coverage of the issues.

Joanna Russ, 'Anomalousness' and 'Aesthetics' (from *How to Suppress Women's Writing*), in Warhol and Herndl (ed.), Feminisms, pp. 194–202.

Dale Spender, 'Women and Literary Theory', in Belsey and Moore (eds), *The Feminist Reader*, pp. 21–33.

Notes

1   Ellmann, *Thinking about Women*, pp. 27–54.
2   Irving Howe, *Thomas Hardy*, p. 84, quoted in Showalter, 'Towards a Feminist Poetics', in Showalter (ed.), *The New Feminist Criticism*, p. 129.
3   Ibid.
4   Fetterley, *The Resisting Reader*, pp. 107–8.
5   Ibid., p. 109.
6   For an informed discussion of the attitudes to friendships between women in Boston at the time of James's novel see Faderman, *Surpassing the Love of Men*, pp. 190–203.
7   Fetterley, *The Resisting Reader*, p. 115.
8   Ibid.
9   In Lawrence, *The Ladybird*.
10   Moynahan, *The Deed of Life*, p. 199.
11   Ibid., p. 200.
12   Ibid., p. 201.
13   Heilman, 'Hardy's Sue Bridehead', *Nineteenth Century Fiction*, 20 (1965–6), reprinted in Draper (ed.), *Hardy: The Tragic Novels*, p. 211.

14   Ibid., p. 210.

15   Ibid., p. 226. For a male feminist reading of the character of Sue Bridehead in relation to critical accounts of her representativeness see John Goode, 'Sue Bridehead and the New Woman', in Jacobus (ed.), *Women Writing and Writing about Women*, pp. 100–13.

16   Heilbrun, *Hamlet's Mother and Other Women*, p. 177.

17   T. S. Eliot, 'Hamlet and his Problems', in *Selected Prose*, pp. 45–9.

18   Rose, 'Sexuality in the Reading of Shakespeare: *Hamlet* and *Measure for Measure*', in Drakakis (ed.), *Alternative Shakespeares*, p. 98. For an earlier, less theoretical, reading of Gertrude in the play, see Heilbrun, 'The Character of Hamlet's Mother', in *Hamlet's Mother and Other Women*, pp. 9–17.

19   Ellmann, *Thinking about Women*, pp. 32–3.

20   Ibid., p. 150.

21   *The Journals of Arnold Bennett*, comp. Newman Flower (New York, 1982), pp. 5–6; quoted in Gillian Beer, 'Beyond Determinism: George Eliot and Virginia Woolf', in Jacobus (ed.), *Women Writing and Writing about Women*, p. 96.

22   Woolf, *A Room of One's Own*, p. 74.

23   Showalter, *A Literature of their Own*, p. 73.

24   Ibid., p. 76.

25   Quoted ibid., p. 85.

26   Quoted in Ellmann, *Thinking about Women*, p. 33.

27   Rose, *The Haunting of Sylvia Plath*, examines the mythicizing of Plath, utilizing a biographical and theoretical approach.

28   Hartman, *Criticism in the Wilderness*, p. 126.

29   Ibid., p. 201.

30   Quoted in Olsen, *Silences*, p. 229.

31   Gilbert and Gubar, *No Man's Land*, vol. 1, p. 154.

32   Bloom, *The Anxiety of Influence*, p. 11.

33   Ibid., p. 12.

34   Ibid., p. 43. It must be said that elsewhere Bloom praises Dickinson highly, but she is not mentioned in this his most influential work.

35   Ibid., p. 61.

36   Ibid., p. 95.

37   Hartman, *Criticism in the Wilderness*, p. 288. Ironically, just before Hartman's book was published, Carolyn Heilbrun diagnosed a similar state of crisis in English studies but her proposal for 'Bringing the Spirit Back to English Studies' (1979) advocates the 'hope in the midst of this, a hope whose name is feminist, or women's studies' (*Hamlet's Mother and Other Women*, p. 175).

38 Hartman, *Criticism in the Wilderness*, p. 201.

39 Ibid., p. 175.

40 Ibid., p. 301.

41 Fiedler and Baker (eds), *English Literature*, p. xi.

42 Ibid., p. xii.

43 LeClair, *The Art of Excess*, p. 31.

44 Ibid., p. 30.

45 Olsen, *Silences*, pp. 186–9.

46 Lauter, *Canons and Contexts*, p. 8.

47 Olsen, *Silences*, pp. 186–9.

48 Russ, *How to Suppress Women's Writing*, p. 79.

49 Christine Fitton, 'From Reactive to Self-Referencing Poet' Jan Montefiore, *Feminism and Poetry*, also documents the exclusions operating in male constructions of the literary history of British literature in the 1930s (pp. 20–5).

50 Wain (ed.), *Oxford Anthology of English Poetry*, vol. 1, p. xix.

51 Rich, *On Lies, Secrets, Silence*, p. 35.

52 Robinson, 'Treason our Text', in Showalter (ed.), *The New Feminist Criticism*, p. 112.

53 Reader-response or reception theory has developed the idea of the reader 'writing' the text as she or he reads, but this has not so far incorporated a feminist approach. For introductory accounts see Terry Eagleton, *Literary Theory*; Selden, *A Reader's Guide to Contemporary Literary Theory*.

54 Lauter, *Canons and Contexts*, p. 160.

55 McGrath, 'Behind the Cliches of Contemporary Theatre', in Walder (ed.), *Literature in the Modern World*, p. 259.

56 Robinson, 'Treason our Text', p. 114.

Writing by Women

'If you please no references to examples in books. Men have had every advantage of us in telling their own story. Education has been theirs in so much higher degree; the pen has been in their hands. I will not allow books to prove anything.'

Jane Austen, *Persuasion*

Many years after that protest by Austen's heroine, Anne Elliot, Simone de Beauvoir made a similar statement: 'Women still dream through the dreams of men.'[1] More recently, the feminist critic Carolyn Heilbrun reread the classic story of Penelope, the wife of Ulysses, as a metaphor for the newly emergent woman writer. During her husband's ten-year absence after the Trojan Wars, Penelope kept at bay her clamorous suitors by unweaving each night the portion of her father-in-law's shroud she had woven by day, promising to choose one from among her many suitors when the work was finished. Heilbrun writes:

> I would like to suggest, Penelope is faced . . . with an as-yet-unwritten story: how a woman may manage her own destiny when she has no plot, no narrative, no tale to guide her. Imagining, inventing she weaves and unweaves . . . Why do I say Penelope is without a story. Because all women, having been restricted to only one plot, are without story. In literature and out, through all recorded history, women have lived by a script they did not write.[2]

In *A Room of One's Own* Virginia Woolf, too, made the difficulties of the emergent woman writer her main theme, outlining the insurmountable problems that would have faced Shakespeare's equally brilliant fictional sister Judith. There would have been the difficulties of lack of education, money and opportunity, of male hostility and, perhaps most serious of all, the absence of any nurturing female tradition. For, wrote Woolf, 'we think back through our mothers if we are women'.[3]

Actually, women writers have not been quite so non-existent as Austen, de Beauvoir, Heilbrun and Woolf all imply. Nevertheless, the concord of their views provides strong testimony to the near-invisibility of women's literary presence. Feminist research is steadily discovering and making available far more writing by women from previous eras of history and from a great variety of cultures. New anthologies and new editions of women's writing have made the presence of women's literary productivity an indisputable fact. This inevitably raises new questions for literary studies. How should we respond to all this women's writing? For what reasons should we welcome it? Do we need to develop new critical skills to read it? Is it essentially different from writing by men? These are complex issues, still the subject of debate. In the course of the chapter I shall outline some of the main responses of feminist critics.

Recognizing a Shared Tradition

First, then, what are the advantages of the availability of more writing by women? Catherine Kerrigan, the editor of a recent anthology of *Scottish Women Poets* (1991), states clearly one major reason for welcoming collections of women's writing. Often it is only when an individual female writer is evaluated within the context of a woman's tradition that her work can be fully appreciated: 'Although critics (including myself) have tended to treat the work of these women as minor ripples . . . I now believe that this interpretation is based on a failure to look at their work in the appropriate context . . . These poems need to be read – not in contrast to . . . a traditional male canon – but in terms of women's work and experience.'[4]

In a pioneering work of feminist criticism, *Literary Women* (1976), Ellen Moers set about bringing to light the submerged tradition of women's creativity, showing the importance of the mutual influence of woman writers on one another. She observes how appreciatively they listened to each other's voices and stories, an interaction little recognized in canonical histories. Moers traces supportive literary interrelationships between George Eliot and Harriet Beecher Stowe, and between Emily Dickinson and Elizabeth Barrett Browning, and recounts Charlotte Brontë's eagerness to meet Harriet Martineau as 'one whose works have so often made her the subject of my thoughts'.[5] She sums up the value of these literary intimacies: 'Each of these gifted writers had her distinctive style; none imitated the others. But their sense of encountering in another woman's voice what they believed was the sound of their own is, I think, something special to literary women.'[6]

This sense of encountering a felt kinship with another woman's voice is a more general reason for welcoming the increasing availability of a variety of women's writing. Women's stories help us live and dream as women. Many of the consciousness-raising groups of early feminism used female-authored texts to combat women's feelings of isolation and in-adequacy. Finding their own emotions, circumstances, frustrations and desires shared, named and shaped into literary form gave (and continues to give) many women, some for the first time, a sense that their own existence was meaningful, that their view of things was valid and intelligent, that their suffering was imposed and unnecessary, and a belief in women's collective strength to resist and remake their own lives. Writing by women can tell the story of the aspects of women's lives that have been erased, ignored, demeaned, mystified and even idealized in the majority of traditional texts.

In this short extract from Agnes Smedley's autobiographical novel *Daughter of Earth* (1929), the heroine Marie describes her mother's struggle to survive after her father deserted the family. Is it possible to recognize features and qualities of women's experiences articulated here which are not often found in canonical texts?

There were days when my mother did washing at home. She started with the dawn and the kitchen was filled with steam and soapsuds. In the afternoon her face was thin and drawn and she complained of pains in her back. I wrung and hung out clothes or carried water from the hydrant outside. She and I were now friends and comrades, planning to buy a washing machine as we worked. We charged thirty cents a dozen pieces for washing and ironing, but the women always gave us their biggest pieces – sheets, tablecloths, overalls, shirts, and generally they threw in the thirteenth piece just for good measure. Thirteen is unlucky, but for washerwomen it is supposed to be lucky – at least they thought so.

Our house was one mass of steaming sheets, underwear and shirts, and to get from one room to the other we had to crawl on the floor. We stretched lines in all but one sleeping room and we could afford a fire only in the kitchen stove. Each day Beatrice and I, beating our hands to keep them warm, ran along the railway track picking up coal that had fallen from passing engines, and after it was dark we 'snitched' as much wood as we could carry from a near-by lumber yard. At night my mother and I prepared a dinner of potatoes and a gravy made from flour and water, and sometimes flour and milk. We still had our cow, but we sold all the milk. We ate in silence about the kitchen table, and the air was laden with the smell of soapsuds. We never ceased dreaming of a washing machine to save her back from so much pain.[7]

What I like about this passage is the seriousness with which typically mundane and gruelling women's work is treated. Women as workers in some of the most lowly paid and despised jobs are rarely represented as a large part of a woman's story — even in the most realist of literary texts. Here we get an insider's account of the economics, the drudgery, the pain and even the smell of soap and laundry. This kind of near-invisible domestic labour, one of the few possible sources of family subsistence, has worn down the health and lives of countless women like Marie's mother. Secondly, as well as representing women as workers, the text avoids the attendant danger of presenting them as stereotyped victims, drawing on the easy pathos of helpless suffering. Marie's mother is being exploited, but Smedley's language communicates their resilient and humorous energy, their determined courage to prevail against hardship by their own wits, work and willingness to snitch as much wood as they could carry. The women are presented as refusing to accept passively an imposition of suffering as destiny.

Finally, it should be noted that this resilience of spirit emanates from a sense of community in shared work, pain and dreams. Marie and her mother 'were now friends and comrades, planning to buy a washing machine as we worked'. Perhaps the most persistent positive feature of women's writing is its recognition of the bonds of friendship, loyalty and love existing between women.[8] In this it strongly contests the many male-authored texts that have presented relationships between women primarily in terms of sexual rivalry and betrayal. Virginia Woolf recognized the representation of affection between women as a near-revolutionary quality in women's writing: ' "Chloe liked Olivia", I read. And it struck me how immense a change was there. Chloe liked Olivia perhaps for the first time in literature.'[9] Woolf suggests that the representation of women's mutual affection and trust 'will light a torch in that vast chamber where nobody has yet been'.[10]

The sense of solidarity with other women has led many women writers to feel the need to 'bear witness'; to use their work deliberately to testify to and protest against oppression and suffering inflicted on women by particularly brutal regimes or events. One example is the sequence of poems 'Requiem' written by Anna Akhmatova to give a voice to all the anonymous women who, with her, waited daily outside prisons during the years of the Stalinist terror for news of loved ones inside. The poems are a response to a woman in the crowd who recognizes the poet and whispers, 'Can you describe this?' Akhmatova writes: 'I see you, hear you, feel you./ . . . I would like to call them all by name, / but the list was taken away. . . For them I have woven a wide shroud / from the humble words I heard among them.'[11]

A similar sense of the need to testify against specific injustice impassions *Woman at Point Zero*, a powerful poetic novel by the Egyptian writer Nawal El Saadawi. The narrative bears witness, in fictional form, to a prisoner El Saadawi met who was condemned to death for killing a man after she had suffered years of victimization within a brutal political and religious system. In her introduction to the novel El Saadawi tells of how Firdaus 'vibrated within, me . . . until the day when I put her down in ink on paper and gave her life after she had died. For at the end of 1974 Firdaus was executed, and I never saw her again. And yet somehow she was always before my eyes.'[12] Despite the immediate ban on the novel in Egypt and several other Middle Eastern countries, it is now in its seventh printing in Arabic. Obviously, it is not only women who suffer oppression and injustice. What is perhaps distinctive about the need women writers feel to bear witness is the greater obscurity of the women victims they commemorate, and their willingness to speak out defiantly in a woman's voice in the predominantly male domain of politics and protest.

Of course, not all women's writing is a record of unacknowledged work and suffering; equally important is its power to celebrate. The novel *Song of Solomon* by Toni Morrison reconstructs the silenced history of black America. Unlike most official histories, Morrison's mythic and folk-tale form of history records the winding roots and routes from past to present of the lives of ordinary black people, and in her history women are central and powerful figures. Here is a passage from the novel in which a male character, Macon, looks in through a window at his rejected sister Pilate, with her daughter and granddaughter.

Again it gives expression to a sense of a woman's community based on closely shared affections and experience, but is it possible to recognize yet another quality associated with these women and celebrated by Morrison here?

> He turned back and walked slowly toward Pilate's house. They were singing some melody that Pilate was leading. A phrase that the other two were taking up and building on. Her powerful contralto, Reba's piercing soprano in counterpoint and the soft voice of the girl Hagar, who must be about ten or eleven now, pulled him like a carpet tack under the influence of a magnet.
>
> Surrendering to the sound, Macon moved closer. He wanted no conversation, no witness, only to listen and perhaps to see the three of them, the source of that music that made him think of fields and wild turkey and calico. Treading as lightly as he could he crept up to the side window where the candlelight flickered lowest, and peeped in. Reba was cutting her toenails with a kitchen knife or a switchblade, her long neck bent almost to her knees. The girl Hagar was braiding her hair, while Pilate, whose face he could not see because her back was to the window was stirring something in a pot. Wine pulp, perhaps . . .
>
> Near the window, hidden by the dark, he felt the irritability of the day drain from him and relished the effortless beauty of the women singing in the candlelight. Reba's soft profile. Hagar's hands moving, moving in her heavy hair, and Pilate. He knew her face better than he knew his own. Singing now her face would be a mask; all emotion and passion would have left her features and entered her voice.[13]

It's difficult to define precisely the quality Morrison is celebrating here. I think it is her sense of the creativity that women bring to everyday life; the capacity they have developed to bestow grace and a form of beauty on the commonplace. Morrison's trick is to narrate the scene from the point of view of a man, an outsider, and by this technique of estrangement allow us to perceive women's intimate creativity as if it were a magical charm or power. Virginia Woolf recognized and paid tribute to this 'intricacy and . . . power of highly developed creative faculty in women': 'Women have sat indoors all these millions of years, so that by this time the very walls are permeated by their creative force.'[14]

We saw, in chapter 1, that male-authored texts tend to construct female characters as passive objects of a masculine gaze, which is frequently voyeuristic and almost invariably judgemental. In such works women are taught to be ashamed of their own bodies, to deny their sexuality as unfeminine, unlawful, shameful. Writing by women can redress this balance, celebrating women's sexuality and articulating the pleasure and beauty of the female body without shame or apology. Here, then is the openly narcissistic conclusion of a short story by Bharati Mukherjee, 'The Wife's Story':

> In the mirror that hangs on the bathroom door, I watch my naked body turn, the breasts, the thigh glow. The body's beauty amazes. I stand here shameless, in ways he has never seen me. I am free afloat, watching somebody else.[15]

Most, if not all, women readers have probably felt the special pleasure of recognition that comes from finding their own feelings and experience given shape in literary form. That so many women writers choose to use autobiographical or first-person narrative no doubt facilitates the sense of reading as interpersonal communication.[16] Women readers as much as women writers seem to desire the sense of community that comes from 'encountering in another woman's voice what they believed [is] the sound of their own'. There are many obvious reasons why this should be so, and it seems likely that women will continue to come to writing by women with this need and this response. Any attempt to construct a feminist poetics has to recognize and accommodate this affective element in the reading–writing relationship of women.

However, it is equally important to recognize that there are serious questions to be asked about the approach to writing I have taken so far in this chapter. I have tended to imply that literary texts can be identified unproblematically with real life, that writing not only should but can tell it like it is. The underlying assumption is that words reflect reality, that language acts as an objective mirror to life. Such a view of language is most consistently maintained in the kind of writing known as 'realism'. The passage from *Daughter of Earth* provides a good example of realist writing: the characters are lifelike, believably shaped by social and personal circumstances; the events of the narrative are similarly credible, represented as a convincing sequence of everyday cause and effect; the language used and the syntax are unobtrusive, the self-effacing style preserving the illusion that what is offered is direct, unmediated access to real people and their lives. The autobiographical form seems the final guarantee that what we read is a true account. However, as we saw in earlier chapters, language is never a neutral transmitter of experience; it is always implicated in value systems. Works of literature cannot simply reflect. Of necessity they must select: there is always choice of details, words and structure, of what to put in and what to leave out, and that choice will inevitably stem from the writers' subjective perceptions and values.

Traditionally, a 'reflectionist' way of perceiving literature, as offering unmediated truth about human experiences, has functioned to make biased, even misogynistic, views seem universal or natural (to naturalize them), as just the way things are. An important reason for welcoming the increasing availability of writing by women is that it offers an alternative perspective, which frequently contests the demeaning or restricted thinking about women that has prevailed. However, to acknowledge this is to acknowledge that it is a perspective, a point of view, not guaranteed truth. No representation tells it as it is; all representation has to be seen as the site of ideological contestation – a linguistic space where opposing views engage in a struggle for dominance. The complex relationship of language and reality will be elaborated more fully in Part II.

Meanwhile, there is another problem in perceiving women's writing as simply reflecting women's experiences. For much of the time and in many places women have not been or have not felt free to tell it like it is. Even now, women writers in western democracies have to operate in a far from sympathetic environment. For earlier generations of literary women and for those living in many parts of the world the situation was and is even more difficult. Much of the scholarly work on women's writing conducted since the late 1970s has concentrated not just on establishing a separate tradition of women's writing, but also on answering two important questions related to the project. What were and are the problems facing women who want to write, and what literary and stylistic methods and techniques have they evolved or constructed to overcome these difficulties? We need to understand these probems in order to develop adequate ways of reading women's writing and of fully recognizing their achievements.

Reading as 'Gynocriticism'

Elaine Showalter, more than any other individual critic, has been responsible for encouraging the focus on women's writing which can be seen as the second phase of feminist criticism, especially in the United States. This is the positive critical project which she called 'gynocriticism' in opposition to the negative 'feminist critique' of male texts.[17] Her influential book *A Literature of their Own* (1977) traces the development of a tradition of women's fiction from the early nineteenth century to the 1960s. It pays detailed attention to many largely forgotten novelists who contributed to the rich pattern of women's developing consciousness of their craft of fiction. In the opening chapter Showalter writes: 'Having lost sight of the minor novelists, who were the links in the chain that bound one generation to the next, we have not had a very clear understanding of the continuities in women's writing, nor any reliable information about the relationships between the writers' lives and the changes in the legal, economic and social status of women.'[18] Showalter documents this process of women's literary history and their struggle for recognition as artists, and suggests that women's fictional writing can be seen as enacting three major phases in response to the changing cultural conditions in which they worked.

The earliest, most difficult, phase, which lasted for most of the nineteenth century, was characterized by male insistence on women's inferior creative powers in keeping with their frailer bodies. Showalter sees women's writing during this phase as generally imitating the dominant male modes and internalizing their aesthetic and social values. Typically, women writers adopted male names like George Eliot or signalled their acceptance of conventional attitudes by foregrounding their marital status: Mrs Gaskell, Mrs Craik, Mrs Oliphant. The late 1880s and 1890s saw the emergence of a more militant political consciousness among women, which Showalter considers as initiating the second phase of women's fictional writing. This was characterized by protest against prevailing attitudes and conditions, and advocacy of greater autonomy in women's lives.[19] This phase predominated from around 1880 to 1920, when the final phase of self-discovery began. At last, women writers were able to free themselves from reacting to patriarchal values and to turn inward, searching for their own independent female identity. Showalter calls the three phases 'Feminine', 'Feminist' and 'Female', and suggests that the Female phase has entered a new stage of self-awareness in women's writing since the 1960s. The categorization of the development of women's writing into just three phases is rather sweeping, and I shall return to more critical evaluation of her work at the end of the chapter. However, the value of her study lies particularly in her careful documentation of a previously unrecognized complex, continuously developing literary consciousness shared and enhanced by many women writers from the Brontës through to Doris Lessing. Showalter demonstrates the insights to be gained from reading women's writing within its own tradition rather than as isolated special cases.[20]

Sandra Gilbert and Susan Gubar's *The Madwoman in the Attic: The Woman Writer and the Nineteenth-Century Literary Imagination* (1979) quickly became another classic study of women's writing. Unlike Showalter, Gilbert and Gubar concentrate on the work of well-known women writers: Jane Austen, Mary Shelley, the Brontës, George Eliot and Emily Dickinson. They analyse the sense of anxiety and the debilitation and distortion imposed on women's literary productivity by masculine insistence that artistic creativity is male – the phallus equated with the pen – while female writing was inevitably linked to pathology and madness. Furthermore, when women writers looked to the most revered literary texts they could find only images of female monsters and whores or, alternatively, idealized figures of angelic submission.

Gilbert and Gubar follow Showalter in recognizing women writers' need, especially during the nineteenth century, to conciliate a suspicious and largely hostile patriarchal culture, but they develop further Showalter's suggestion that beneath this apparently conforming surface women's narratives may tell a different story – a woman's story. Women's writing, they argue, must be seen as constructing techniques of evasion and concealment, 'But what is this other plot? . . . What is the secret message of literature by women?'[21] Their answer is:

As we explore nineteenth-century literature, we will find that this madwoman emerges over and over again from the mirrors women writers hold up both to their own natures and to their own visions of nature. Even the most apparently conservative and decorous women writers obsessively create fiercely independent characters who seek to destroy all patriarchal structures which both their authors and their authors' submissive heroines seem to accept as inevitable. Of course, by projecting their rebellious impulses not into their heroines but into mad or monstrous women (who are suitably punished in the course of the novel or poem), female authors dramatise their own self-division, their desire both to accept the structures of patriarchal society and to reject them.[22]

Gilbert and Gubar take their title from Charlotte Brontë's *Jane Eyre*, in which the rejected mad wife, Bertha Mason, sets fire to the patriarchal home which has confined her. Recognizing this archetypal figure in women's texts as signifying confinement and revolt has proved an extremely productive way of decoding many other texts written by women has offered a productive insight into many texts written by women. It suggests a way of decoding women's writing to reveal hidden sources of creative imagination and subversive energy.

From this perspective even stories by twentieth-century writers may be found to conceal artistic rage beneath deceptively quiet surfaces. The American writer Eudora Welty, for example, appears to have little interest in articulating any overt feminist protest. Her stories, set in the small communities of Mississippi, are often told sympathetically from the point of view of a male character and seem concerned only with small-scale individual dramas. Welty herself has claimed that she writes only out of love and that anger is entirely absent from her creative processes: 'Of all my strong emotions, anger is the least responsible for any of my work. I don't write out of anger.'[23] However, in her narrative sequence *The Golden Apples* the central and key story, 'June Recital', focuses on a lonely ageing piano teacher, Miss Eckhart, who is rejected and eventually expelled by the narrow little community she tries to approach and conciliate. They cannot accept her unmarried status and independent life, and unconsciously they fear her artistic intensity, her visionary dedication to creative inspiration – the fire in her head. 'Cassie thought as she listened, had to listen, to the music that perhaps more than anything it was the terrible fate that came on her that people could not forgive Miss Eckhart for.'[24] Ostracized and finally cast out, Miss Eckhart secretly returns to Morgana, locks herself into the old music room and constructs an elaborate pyre around the disused piano. She is watched all the time by a young boy, Loch, hidden in a tree. Much of the narrative is from his uncomprehending boy's perspective:

> Her hair he saw was cropped and white and lighted up all round. . . . he could see how bright her eyes were under their black circling brows, and how seldom they blinked. They were owl eyes.
>
> She bent over painfully, he felt, and laid the candle in the paper nest she had built in the piano . . . The newspaper caught, it was ablaze, and the old woman threw in the candle. Hands to thighs she raised up, her work done.

Flames arrowed out so noiselessly. They ran down the streamers of
paper, as double-quick as freshets from a loud gulley-washer of rain. The
room was criss-crossed with quick dying yellow fire, there were pinwheels
falling and fading from the ceiling.[25]

Poignantly, even this final artistic inspiration of revenge is frustrated,
her flames quenched, but not before 'the fire caught her own hair. The
little short white frill turned to flame.' Welty claims to write without
anger, but nevertheless she acknowledges a sense of identity with Miss
Eckhart, the artist madwoman who returns to consume the framework of
convention and petty gentillity that smothered her vision and denied her
need for love.[26]

It is not just novels that can be read in the light of Gilbert and
Gubar's model of a conforming surface narrative concealing a hidden
plot of subversive female rage. It also offers a productive way of thinking
about a poem like 'Mirror' by Sylvia Plath.

Mirror

I am silver and exact. I have no preconceptions.
Whatever I see I swallow immediately
Just as it is, unmisted by love or dislike.
I am not cruel, only truthful –
The eye of a little god, four-cornered.
Most of the time I meditate on the opposite wall.
It is pink with speckles.
I have looked at it so long
I think it is a part of my heart. But it flickers.
Faces and darkness separate us over and over.

Now I am a lake. A woman bends over me,
Searching my reaches for what she really is.
I see her back, and reflect it faithfully.
She rewards me with tears and an agitation of hands.
I am important to her. She comes and goes.
Each morning it is her face that replaces the darkness.
In me she has drowned a young girl, and in me an old woman
Rises toward her day after day, like a terrible fish.[27]

Conventionally, the poem reads like a sad narrative of a woman's
process of growing old, moving inexorably and helplessly from youth

towards old age. The apparently dispassionate perspective and voice of the mirror allows us to watch the woman's tears and agitation as if from outside her situation. However, Gilbert and Gubar point out that in women's writing a mirror often serves as image of self-division – of a 'desire both to accept the structures of patriarchal society and to reject them'. There seems to me a rather irritating smugness conveyed in this mirror's tone of voice. Its boast of exactness and truthfulness, its rejection of emotion and its claim to godlike status suggests the voice of a judgemental patriarchy in which the woman strives to find an acceptable and accepted self-image. While the poem seems to distance itself rather complacently from the woman's anxiety and distress at her inevitable loss of attractiveness as she ages, what it actually constructs is a very unflattering sense of the male mirror. However, in the second part of the poem the brittle silver surface is transformed into a lake conveying a sense of hidden depths. In these 'reaches' the woman searches 'for what she really is'. Could it be an unconforming unconciliatory image of rage that she finds there, flashing up to the surface like a dangerous 'terrible fish'?

Gilbert and Gubar's ambitious sequel to *The Madwoman in the Attic* is a planned three-volume study entitled *No Man's Land: The Place of the Woman Writer in the Twentieth Century* (1988–). It is a project equal in ambition to the canonical works by male literary critics like Harold Bloom which we considered in chapter 2. As the title suggests, their study continues their detailed analysis of the interaction – frequently embattled but creatively productive – of male and female writers from the nineteenth century into the twentieth. Their focus is on Modernist literature and the anxieties and conflicts that have arisen in both literary men and women with the increasing influence and success of women entering the literary market-place.

They suggest that for women writers this success results in complex and ambivalent feelings. Unlike previous generations of literary women, twentieth-century female writers can look back on powerful precursors of the same gender. At last, literary daughters can think back through literary mothers. A female tradition has been established. Gilbert and Gubar use a Freudian model of psychic development to analyse the difficulties of choice this presents for women writers. They follow Freud in labelling this the 'affiliation complex', that is the need to identify either with the father or with the mother. Earlier writers, as Showalter argued, could identify or affiliate only with a patriarchal literary tradition, internalizing its values and seeking to imitate its forms. According to the Freudian model of maturation, this is the 'normal' path of psychic development for girls. Discovering that their mother, like themselves, has been 'castrated', they reject their first loving identification with her, turning instead to the father as source of potency and authority.[28] For nineteenth-century women writers the necessary paternal affiliation was, at least, uncomplicated; whereas for the modern woman writer, Gilbert and Gubar argue, the issue has become more troubling. The arrival of powerful literary mothers on the scene not only suggests for the first time the vulnerability of the once great literary fathers, but it also brings anxiety about the possible castrating power of the mother. Gilbert and Gubar write, 'we are now convinced that female artists, looking at and revering such precursors, are also haunted and daunted by the autonomy of these figures. In fact we suspect that the love women writers send forward into the past is, in patriarchal culture, inexorably contaminated by mingled feelings of rivalry and anxiety.'[29] Personally, I find this analysis of women's anxiety in the face of a female literary tradition, established at last, less convincing than the ideas in *The Madwoman in the Attic*.

Here is a poem from a cycle written by the Russian poet Marina Tsvetayeva to her older contemporary Anna Akhmatova, which certainly expresses ambivalent feeling towards its subject. Does it contain a sense of the self-divisive 'affiliation complex' in which the woman writer turns towards a maternal precursor for nurture and love, but with a strong fear of her daunting power?

From 'Poems to Akhmatova'

My hands grasping my head, I stand.
What of human scheming!
I sing, my head grasped in my hands.
In the dawn's late gleaming.

Ah, a violent breaker threw
Me to sixes and sevens.
I sing you, because we've one of you,
As we've one moon in the heavens.

Because a raven you flew into a heart
Piercing the grey clouds' blindness.

You're hook-nosed, and your anger's a dart
Of death, as is your kindness.

Because you covered with your night
My Kremlin's pure gold ringing,
Winding a strap around my throat
You choked me with your singing.

Ah, I am fortunate! Never yet
Has any dawn burnt fiercer.
I'm fortunate! Making a gift
Of you, I leave – a beggar.

And you whose voice – dark vertigo –
Drew all my breathing tighter,
I called you Muse of Tsarskoye Selo,
And first gave you that title.[30]

I think the idea of an affiliation complex can offer some helpful insight into what is a difficult yet passionate poem. There is a clear sense, even through translation, of admiration, even adoration, for Akhmatova's poetic power: its force of honesty pierces into the heart, its anger is 'a dart of death'. As the influence of the moon was thought to inspire poetic inspiration, even divine frenzy, so Akhmatova is like the 'one moon in the heavens'. The poem also suggests that Akhmatova has created the conditions that made Tsvetayeva's own poetic voice possible; it is the older poet's night that has produced the younger poet's day: 'Ah, I am fortunate! Never Yet / Has any dawn burnt fiercer.' Nevertheless, the praise and recognition of indebtedness is shadowed by a sense of fear and vulnerability in the face of Akhmatova's strength. The older poet's voice is a 'dark vertigo', drawing 'all my breathing tighter': 'You choked me with your singing.' However, despite the ambivalence, the younger poet is not finally overwhelmed. The poem ends with a claim in which both love and rivalry are completely fused: 'I called you Muse of Tsarskoye Selo, / And first gave you that title.' In effect, Tsvetayeva is saying, my voice – which you gave me – gave poetic identity to you.

So it seems that the notion of an affiliation complex can be a useful way of reading at least some writing by women. Nevertheless, it would surely be a disheartening paradox if all the scholarly work to establish a female tradition or canon simply replaced the sense women writers have of vulnerability and isolation within a male canon with anxiety and self-division in regard to newly recovered maternal precursors. What has happened to Moers's sense of the kinship responded to in another woman's voice? Is it so easily extinguished by rivalry and competition? Gilbert and Gubar's analysis of the affiliation complex is useful in warning against any complacent or over-idealistic view of the likely relationship between women writers. Woolf is probably right in saying that women think back through their mothers, but their influence is always an intensely complicated one and by no means always benign.

We also need to be aware of a powerful influence on the thinking of American feminist critics like Gilbert and Gubar: the influence of male precursor critics like Harold Bloom. As we saw in chapter 2, Bloom theorizes literary creativity as the outcome of a writer's antagonistic anxiety about a powerful precursor. It is the need to supersede or overcome the creative word of the rival that produces the new text, or, as Bloom sees it, a powerful misreading or de/re-formation of the earlier work. Gilbert and Gubar demonstrate how the anxiety women writers experience faced with a powerful male tradition, depicting alternative 'monster' and 'angel' women, has produced creative misreadings of those precursor texts to articulate hidden plots of anger, confinement, madness and self-division. A reading practice based on recognition of this sense of creative anxiety and antagonism at work in women's writing has taught us to approach their work with a responsiveness to its possible duplicities, tangential telling and techniques of concealment. Nevertheless, feminist critics should be wary of adopting too readily a poetics based on a masculine model of rivalry and competition as the mainspring of artistic energy. Moreover, there is a danger that a 'gynocriticism' that emphasizes the pathology of women writers' interaction with a patriarchal canon (or even a maternal one) in terms of self-division and madness becomes a poetics of suffering and victimization. We also need to ask whether there are other more positive ways in which women writers may respond to an intimidating male tradition of misogynistic myths and monstrous women that threatens the creative fire in their heads? Is there hidden laughter as well as anger, a subversive spirit of feminine mischief able to parody or appropriate or reshape male stories, masculine modes and forms?

Beyond Anxiety: Writing as Appropriation

The most obvious example of mischievous woman's laughter is the parody and mockery of Virginia's Woolf's *A Room of One's Own*, originally delivered as two lectures at the new women's colleges of Newnham and

Girton. Throughout, Woolf adopts a tone of mock humility and reverence towards the institutions and traditions of the male colleges in order to make fun of their patriarchal assumptions of authority and knowledge. She begins by describing her encounter with this world of privileged elitism as she is chased back on to the gravel path by an indignant beadle who has found her venturing on to the smooth turf preserved for the feet of Fellows and Scholars. Finding herself in the enclosed quadrangles of 'ancient halls', she notes with subversive innocence how 'the roughness of the present seemed smoothed away; the body seemed contained in a miraculous glass cabinet through which no sound could penetrate and the mind [was] freed from any contact with facts'.[31] She parodies the erudite forms of discourse nurtured in these academic glass cabinets, playing games with scholarly footnotes and learned references. However, even while she thus mocks time-honoured pedagogic forms, her references and statistics are aimed at bringing those minds long 'smoothed' and 'freed from any contact with facts' sharply up against the rough justice of women's economic and social inequality.

Coincidentally, another female wolf in sheep's clothing, the German writer Christa Wolf, has also appropriated and reshaped the prestigious lecture form as it is associated with notions of authoritative impersonal veridical discourse. In 1982 Wolf was awarded a guest lectureship at the University of Frankfurt where she was asked to give five 'Lectures on Poetics'. She began the series with a parodic adoption of the 'lecture' tone only to deny its claims to authority: "Ladies and gentlemen: This enterprise bears the title "Lectures of Poetics" but I will tell you at once that I cannot offer you a poetics. One glance at the *Classixcal Antiquity Lexicon* was enough to confirm my suspicion that I myself had none.'[32] She goes on to assert her need to take 'a personal approach' and to 'employ various subjective forms of expression'.[33] The 'subjective forms' she deploys to appropriate the lecture form to a woman's voice and purpose are two informal travelogues recounting her personal responses to leaving the German Democratic Republic for the first time to visit Greece; a series of work-diary extracts 'about the stuff life and dreams are made of'[34] which form an intricate interweaving of her thoughts on daily domestic occurrences, international politics (the arms talks) and past history (the Trojan Wars, Minoan culture); and a letter to a friend similarly inclusive, richly allusive and open-ended. The final and fifth lecture is in the form of a draft for a novel called *Cassandra*.

Cassandra in its turn becomes another mode of appropriation, for in it Wolf reshapes the classic myths of the fall of Troy, refocusing them imaginatively from the feminine perspective of Cassandra, the Trojan princess and prophet punished for disobedience to Apollo with the woman's fate of being always disbelieved as mad. The first-person narrative Wolf uses is intensely subjective so that readers are drawn wholly into Cassandra's position, made to feel the impassioned powerlessness of a woman's voice and vision mocked and disregarded in a world dominated by male violence, war and power politics.

I shall return to women's use of parody and appropriation in chapter 6, but as a final example of a woman writer's audacious trespassing on the turf of revered male precincts, seizing sacred myths as her own literary space, let us look again at Eudora Welty's *The Golden Apples*. Welty takes a poem by one of the great male figures of twentieth-century poetry, W. B. Yeats's 'The Song of Wandering Aengus', and weaves its lines and images in and out of her own prose. Yeats's poem uses an Irish myth to represent the familiar literary notion of the male poet haunted by his muse in tantalizing female form. Aengus driven by a creative 'fire . . . in [his] head', hears his name called by 'a glimmering girl' who then 'faded through the brightening air'. Thus begins his lifelong poetic quest, wandering in search of this glimpsed vision of beauty, determined at last to pluck 'The silver apples of the moon, / The golden apples of the sun'.

The implicit question that runs through Welty's series of stories is: what happens when it is a heroine and not a hero who is driven by a creative impulse? What happens when the 'glimmering girl' herself has the fire in her head – a girl who will not easily be allowed the freedom to spend her life in wandering after visions? Throughout *The Golden Apples* we glimpse these glimmering girls fading into the air because, as the boy Loch notes of Miss Eckhart's doomed fire, 'What she really wanted was a draught . . . let her try to make fire burn in that airless room. That was the conceited thing girls and women would try.'[35] Welty seizes the beauty and poignancy of Yeats's poem and reshapes it into a sense of wonder and pain for the spirit of poetic freedom and vision which kindles in her series of heroines only to fade, extinguish and then flicker into brightness all over again.

Welty's image of the resilient fire of the female imagination may be a more apt metaphor for the creative energy of women writers than that of the madwoman in the attic. As understanding and knowledge of women as writers increases it becomes clear that, despite all the difficulties of their position and all the obstacles in their way, their productivity and artistic invention has consistently resisted confinement. A recent study by Jane Spencer, *The Rise of the Woman Novelist* (1986), provides a good example of how even the apparently most conservative forms may be put to progressive purposes in the hands of women writers. At first sight the didactic narratives developed during the eighteenth century, dealing with the reformation of an initially wayward heroine who is brought to see the folly of her unconventional or 'unfeminine' views would seem wholly complicit with patriarchal authority, typical examples of Showalter's phase of internalization and imitation of male values. However, Spencer argues convincingly that these female-authored works not only produced some of the novel's most impressive formal achievements, but also contain implications which undermine their overt moral conservatism.

Although a plot tracing the heroine's gradual development of self-awareness, as she learns the error of her earlier vanity and foolishness, usually by means of earnest moral guidance from her future husband, enacts a message of submissive conformity, it also brought about an increasing artistic concern with the heroine's inner consciousness. Spencer demonstrates that the psychological realism that became the central and celebrated feature of the nineteenth-century novel was almost entirely the achievement of a tradition of women novelists. This tradition reached its maturity in the work of Jane Austen. The construction of the heroine's inner life as complex, discriminating and sensitive was at odds, even if only implicitly, with commonly held assumptions of the time which denied women any responsibility in the choice of marital partner and insisted on the inherent inferiority of the female mind. Spencer writes, 'The tradition of the reformed heroine, however much its basic fable worked in the opposite direction to feminist protest, did contain the implicit assumption that women's moral growth was both more important and interesting than had usually been thought . . . [Emma] is the first character in English fiction, male or femal, to have a moral life so richly created yet ironically analysed. Characterisation of men in the novel only reached a comparable level after Austen's example had shown the way.'[36]

As Spencer's study demonstrates, eighteenth-century women novelists, many of whom are now forgotten, played a central role in developing the complex sense of inner psychology that for many readers is the finest achievement of nineteenth-century realist fiction. Such novels aim to represent the detailed interaction of the moral and psychic development of the central characters with their determining social world. However, for this very reason, realist form has to stay within the bounds of the actual if it is to maintain its illusion of being true to life. For the female writer this can present problems: since the actuality of women's lives has been restricted in range, so too must be the experience allowed to the heroine of a realist novel. The problem is even more acute for a woman writer who wants to suggest alternative destinies and different modes of existence for women. For this reason the tradition of romance has always attracted women writers as offering a licensed evasion of confining conventions.

In contrast to the claims of realism, the romance and gothic traditions have always espoused magical transformations of identity, narrative leaps in space and time, and an interest in the irrational, the passionate and the violent. Early women novelists, like Ann Radcliffe and even Emily Brontë, may have utilized the popular form of the gothic novel because it afforded them fictional space to explore extremes of obsessive emotion otherwise forbidden to both heroines and their female authors. In *Literary Women* Ellen Moers makes an intriguing case for seeing Mary Shelley's gothic novel *Frankenstein* as a covert exploration of the feelings of pain and horror women may experience in childbirth which can find no legitimate expression within the sanitized and idealized discourse of maternal love. Shelley was only 16 when she gave birth to an illegitimate daughter. Premature and sickly, it lived for a month by which time she was again pregnant. Moers writes, 'It is in her journals and her letters that Mary Shelley reveals the workshop of her own creation, where she pieced together the materials for a new species of romantic mythology. They record a horror story of maternity of the kind that literary biography does not provide again until Sylvia Plath.'[37]

Moers also points out the more positive attraction offered by the exotic settings of many gothic romances for women writers whose own freedom of movement was often severely restricted.[38] This transformational removal from the familiar domestic world continues to exert a strong attraction for women writers and not only as the exotic background favoured by popular romance fiction of the Mills and Boon type. Serious women writers also resort to it to construct utopian fictions, often feminist-inspired, in which to explore wholly new possibilities of female destiny. Women writers like Marge Piercy, Margaret Atwood, Doris Lessing and Ursula Le Guin have turned to non-naturalist genres such as science fiction and fantasy to free themselves from the limitations of realist plots and characterization. In her book on *Doris Lessing* (1989) Jeannette King traces Lessing's growing dissatisfaction with the restrictions that realist conventions imposed on her ability to explore and realize alternative women's stories, and her movement towards forms of science fiction to find greater freedom for her artistic vision. In these ways women writers have had an important influence in breaking down some of the restrictive boundaries between high and popular culture, challenging some of the hierarchical divisions within the league table of canonical literature.

Feminist critics, too, have pioneered eclecticism in literary studies. They have brought serious critical attention to gothic and romance genres; they have insisted on the imaginative energy of writers like Louisa May Alcott and Harriet Beecher Stowe, who were previously disdained by male critics despite or even because of their record-breaking sales.[39]

As this chapter suggests, feminist critics' endeavour to establish and analyse a women's tradition of writing tended to look first to the novel genre. There are two obvious reasons for this. The early concern of feminist criticism with male representations of women made it natural to look to novels and short stories by women for positive counter-images of women's lives. More importantly, the novel seemed to be the literary form women writers first and most successfully made their own. There was already a great tradition of women writers there – Austen, the Brontës, George Eliot – for feminist critics to build on, largely because, as a relatively new genre, the novel was the least prestigious of literary forms. Without classical origins, it was regarded for most of the eighteenth century and even into the nineteenth as mainly suited for the light entertainment of women readers. Thus there was less resistance to women taking up this literary form than any other. Woolf also suggests a more positive reason: 'All the older forms of literature were hardened and set by the time she became a writer. The novel alone was young enough to be soft in her hands – another reason perhaps why she wrote novels.'[40]

Appropriating the Poetic Tradition

It now seems likely that this view of women's literary history will need revision. Further research is revealing that women have been equally involved, if even more out of sight, in the long history of poetry, especially in the poetic traditions associated with spoken or sung forms – with orality: ballads, children's rhymes, charms, riddles and folk-songs.[41] More work in this area seems likely to show not just the centrality of women to these forms, but also the way in which the oral tradition has functioned as a regenerative source of imaginative vitality for the more prestigious forms of national literature. Women writers at least up to the time of Woolf were made to feel disadvantaged, even inadequate, due to their lack of a classical education. In *A Room of One's Own* Woolf expresses her sense of unjust denial through her suppositious account of the fate of Shakespeare's gifted sister Judith: 'She was as adventurous, as imaginative, as agog to see the world as he was. But she was not sent to school. She had no chance of learning grammar and logic, let alone of reading Horace and Virgil.'[42] Yet despite men's advantaged access to the rich heritage of classical literature, what we frequently sense in reading Spenser, Shakespeare, Milton, Wordsworth and most of the notable male poets is the presence in their work of the imaginative vitality of a popular oral tradition – a tradition that may have been shaped, nurtured and renewed by invisible women poets.

Many of the ways of reading women's writing considered so far can apply to poetry as well as to prose. Are there any specific problems, though, facing women as poets?[43] I think the answer is implied in what Woolf says on women's exclusion from a classical education. Poetry has always been accorded a privileged status and function as a high language within western culture. More than any other genre, poetry is associated with notions of literature as universal, as the form most suited to the lofty treatment of the great and timeless human themes. Women have undoubtedly found it particularly intimidating to claim entry into this elevated discourse.[44] In many cultures, including western ones, public rhetorical forms have been perceived as a male preserve, while women's speech has been restricted to the domestic and private spheres.[45] This linguistic division increases women's sense of distance from the 'universal' language of poetry. One woman poet who consistently and fearlessly breached the barrier of 'high' culture was Elizabeth Barrett Browning, especially in her epic poem *Aurora Leigh*. In her introduction to the poem Cora Kaplan writes: 'In the first person epic voice of a major poet, it breaks a very specific silence, almost a gentlemen's agreement between women authors and the arbiters of high culture in Victorian England, that allowed women to write if only they would shut up about it.'[46] *Aurora Leigh* made it impossible to claim that women cannot attain an epic voice and vision; it is considerbly longer than *Paradise Lost*, takes on Wordsworth's great personal theme of the making of the poet's mind from a woman's perspective and speaks out passionately on the great public debates of the time.

We saw in chapter 1 that the so-called universality of poetic language not infrequently elevates the expression of an exclusively male-centred view. Even when the male poet deliberately sets out to write in praise of a woman, the female figure constructed is usually a passive one, serving either as muse or functioning narcissistically to mirror back a sense of the poet's sensibility, the intensity of *his* emotions, the fineness of *his* judgements and the anguish of *his* loss. Nowhere is this more evident than in the celebrated tradition of love poetry. This too causes considerable problems for the woman poet. How is she to inhabit the linguistic space of the 'I' who speaks the poetic discourse of love? Again, Elizabeth Barrett Browning not only refused to be daunted by the challenge; she appropriated the most prestigious of all forms of love poetry – the sonnet – to speak of her passion.

Here is one of her *Sonnets from the Portugese*. It might be interesting to read it bearing in mind the discussion of Wordsworth's 'Lucy' poem in chapter 1. Does Barrett Browning's language foreground *her* sensibility and subjectivity as poet-lover rather than the presence of Robert Browning as the subject of the poem and one who is loved?

Sonnet XXIX

I think of thee! – my thoughts do twine and bud
About thee, as wild vines, about a tree,
Put out broad leaves, and soon there's nought to see
Except the straggling green which hides the wood.
Yet, O my palm-tree, be it understood
I will not have my thoughts instead of thee
Who art dearer, better! Rather, instantly
Renew thy presence; as a strong tree should,

Rustle thy boughs and set thy trunk all bare,
And let these bands of greenery which insphere thee
Drop heavily down, – burst, shattered, everywhere!
Because in this deep joy to see and hear thee
And breathe within thy shadow a new air,
I do not think of thee – I am too near thee.[47]

The poem expresses a consciousness of this danger of poetic egoism in
love poetry. Barrett Browning castigates her thoughts (the poem) as a
'straggling green' vine whose wild twining and budding risks obscuring
the stronger beauty of the tree. She invokes the 'presence' of 'thee / Who
art dearer, better' in place of her poem. If Robert Browning is perceived
as male muse to female poet, then it is in reversal to the usual relation of
poet to muse. This muse gives such 'deep joy' to the poet that his
presence puts a stop to poetic inspiration: 'I do not think of thee – I am
too near thee.'

But does this escape the egoistic assertion of self as lover that is
characteristic of male love poetry only by conforming to a stereotypical
feminine submissiveness? Does Barrett Browning take masochistic pleasure in expressing her subservience and inferiority to her lover, Robert
Browning. I think this is to ignore the confident tone of the poem, the
imperatives she addresses to the loved one: 'be it understood / I will not
have', 'Rather, instantly / Renew thy presence'. These are not the words
of a submissive and passive woman but of an authoritative poet. There is
also an almost overt declaration of joyful feminine eroticism and orgasm:
'Rustle thy boughs and set thy trunk all bare, / And let these bands of
greenery which insphere thee / Drop heavily down, – burst, shattered,
everywhere!' Finally, we should note the implicit self-humour of the
poem. Although it deprecates its 'wild vines' of words which threaten to
hide the loved one's presence, that presence is, of course, constructed
entirely by those words. Moreover, the 'straggling green' is pruned by
the poet into that most disciplined of forms, a sonnet. Angela Leighton,
to whose excellent chapter on Barrett Browning's love poetry I am
indebted, writes:

Thus for all their self-abasement, the *Sonnets* betray a knowledge of the
power of their own writing. Barrett Browning knows that to be mistress
of 'the power at the end of my pen' is to enter into a political game of

subject and object in which the one is gained at the other's expense. For all her protestations, she does not, in *practice*, give up her woman's right to speak.[48]

Moers claims that with her Portugese sonnets sequence Barrett Browning empowered a rich tradition of women's poetry: 'All the way to Anna Akhmatova and beyond, the tradition of women's love poetry appears dominated by the creative presence of Mrs Browning.'[49]

Since the early twentieth century another prestigious literary tradition has been asserting its claim to a universal and impersonal language of poetry. This is the avant-garde tradition of Modernism, particularly as expounded by T. S. Eliot in his highly influential essay 'Tradition and the Individual Talent', in which he declared that the true poet must write not from personal feeling but from an awareness of 'the mind of Europe', a historical consciousness which 'abandons nothing *en route*, which does not superannuate either Shakespeare, or Homer, or the rock drawing of the Magdalenian draughtsmen'.[50] Eliot, critics claim, achieved the impersonal voice of history in the innovative form of his poem *The Waste Land*, largely by means of his use of classical and literary allusion and personae. In *No Man's Land* Gilbert and Gubar argue that Modernist writers like Eliot, Ezra Pound and James Joyce constructed ideological notions of history and culture as a reaction to their fears of women writers. The Modernists' insistence on the 'impersonality' of the poet elevates as universal a male tradition which excludes women from 'the mind of Europe'. Eliot's allusions, for example, are drawn entirely from a male canon – Shakespeare, Spenser, Dante, St Augustine, Greek myth – to construct a tradition that is elitist and patriarchal.

However, as we have seen with the novel form, women writers are as likely to challenge and appropriate male traditions as to be intimidated by them. As readers of women writers we have to be ready to recognize the scale and ambition of women's literary projects, because they may not always make those claims for themselves. For example, the Guyanese poet Grace Nichols has written cycles of poems with titles like *i is a long memoried woman*, *Fat Black Woman's Poems*, *Lazy Thoughts of a Lazy Woman*. What such titles might suggest to feminist critics is that Nichols is constructing personae. In this case, each cycle of poems should be read as an interconnected whole, perceived as a dramatic articulation of a collective culture, the interwoven tragic history of the Caribbean, the resilience, laughter and anger of black women who were once slaves. To read one or two anthologized poems outside the context of the whole sequence inevitably diminishes their full resonance. Only by recognizing the cultural stakes of a poet like Nichols can we read her work with the same degree of attentiveness demanded by male writers like the Caribbean poet Derek Walcott, who overtly claims his place in the Modernist canon, outdoing even Eliot in his use of arcane allusion.

In her poem 'Culture and Anarchy' Adrienne Rich challenges Modernism more overtly than Nichols. Its title alludes ironically to Matthew Arnold's work of that name, and sets out to reverse Arnold's elevation of high culture over what he termed the 'anarchy' of those excluded from its privileges. Eliot's view of 'culture' as represented in *The Waste Land* reproduces Arnold's traditional values; his allusions to history, myth and literature are represented as fragments of the lost greatness, contrasted nostalgically with a tawdry present. Rich's use of allusions draws on the imagery of quilting. In her poem, in contrast to Eliot and Arnold, the past is stitched lovingly and creatively into the present by a womanly craft, like that of the old 'Alabama woman still quilting in her nineties'. Whereas Eliot's allusions are to great canonical figures, Rich's fragments are from the silenced and excluded history of women; from those 'records usually not considered / of sufficient value to be / officially preserved'. The tradition this poem elevates is 'THE HISTORY OF HUMAN SUFFERING: borne, / tended, soothed, cauterized, / staunched, cleansed, absorbed, endured / by women'.[51]

The image of Penelope turns out to be most apposite for the woman writer, encompassing as it does the endless resourcefulness, productivity, cunning and daring of literary women. Working within an unsympathetic cultural tradition, women writers have turned their very anger into a source of creativity, have laughed away the female monsters threatening them in male texts, wittily reshaped male canonical forms, reworked old myths, turned apparent conformity into artistic innovation and boldly challenged high culture on its own ground. We read women writers adequately by recognizing and responding fully to these multiple achievements.

A Woman's Aesthetic?

In this chapter I have outlined some answers to the questions raised at the beginning: why should we welcome the increasing availability of women's writing and what kinds of reading practices should we bring to it? The field is still a very productive one within feminist critical writing and I can offer only a selective survey of all the work currently published on the subject. However, I have not as yet addressed the final question: is writing by women essentially different from writing by men? Our discussion has suggested aspects of style, form and theme to look for in women's writing. Are these to be seen as constituting an inherent and identifiable female aesthetic, or should they be regarded more as an oppositional aesthetic? Are the literary qualities discussed in this chapter the kind of strategies we would expect to find in the literature of any subculture responding to a largely hostile dominant group, even though in the case of women the subculture is half the human species? The answer to this question has to be yes, I think. What we have been noting in this chapter are literary forms, themes and preoccupations that are more accurately perceived as an aesthetics of opposition than features universally and eternally present in women's writing.

There have been attempts to construct an essentially female aesthetics on intimate and exclusive female experience and biology, for example themes like childbirth, breast-feeding, menstruation, rape and sexual violation. The problem is that it tends to reproduce a female aesthetic as an aesthetic of suffering.[52] It also produces an over-emphasis on content as opposed to style and form. A more interesting line of approach has been the linking of women's imagery to the female body. Kaplan has pointed to recurrent images of menstruation in *Aurora Leigh*, an imagery that is also predominant in the poetry of Sylvia Plath. Women writers' frequent use of sea and tidal imagery has likewise been linked to their experience of menstrual cycles. Moers draws attention to the frequency with which secret and symbolic landscape is associated with the female body in women's texts, as for example Maggie Tulliver's attachment to the 'Red Deeps' in *The Mill on the Floss*. From analysing several examples of such symbolic female terrain, Moers concludes that it is typically 'harsh and upswelling', stony, 'wind-swept', cut with 'ravines and declivities'.[53]

This approach to women's writing and imagery suggests intriguing possibilities, but it is also fraught with difficulties. For example, here is a short poem by the Scottish poet Hugh MacDiarmid, but just suppose for a moment it were read in the belief that it was a woman's work. What aspects of an essential female aesthetic might then be discovered in its themes and imagery?

Empty Vessel
I met ayont the cairney
A lass wi' tousie hair
Singin' till a bairnie
That was nae longer there

Wunds wi' warlds to swing
Dinna sing sae sweet
The licht that bends owre a' thing
Is less ta'en up wi' t.[54]

Most obviously there is the woman's subject of the poem – the anguished sense of loss felt by a mother whose baby is stillborn. The poem implies a sympathetic oppositional attitude to a judgemental society; the woman's desolate situation and the term 'lass' suggest that she is young and unmarried. Her grief is linked to the theme of madness which Gilbert and Gubar identify in women's writing as a reworking of masculine images of women's sexual depravity. Implicit in the term 'cairney' is the 'harsh', 'windswept' landscape sought out by women as secret symbolic places.

My intention here is not to make light of the kinds of ideas articulated by Moers and other feminist critics, and certainly not to make fun of the poem, which is finely imagined in its juxtaposing and reversal of cosmic force with the power of a young mother's grief and love. The reading does, however, illustrate the difficulty of relating writing in any simple way to biological sex. Would we want to claim that a woman's poem on such a topic would be truer in some essential way? I think not, but this kind of thinking seems to have crept into some of the feminist criticism we have encountered in this chapter. Despite Showalter's concern with the material and historical conditions effecting women's creativity, she implies at times that her categories – Feminine, Feminist, Female – are universally applicable to all women writing in each historical period, and that there is a progression towards 'truth' in women's fiction. As women liberate themselves from reaction to patriarchal pressures they will become more free to find within themselves, and thus express, the 'true' reality of 'Female' experience. So, too, Gilbert and Gubar suggest that there is an unmediated 'truth' hidden beneath the surface of women's writing. The perceived self-division of the female writer is reflected in the self-division of the heroines and language of female-authored texts.

This reflectionist view of literature ignores the way language is always the site of ideological contestation. It also has difficulty in dealing adequately with writing by women which, quite deliberately, sets out to tell it like it is not, of the attraction for many women writers and women readers of non-realist forms: fantasy, science fiction, surrealism and linguistic experimentation.[55] Neither does all 'gynocriticism' acknowledge how complex is the issue of authorial intention. Not all women-centred texts can be assumed to be consciously feminist texts in the sense of the definition of a political agenda (see introduction).[56] Clearly, it would be anachronistic to claim that many earlier writers were feminists; in addition, many writers would reject such a label. Nevertheless, we have seen that even texts with overtly conservative aims can function in progressive ways. How does one position authorial intention in such cases? The term 'author' can seem too unitary to cover the often conflicting plurality of meaning contained within a literary text.[57]

Feminist criticism can rightly claim to have launched a fundamental challenge to the cultural prestige of 'literature' as embodying revered and universal values of human existence by unveiling its pervasive investment in the structures of patriarchal power. In their turn, literary texts as 'writing' challenge any simple assumptions feminists may want to stake on the inherent nature and identity of women's creativity, insisting we pay attention to the complex interrelationship between language, gender and identity.

Summary of Main Points

1 One positive effect of the availability of a women's tradition of writing is that it makes visible women's experience which has been excluded or misrepresented in mainstream traditions.

2 This visibility provides women with a means of self-recognition, a shared voice and identity; but writing cannot mirror reality – it is always selective verbal construction.

3 Gynocriticism: the study of women's writing and their professional problems within a male-dominated tradition. Showalter's three developmental phases: Feminine (imitative), Feminist (protest), Female (self-discovery).

4 Gilbert and Gubar diagnose repressed anger and anxiety, produced in

women writers by a misogynistic literary tradition, in terms of imagery of madness, confinement and disease prevalent in women's texts. With the establishment of a women's cannon, women writers are now experiencing anxiety about powerful literary mothers, which produces an 'affiliation complex'.

5 Gynocriticism is in danger of constructing a poetics of suffering and victimization. Positive responses of women to a dominant male tradition include parody, mockery, appropriation of male forms and stories. Women writers are eclectic: they make use of conservative forms, gothic and romance novels and popular fiction for their own purposes.

6 Despite the inhibiting reputation of poetry as a high culture form, Elizabeth Barrett Browning appropriates the epic and love tradition for a woman's voice.

7 Modernist poets claim to express a universal historical consciousness in order to exclude women; however, women poets assert a woman's poetic articulation of culture and history.

8 Are the qualities in women's writing noted in the chapter essential characteristics of a female aesthetics or an 'oppositional aesthetics'? It is difficult to establish an essential link between femaleness and forms of writing.

Suggestions for Further Reading

Sara Mills et al., *Feminist Readings/Feminists Reading*. Chs 2–4 (pp. 51–153) are particularly useful in giving practical readings of well-known women's novels using the ideas of Showalter and Gilbert and Gubar, and an approach to realism.

Toril Moi, *Sexual/Textual Politics*, pp. 50–88, provide clear outlines of the classic texts of 'gynocriticism' and a rigorous analysis of their conceptual problems. However, Moi tends to underestimate their positive insights.

Elaine Showalter, 'Towards a Feminist Poetics', in Showalter (ed.), *The New Feminist Criticism*, pp. 125–43. A succinct and useful summary of Showalter's views.

Virginia Woolf, *A Room of One's Own*. The classic account of women writers' difficulties; essential reading.

Notes

1 De Beauvoir, *The Second Sex*, p. 174.
2 Heilbrun, *Hamlet's Mother and Other Women*, p. 108.

3   Woolf, *A Room of One's Own*, p. 76.

4   Kerrigan (ed.), *An Anthology of Scottish Women Poets*, p. 8.

5   Moers, *Literary Women*, p. 43.

6   Ibid., p. 66. Recently, important supportive networks among Modernist women at the beginning of the twentieth century have been studied. See e.g. Benstock, *Women of the Left Bank*; Hanscombe and Smyers, *Writing for their Lives*.

7   Smedley, *Daughter of Earth*, pp. 54–5.

8   For more extensive studies of this theme see Auerbach, *Communities of Women*; Todd; *Women's Friendship in Literature*.

9   Woolf, *A Room of One's Own*, p. 81.

10   Ibid., p. 84.

11   Akhmatova, *Selected Poems*, pp. 90, 104.

12   El Saadawi, *Woman at Point Zero*, p. iii.

13   Morrison, *Song of Solomon*, pp. 34–5.

14   Woolf, *A Room of One's Own*, p. 87.

15   Mukherjee, *The Middleman and Other Stories*, p. 40.

16   For studies of women's use of this form see Jelinck (ed.), *Women's Autobiography*; Benstock (ed.), *The Private Self*; Felski, *Beyond Feminist Aesthetics*, pp. 86–153.

17   Showalter, 'Towards a Feminist Poetics', in Showalter (ed.), *The New Feminist Criticism*, p. 131.

18   Showalter, *A Literature of their Own*, p. 7.

19   Typical of writers of this phase are Charlotte Perkins Gilman and Kate Chopin. See bibliography for titles of their fiction. See ch. 6 for a discussion of Chopin's *The Awakening*.

20   For a similar recent empirical approach which considers primarily twentieth-century women writers see Miles, *The Female Form*.

21   Gilbert and Gubar, *The Madwoman in the Attic*, p. 75.

22   Ibid., pp. 77–8.

23   Welty, *One Writer's Beginnings*, pp. 38, 21.

24   *The Collected Stories of Eudora Welty*, p. 302.

25   Ibid., pp. 317–18.

26   Welty, *One Writer's Beginnings*, p. 101. Welty writes, 'I realized that Miss Eckhart came from me.'

27   Plath, *Collected Poems*, p. 173.

28   Freud's theories are set out more fully in ch. 4.

29   Gilbert and Gubar, *No Man's Land*, vol. 1, p. 195.

30   Tsvetayeva, *Selected Poems*, p. 53.

31   Woolf, *A Room of One's Own*, p. 8.

32   Wolf, *Cassandra*, p. 141.

33   Ibid., p. 142.

34   Ibid., p. 225.

35   *The Collected Stories of Eudora Welty*, p. 284.

36   Spencer, *The Rise of the Woman Novelist*, p. 177. For further studies of pre-nineteenth-century writing by women see Todd, *The Sign of Angellica*; Hobby, *Virtue of Necessity*.

37   Moers, *Literary Women*, p. 95. Gilbert and Gubar, *The Madwoman in the Attic*, has an extensive discussion of *Frankenstein* in relation to Mary Shelley's response to *Paradise Lost* (pp. 221–47).

38   The point should not be exaggerated, however. Recent publications of travel writing by nineteenth-century women challenge notions of a totally confined female population.

39   See e.g. Kaplan on *The Thorn Birds* in *Sea Changes*, pp. 117–46; Spacks, *The Female Imagination*, writes on *Little Women*, as does Heilbrun (*Hamlet's Mother and Other Women*, pp. 140–7).

40   Woolf, *A Room of One's Own*, p. 77.

41   See Kerrigan's introduction to *An Anthology of Scottish Women Poets*. Katherine Raine has written of the inheritance from her mother of 'Scotland's songs and ballads . . . sung or recited by my mother, aunts and grandmothers, who had learned them from *their* mothers and grandmothers'. Jenni Couzyn describes the influence of her African childhood on her poetry: 'Africa for me was full of music. I remember sitting in my mother's kitchen peeling wild mushrooms, or shelling great mounds of green peas, with my mother and our servants and my sisters, singing songs in four harmonies.' These quotations come from Couzyn (ed.), *Contemporary Women Poets*, pp. 57, 217.

42   Woolf, *A Room of One's Own*, pp. 48–9.

43   An extremely useful introduction to feminist approaches to poetry is Jan Montefiore, *Feminism and Poetry*.

44   For a discussion of this see Kaplan, 'Language and Gender', in *Sea Changes*, pp. 69–93.

45   An interesting, fairly recent, example of this in Britain was the strong resistance to women presenters of the national news on television.

46   Barrett Browning, *Aurora Leigh and Other Poems*, p. 10.

47   Barrett Browning, *Selected Poems*, p. 230.

48   Leighton, *Elizabeth Barrett Browning*, p. 110.

49   Moers, *Literary Women*, p. 55.

50   T. S. Eliot, 'Tradition and the Individual Talent', in *Selected Prose*, p. 39.

51   Rich, *The Fact of a Doorframe*, p. 275. Although I have discussed Nichols and Rich here as providing less obvious challenges to male Modernist claims, there were, of course, many women writing at the same time as

Pound and Eliot whose work is often overlooked in accounts of Modernism. See Scott (ed.), *The Gender of Modernism*.

52 It seems to me that Spacks, *The Female Imagination*, does not avoid this danger in her thesis that the welcoming of unhappiness and suffering by the heroines of female-authored novels results in an affirmation 'in far-reaching ways of the significance of their inner freedom' (p. 320). For a more recent development of a female aesthetics of suffering see Lawrence Lipking, 'Aristotle's Sister: A Poetics of Abandonment', *Critical Inquiry*, 10 (Sept. 1983), pp. 61–88.

53 Moers, *Literary Women*, p. 262.

54 *The Hugh MacDiarmid Anthology*, p. 15.

55 Moi, *Sexual/Textual Politics*, pp. 50–88, elaborates this criticism in more detail.

56 See Coward, 'Are Women's Novels Feminist Novels?', in Showalter (ed.), *The New Feminist Criticism*, pp. 225–39.

57 The idea of the pluralized identity of the writer is dealt with in Part II.

Part II

Feminism?

4

The Construction of Gender:
Sigmund Freud and Jacques Lacan

In the previous chapters I tended to discuss writing by women separately from writing by men as if there were a natural and self-evident distinction between the sexes. We saw that there is one clear difference in the position of men and women as writers: across time and cultures women writers have had to operate against the grain of greater or lesser male prejudice and hostility. For this reason I suggested that many of the qualities and achievements recognized in women's writing can best be seen in terms of an oppositional aesthetics. Beyond this, however, any attempt to link a writer's subjective sense of gender identity with the form or content of her or his writing is fraught with difficulty and contention. Many women writers fiercely resist categorization of their work as 'women's writing', insisting that their creative imagination transcends a purely female point of view. The poet Anne Stevenson, for example, is 'not convinced that women need a specifically female language to describe female experience . . . A good writer's imagination should be bisexual or trans-sexual.'[1] In a similar way, male writers claim access to the feminine in their work. Perhaps the most succinct and famous statement of this is Flaubert's identification with his heroine: 'Madame Bovary, c'est moi.' Adding to these complications are the large number of women who write romantic fiction of the kind that seems to conform to the conventional ideals of femininity and masculinity and who passionately assert their identification as women with these ideals. Clearly, if we are to discuss writers in relation to gender issues, we need a more complex way of understanding gender identity than the automatic assumpation that to be female ensures a feminine sensibility. Even supposing we could agree as to what a 'feminine sensibility' would entail!

Feminists have been very reluctant to associate any qualities culturally identified as feminine with female biology. As we saw in Part I, biological essentialism has been the bedrock of most traditional thinking about women, used both to denigrate and to idealize them, but always to justify the existing status quo of power structures. Feminine attributes naturalized as biology become destiny: what is inborn must be borne since it cannot be changed. However, purely sociological explanations of gender as resulting from imposed social training fail to provide powerful or complex enough accounts of sexuality as identity.[2] They fail to explain the indivisibility of gender from the subjective 'inner' sense of self most people experience. Neither can they offer an adequate understanding of the equally strong feeling many people have that their sexuality cannot be neatly compartmentalized into the simple opposition of masculine and feminine. Finally, social theories of gender in terms of social training and role models cannot account for the universality of patriarchal configurations, despite the diversity of their forms within otherwise different cultures, or for their capacity to adapt and survive other radical social transformations. Feudalism may have given way to capitalism, but patriarchal power reinhabits the new structures and institutions.

For these reasons many feminists have turned to psychoanalytic theories as offering the most powerful explanation currently available of how our subjective sense of gender identity comes into being. This 'turn' to psychoanalysis has not been made without a good deal of reluctance, suspicion and resistance, a fair degree of which still exists. Sigmund Freud figured largely in Kate Millett's *Sexual Politics* as the propagator of a reactionary theory of sexuality functioning to confirm and sustain masculine dominance and prescribe women's inherent inferiority. Such was the success of Millett's polemic that many feminists, especially in the United States, perceived him simply as an enemy to be rejected on all fronts. Juliet Mitchell's *Psychoanalysis and Feminism* (1974) was the first influential attempt to counter this hostility: 'The greater part of the feminist movement has identified Freud as the enemy. It is held that psychoanalysis claims women are inferior and that they can achieve true femininity only as wives and mothers . . . but the argument of this book is that a rejection of psychoanalysis and of Freud's works is fatal for feminism. However it may have been used, psychoanalysis is not a recommendation *for* a patriarchal society, but an analysis *of* one. If we are interested in understanding and challenging the oppression of women, we cannot afford to neglect it.'[3] The distinction Mitchell pin-points here as to whether Freudian theory and psychoanalysis generally should be read as a *de*scription of or a *pre*scription for patriarchal structure remains at the centre of the debate between psychoanalysis and feminism.

Mitchell's early academic affiliation was to the English Marxist tradition which has remained an important element in British feminism whereas American feminism has tended to be more individualistic in its focus. Mitchell was much influenced by the new intellectual ideas coming from France in the late 1960s and early 1970s, especially the conjoining of Marxism, psychoanalysis and feminism projected by a radical group of women associated with the name 'Psychanalyse et Politique', usually shortened to 'Psych et Po'.[4] Accounts of feminist literary criticism and theory sometimes suggest a rather hostile opposition between American feminism on the one hand and French feminism on the other. While there are important differences of cultural orientation, as one would expect, such a view risks over-simplification.[5] There has always been cross-fertilization of ideas between American and French feminists, and within each country many approaches to feminism have been in debate rather than any monolithic national version of feminism holding sway. Nevertheless, it has to be said that French feminism is strongly influenced by the speculative intellectualism of French academic culture and so the chapters in Part II deal with complex theoretical frameworks.

Sigmund Freud

Freud's writing on sexuality is so influential that some knowledge of his work is essential for an understanding of current feminist thinking. Mitchell identifies two aspects of Freudian theory as particularly important to feminism: his account of sexuality as socially and not biologically constructed, and his theory of the unconscious. Freud's most radical and, for many of his contemporaries, most scandalous claim was that sexuality is not an inborn instinct which remains dormant until puberty; children are born bisexual and, as he put it, are 'polymorphously perverse'. In other words, a ready-gendered sexuality is not a biological urge that develops 'normally' in response to the needs of heterosexual reproduction, ensuring that men are attracted to women and vice versa. Mitchell explains that Freud 'found that "normal" sexuality itself assumed its form only as it travelled over a long and tortuous path, maybe eventually, and even then only precariously, establishing itself . . . unification [from bisexuality into one gender] and "normality" are the effort we must make on our entry into human society'.[6] This is undoubtedly the single most significant aspect of Freudian theory for women. According to Freud, we are born biologically female or male but not with a corresponding ready-made feminine or masculine gender identity; our first infant experience is of bisexuality and our eroticism is polymorphous, unconfined to a specific bodily zone. Attributes of what are considered 'normal' feminine and masculine sexuality are by no means natural or inherent but constructed painfully from the child's interaction with its social world. Far from immutable, our subjective gender identity is always fragile and unstable.

It is Freud's account of the 'tortuous' path from infant bisexuality to adult gender identity that causes problems for feminists. The central mechanism of this psychic process, according to Freud, is the idea of castration. For both male and female infants the first and absolute love is the mother. In this earliest, pre-Oedipal, phase of life the child has no sense of corporate or psychic identity; the maternal body is experienced as coextensive with its own, as a continuum of auto-erotic pleasure and plenitude. Thus the child's sexuality is simultaneously passive and active. Held within this all-emcompassing unity the child could never acquire a sense of its own individual identity. Subjectivity has to be constructed in relation to objectivity: for a sense of 'me' to be conceived there has to be a sense of a separate 'other'. Therefore some mechanism is needed to cut the child off from its narcissistic first love.

According to Freud, it is the Oedipal complex that resolves this problem. Little boys discover that not every human being has a penis and this leads to traumatic fears of castration to be enacted by the father as punishment for incestuous desire for the maternal body. Under pressure of these castration fantasies the boy represses the forbidden desire and identifies with the father as figure of authority and moral law. In so doing the son enters into the paternal heritage; when he is big like his father he can hope for a woman of his own and the authority to possess her. According to Freud, this identification with the father resolves the

Oedipal complex for little boys. They have constructed an active masculine identity and can continue to desire a sexual partner of the opposite sex.

For little girls the problem is altogether more complicated, Freud admitted. What they discover is that they have already been 'castrated', that they have no penis. According to Freud, this is a traumatic realization of lack: 'She makes her judgement and her decision in a flash. She has seen it and knows that she is without it, and wants to have it.'[7] The little girl, Freud suggests, blames her mother for inflicting her with this physical inferiority and, discovering that the mother too is 'castrated', turns away from her as primal love-object towards the father. In so doing she assumes the 'normal' passive feminine sexuality, desiring the father to give her a baby as a substitute for a penis. Freud associates the final phase of this replacement of active sexuality by passivity with a shift from clitoral eroticism, a sort of mini-penis, to the vagina as the site of adult female orgasm. Despite her rejection of her mother as inferior, the girl nevertheless continues to identify with her as a rival for the love of the father. Because of this, Freud claims, a woman always suffers from 'the wound to her narcissism, she develops, like a scar, a sense of inferiority'.[8]

Many women's first reaction to these ideas is to explode either with ironic laughter or with outrage. However, we should bear in mind Mitchell's contention that what Freud offers us here is an insight into the psychic mechanism of patriarchal structure, not an advocacy of it. Her very detailed account of his work is at pains to show Freud's own hesitancy in using terms like 'passivity' and 'activity', and his recognition of their inseparability from conventional gender assumptions. Freud also admits that both sexes display a 'mixture of the character-traits . . . belonging to the opposite sex'.[9] What is important for feminists in his theory is his insistence that 'femininity' and 'masculinity' have no basis in biology, but are constructed by the child's familial relationships. Thus the account of the Oedipal struggle and its resolution can be read as description, not prescription, of the social and psychic process whereby the power relations of patriarchal authority, symbolized in the father, reproduce themselves in each new generation as a subjective sense of self is constructed. Only by understanding this process, Mitchell argues, can we begin to find ways of confronting and subverting the mechanism of internalized oppression.

The child's repression of its polymorphous desires, at the Oedipal stage, especially the incestuous desire for the mother, forms the basis of the unconscious. By accepting the paternal law, the child is acknowledging what Freud calls the 'reality principle'; it concedes the necessity of adapting and modifying its libidinal drives so as to find ways of satisfying them, often indirectly, in the real world. At this stage, too, the father's authority is internalized to become the superego, functioning as an inner agency of social and moral prohibition. Beyond the domain of these restricting codes, however, the unconscious remains dominated by primal desire and bisexual drives. Unregulated by the reality principle, unconscious desire is organized by fantasy and imaginary ideas to which powerful libidinal charges become fixed. Thus the unconscious always remains a potentially disruptive force underlying our conscious gender identity.

From his work on dreams Freud discovered two primal mechanisms by which the unconscious organizes its ideas and attempts to find ways of discharging its repressed libidinal energy while avoiding the censorship of the superego. The first of these is the mechanism or process of *condensation* whereby one idea or image in the unconscious becomes a nodal point or intersection for a whole cluster of associated feelings, repressed primal memories and desire. In this way, especially in dreams, a single image, word or sound can evoke throught its compression a whole range of repressed wishes, emotion and thoughts. The other mechanism is that of *displacement* whereby the libidinal energy associated with a particular unconscious desire is displaced through a chain of apparently innocuous images and ideas and can thereby slip through the barrier of censorship. The concepts of displacement and condensation are useful ones for literary criticism generally in that poetic language often seems to function in strikingly similar ways.

For example, the two main images of 'rose' and 'worm' in William Blake's poem 'The Sick Rose', might be seen as evading any explicit naming of forbidden subjects. Moreover, the 'rose' image seems to function mainly by condensing multiple meanings and feelings within itself while the 'worm' image seems more fluid, slipping from change to change.

> O rose, thou art sick:
> The invisible worm

That flies by night,
In the howling storm,
Has found out thy bed
Of crimson joy
And his dark secret love
Does thy life destroy.[10]

It would be difficult not to notice that the ostensible subjects of the poem, the sick rose and the invisible worm, function as metaphoric substitutions for what seems a barely disguised concern with sexual love, and, perhaps, with the female and male genitals. Taken separately, the phallic image of the worm suggests that it is masculine sexuality that threatens the rose, but the sense of menace is evoked not so much by the worm image as by its *displacement* through a series of images which render its meaning ambiguous, shifting and elusive. The adjective 'invisible' associates uneasily with 'worm', then the image shifts to 'That flies by night', suggesting darkness and something insubstantial (but surely worms do not fly?). It flies 'In the howling storm' – a sense of sorrow and violence associating here with darkness – yet it has the power or sight to find out the intimacy of 'thy bed' where again its effect is 'dark secret' and destructive. The strongest effect of the poem, however, lies in its power of *condensation*. The sick rose image is charged with an intensity of compressed feeling. It simultaneously evokes female sexuality, the sensuality of physical love, the female sexual organs and the fullness and beauty of the actual flower, but also hints at the over-sweet scent of sickness, decay and perhaps sin, of the fear of death perceived as concealed in the depths of the female. The poem makes no attempt to deal with these opposing ideas rationally but condenses them into the one intense image of a sick rose.

Poems are never simply the workings of the unconscious, of course; they are highly ordered, carefully crafted structures of words. Nevertheless, this poem does help, I hope, to convey the potential power of the processes of displacement and condensation to generate, discharge and speak the intense libinal forces of the unconscious. It is the presence of these anarchic unconscious energies and the deviousness and subversiveness of their working to evade conscious control that indicates how precariously our sense of stable, single gender identity is maintained. In that sense 'self' is always a plurality of forces sheltering under a unitary name: 'I', 'woman', 'man'.

Nevertheless, while feminists welcome this sense of the instability of our conscious social gender identity within the Freudian theory of sexuality, its account still seems to fall back finally on biological difference – even biological inequality. The mechanism that propels the child towards a social identity is the penis, and a woman's inferior position within the social order is directly linked to her lack of that organ. Reading Freud it is difficult to avoid the conclusion that for him this was the determining factor in sexual relations: not having a penis ensures women's continued subordination to men.

It is for this reason that feminists wanting to pursue a psychoanalytic explanation of gender subjectivity have turned to the work of Jacques Lacan. What makes Lacan important for feminist literary criticism is his translation of Freud's ideas into theories of language. Lacan associates the Oedipal stage with the child's entry into the language system, which, he claims, confers on us our social and gender identity. We can recognize ourselves only in the oppositional terms available (for example boy or girl). So, for Lacan, social identity is always in the nature of an illusion – a restrictive unitary meaning imposed on our actual multiplicity of being. Because language thus subjects us to its law, the term 'subject' is used within this framework of thought in preference to 'individual'. Lacan's work is well known for its complexity. For this reason you may wish to leave the next section for the time being and move straight on to chapters 5 and 6. The feminist ideas outlined there can be read independently, even though Cixous, Irigaray and Kristeva all write in response to Lacan.

Jacques Lacan

Although Mitchell was ostensibly defending Freud in *Psychoanalysis and Feminism*, she had clearly been strongly influenced by the ideas of Lacan. This is not surprising, for the radical French feminists 'Psych et Po' were deeply engaged with Lacanian thinking even if the relationship was often a combative one. Lacan's key innovation is to refocus Freud's ideas through the intense concern with language which has been at the centre of most intellectual activity in France in the past three decades. In *Jacques Lacan: A Feminist Introduction* Elizabeth Grosz explains the attraction of Lacan's work: 'his reading of Freud stresses Freud's originality and subversiveness and helps to vindicate psychoanalysis in feminist terms, enabling it to be used as an explanatory model for social and political relations. Lacan can be utilized to explain such notorious concepts as women's "castration" or "penis envy" in socio-historical and linguistic terms, that is, in terms more politically palatable than Freud's biologism.'[11]

Lacan's view of language develops from the structural linguistics of Ferdinand de Saussure whose work in the early twentieth century initiated an intense interest in language across a wide range of thinking and fields of knowledge.[12] Saussure's concern was to understand how language as a systematic structure of signs produces meaning. All signs, he argues, are comprised of two aspects: a signifier and a signified. Each sign has a visual or a sound element (the signifier) and, attached to it, an idea, image or concept (the signified). For example, the visual signifiers 'd'-'o'-'g', or their phonetic (sound) equivalent, evoke, for English speakers, the signified concept or mental image of a small domestic animal that barks. Saussure points out that there is no natural or necessary relation between signs – words – and the objects in the real world that they represent – the referents. The connection between sign (word) and referent (object) is quite arbitrary; hence the signs 'dog', 'chien' and 'Hund' all refer to the same referent – the actual animal that runs around wagging its tail and barking. If there were a necessary or innate connection between signs and referents there would be just the one sign matching its own one referent the world over.

A radical perception follows from this: there is a separation or gap between the world of reality and the world of language. Reality does not endow language with meaning, but rather our system of language is the means by which we are able to make sense of the world. We place the grid of signs over the continuum of experience. It is from their structural relationship to each other within this grid that signs produce meaning. For example, the concept 'small' signifies only in its differential relationship to 'large'; similarly, 'east' and 'west', 'good' and 'bad' are dependent on their oppositional relationship to each other. Less obviously, 'yellow' has meaning only in so far as it is not blue, not green, not orange and so on. At the level of sound and meaning language functions only as a structure of differences. The meaning of words inheres not in any positive intrinsic quality they possess, but in their difference from other words. As we shall see, the production of meaning through positioning within a signifying structure of difference is at the centre of Lacan's perception of social identity.

However, before continuing with Lacan's ideas it might be useful to consolidate this view of meaning as produced by opposition or difference by looking at a practical illustration in part of a poem by Maya Angelou, 'Caged Bird'. It is not difficult to recognize the binary opposition (the opposing concepts) that structures the poem, but consider also how the poem actually expresses the idea, just discussed, that meaning derives from, is produced by, difference.

> A free bird leaps
> On the back of the wind
> and floats downstream
> till the current ends
> and dips his wing
> in the orange sun rays
> and dares to claim the sky.
>
> But a bird that stalks
> down his narrow cage
> can seldom see through
> his bars of rage
> his wings are clipped and
> his feet are tied
> so he opens his throat to sing.
>
> The caged bird sings
> with a fearful trill
> of things unknown
> but longed for still
> and his tune is heard
> on the distant hill
> for the caged bird
> sings of freedom.[13]

Clearly, 'Caged Bird' is structured on the binary opposition of freedom and confinement, so that the images of space, movement and openness in the first verse are made more intense by and in turn make more poignant the contrasting images of constriction, closure and imprisonment in the second and third stanzas. However, what Angelou is also saying is that while the uncaged bird experiences freedom to the full (it 'leaps' and 'floats'), it cannot conceptualize it, only the bird that has been caged knows the *meaning* of freedom, because it knows it as difference or lack. Only the caged bird can conceptualize and hence 'sing' of freedom.

To return to Lacan, let's begin with his account of the first pre-Oedipal phase of infancy: the stage of narcissistic identification with the maternal body. He renames this the 'Imaginary' to emphasize the fantastical nature of the child's relation to its world before it acquires language, a conception of self, or concedes to the demands of the reality principle. In considering this stage, Lacan elaborates Freud's sense of the tremendously difficult and precarious task the infant faces in constructing a sense of self. How does the child effect that separation of self from m/other necessary for any perception of a distinguishable identity? Lacan suggests that this long process is initiated in what he calls the 'mirror phase', beginning somewhere around six months.[14] During this phase the infant gains an imaginary concept of self as a potentially separate corporate being. This is an intellectual and visual cognizance of self as a specular image which could originate in an actual mirror reflection, or a reflection in its mother's eyes, or even an image of self projected on to another small child.

However, it is always a form of misrecognition since the child's relation to the world is still an imaginary, fantasizing one. It invests this image of self with narcissistic desire and with wishful projections of self-plenitude and omnipotence. All of this is greatly at odds with the child's actual state of total physical dependence on its mother and complete lack of any motor co-ordination. What is achieved in the mirror identification is an imaginary perception of a self, opening up the pathway towards an eventual social identity. But the cost of this is high; a radical split has occurred between the ideal imaginary identity and the actual self which perceived that projected mirror ideal. Thus for Lacan subjective identity from its first intimations is constructed on a mirage, what he terms an Ego-Ideal. This imaginary self, invested with narcissistic desire, thereafter haunts the unconscious as a dream of self-unity and self-sufficiency. Throughout life we will chase this fantasm of a 'real', 'authentic' self, seeking but never finding it in a displaced chain of projected cultural ideals, as good little girls, brave boys, supermums, go-getting men, sexual stars. Identity for Lacan is a series of displacements of desire to reunite with an imaginary narcissistic Ego-Ideal.

However, this process of constructing a self as a social identity, initiated at the mirror stage, is brought to fulfilment only with the resolution of the Oedipal crisis. For Freud the outcome of the child's fear of castration is its submission to the reality principle and hence its entry into the social order. For Lacan this must coincide with the child's entry into the language system since, as Saussurean linguistics suggests, it is the grid of language that imposes order on what would otherwise be an undifferentiated flux of experience. We can know only what we can represent – can symbolize – to ourselves and this is why Lacan calls language the 'symbolic order'. The 'symbolic order' simply means our total structure of meaning.

While the child remains enclosed in a unity with its mother all its needs are satisfied, and so it has no need for speech. The necessity for words is born of deprivation; only loss of the mother will impel the child into language to demand (to symbolize) what it no longer has. While the breast seems part of its coextensive world it has no need to ask for it. Words allow us to represent absent objects. Fear of castration, embodied in paternal authority, separates the child from the maternal body, and so imposes the lack which forces it to speak its needs, forces it into the symbolic order. For this reason Lacan perceives language as based on lack or loss. He argues that the phallus is the signifier (he calls it the transcendental signifier) of this lack since it represents the paternal law which imposes the loss of the mother. Language is thus the Law of the Father; a linguistic system within which our social and gender identity is always already structured. Even before we are born, Lacan says, language 'expects' us; we are already being positioned within its grid of difference as 'son' or 'daughter', 'boy' or 'girl' and so on. To enter the symbolic order is to be placed in a restrictive and repressive subject/ed position within a structure of meaning encoding patriarchal law.

For Lacan the entry into language brings the unconscious into being. Phallic authority represses desire for the mother along with all the anarchic libidinal perversities of the pre-Oedipal phase. Language becomes the means by which forbidden desire is redirected into realistic social goals, but in this sense our words always misname what we want; what we want/desire is henceforth taboo. Unconscious desire flows through the gap in our speech between what we can say and what cannot or must not be named. Lacan associates this gap or split with the Saussurean division of the sign (word) into signifier and signified. Lacan points out that the signifier slides over a chain of signifieds. This provides a linguistic description for Freud's primal mechanisms of displacement and condensation. For example, we could say of 'The Sick Rose' that a chain of signifieds (meanings) are released from the one signifier 'rose'. What the child or adult says it wants names an object in the social order, but unconscious desire has lost its object (the pre-Oedipal maternal body) and so cannot be satisfied. For this reason words (or, more accurately, signifiers) never have a stable unitary meaning; their meanings (signifieds) continuously slide over an endless chain of displacements. When I say 'I' what I signify is not only an apparently cohesive social identity by which I know and name myself, but also the anarchic ambiguous chain of desire that is my unconscious.

Let us turn to literature for an illustration of some of these theoretical ideas. Virginia Woolf's novel *To the Lighthouse* was almost certainly influenced by her awareness of Freudian psychoanalysis, and in many ways it seems prescient of Lacan's linguistic emphasis. In the opening pages of the novel the two central characters, Mr and Mrs Ramsay, are represented as caught up in an Oedipal conflict with their youngest son James. James is still attached to the pre-Oedipal Imaginary maternal phase, and so 'cannot keep this feeling separate from that'; he has not yet firmly established the differentiating grid of language on his world.[15] Equally, although words are already functioning to substitute realistic social goals – 'going to the Lighthouse' – for forbidden incestuous desires, the separation of signifier from signified is still an easily permeable boundary to that desire. For James 'going to the Lighthouse' functions as only the barest displacement for an imaginary incestuous consummation prior to and always beyond the reality principle. For this reason his mother's 'yes' to his expressed wish to go to the lighthouse floods him immediately with 'extraordinary joy'. But this maternal promise of ecstatic fulfilment is blocked at once by paternal prohibition:

> 'But,' said his father, stopping in front of the drawing-room window, 'it won't be fine.'
>
> Had there been an axe handy, a poker, or any weapon that would have gashed a hole in his father's breast and killed him, there and then, James would have seized it.[16]

Throughout the story Woolf elaborates the opposed meaning systems within which Mr and Mrs Ramsay operate, and indicates how authority and power belong only to the form of discourse that Mr Ramsay claims as his own. In the text masculine language continuously asserts its exclusive possession of 'truth', 'rationality', 'the facts' and 'knowledge'. When Mrs Ramsay ventures to question this privileged domain, asking her husband how he can be so sure he knows it will rain tomorrow, she challenges the very basis of patriarchal order — its monopoly of 'truth' and 'knowledge'. Indeed, the violence of Mr Ramsay's response is a measure of the seriousness of her challenge to this authority:

> 'The extraordinary irrationality of her remark, the folly of women's minds enraged him . . . she flew in the face of facts, made his children hope what was utterly out of the question, in effect told lies. He stamped his foot on the stone step. 'Damn you,' he said.[17]

For most of the novel James remains locked in a rivalrous hostility towards his father. This Oedipal conflict is only resolved at the end of the story when it is Mr Ramsay, the father, who fulfils his son's desire, by taking him and his sister Cam to the lighthouse. James embarks on the journey in angry and steadfast opposition to his father and thinks back to his childhood yearning for the lighthouse as an image of seductive desire. It 'was then a silvery, misty-looking tower with a yellow eye that opened suddenly and softly in the evening'. Now, as they approach it, 'He could see . . . the tower, stark and straight; he could see that it was barred with black and white; . . . So that was the Lighthouse, was it? No, the other was also the Lighthouse. For nothing was simply one thing. The other was the Lighthouse too.'[18]

Woolf represents James here as sensing the way in which language is always at least double in the service of the unconscious. The lighthouse signifies his long-repressed desire for the m/other even as it names a physical object in the social world. At this point on his journey James still seems more attracted to the imaginary lighthouse with its 'eye opening and shutting' like a pulse of desire.[19] However, as the crossing to the lighthouse culminates he finally identifies with his father and his relationship to the meaning of the lighthouse simultaneously reorientates itself. The perceived duality of the signifier is repressed again and a sense of unitary, defined, identity for both the object and his self within the symbolic order is achieved:

> So it was like that, James thought, the Lighthouse one had seen across the bay all these years; it was a stark tower on a bare rock. It satisfied

him. It confirmed some obscure feeling of his about his own character . . .
He looked at his father reading fiercely with his legs curled tight. They
shared that knowledge.[20]

From now on, as inheritor of the Law of the Father, James will take
up his position within the symbolic order and affirm his language as the
discourse of truth, of unambivalent fact and a totalizing knowledge,
repressing his perception of the slide of the signifier so that 'nothing was
simply one thing'. But what of Cam, his sister? It is significant that
Woolf provides no words to represent her relationship to the symbolic
order. James can achieve his identification with it through identification
with the father, with the phallus. Lacan argues that for women no such
identification is possible; they remain always marginalized within and by
language. This is what Woolf's text seems to suggest too, since Mrs
Ramsay is given no other name but that of her husband. As a signifier in
the text of *To the Lighthouse*, 'Mrs Ramsay' even more than the 'lighthouse'
is a rich condensation of multiple connotative meanings or signifieds.
However, in the social world of the novel, what her name denotes is
only a position nominated by the paternal order – Mr Ramsay's wife.

We have arrived at a conclusion which seems as negative for women
as that of Freud's. Both Freud and Lacan insist on gender as social
construction, not as inborn destiny. Lacan, even more than Freud,
stresses the unstable and provisional nature of all subjective identity.
However, his theories seem to release women from biology only to lock
them into another form of determinism. Instead of women's lack of a
penis making their inferior status inevitable, Lacan theorizes a symbolic
order that enacts an equally irresistible subordination of women. The
process of constructing a social identity is the process whereby language
positions us into our expected place within the Law of the Father. Lacan
insists that the phallus as symbol or signifier of that order is not to be
identified with the real penis; it merely represents the (maternal) lack
which produces all language. Hence it produces us as subjects. Nevertheless, the concept of castration, on which the idea of lack depends,
seems ultimately to have to be derived from the actual possession of the
male organ.

In the next two chapters I shall outline how feminists have taken
up Lacan's ideas, challenged them and appropriated them. However,
it is useful to remind ourselves that psychoanalytic theory provides

description rather than prescription. Certainly Lacan's account of women's marginalization from the symbolic order may offer insights into the sense of radical alienation from language and culture that many women have expressed. We can bring this insight to our consideration of women's language and writing without necessarily accepting all of Lacan's linguistic determinism. Sylvia Plath's poem 'The Colossus', for example, seems to lend itself to being read as an extended metaphor for women's marginalization from the tradition of patriarchal culture and language. The female speaker of the poem (the persona) articulates a sense of defeated exclusion from a vast and incomprehensible ancient order. Nevertheless, the language and imagery of the poem (that is Plath's language) constructs an irresistibly irreverent view which undercuts the professed despair and complicity of the poem's female persona. While some images and phrases suggest the alienation of the woman in the poem and testify to her desire to conciliate and belong, we recognize also an opposing language and tone of voice which casts the whole enterprise in a mocking and ironic light.

The Colossus

I shall never get you put together entirely,
Pieced, glued, and properly jointed.
Mule-bray, pig-grunt and bawdy cackles
Proceed from your great lips.
It's worse than a barnyard.

Perhaps you consider yourself an oracle,
Mouthpiece of the dead, or of some god or other.
Thirty years now I have labored
To dredge the silt from your throat.
I am none the wiser.

Scaling little ladders with gluepots and pails of Lysol
I crawl like an ant in mourning
Over the weedy acres of your brow
To mend the immense skull-plates and clear
The bald, white tumuli of your eyes.

A blue sky out of the Oresteia
Arches above us. O father, all by yourself
You are pithy and historical as the Roman Forum.
I open my lunch on a hill of black cypress.
Your fluted bones and acanthine hair are littered

In their old anarchy to the horizon-line.
It would take more than a lightning-stroke
To create such a ruin.
Nights, I squat in the cornucopia
Of your left ear, out of the wind,

Counting the red stars and those of plum-color.
The sun rises under the pillar of your tongue.
My hours are married to shadow.
No longer do I listen for the scrape of a keel
On the blank stones of the landing.[21]

The poem certainly articulates a sense of the pygmy scale of the individual woman set against a vast unheeding and excluding order, extending from arching sky to the horizon line. The woman has spent her life (thirty years), the poem suggests, in a dutiful but fruitless attempt to make sense of the oracular language issuing from the 'great lips' of masculine authority, but 'I am none the wiser'. Although her labour has been expended in an attempt to mend and glue the 'old anarchy' together, it affords her only a squatter's lodging 'out of the wind'. However, in opposition to this sense of a conciliatory yearning for communication and attachment, the Colossus, despite its intimidating scale, is perceived as stupid, its language as nothing more than 'mule-bray' and 'pig-grunt'. It belongs to the past and it is time for the woman to stop her repairs, to look for a world elsewhere, no longer listening 'for the scrape of a keel / On the blank stones of the landing'. The ironic poise of the poem lies precisely in the extreme originality of Plath's language to give dramatic utterance to a woman's sense of powerlessness. The persona may feel ineffectual, the poet certainly is not. Thus the poem simultaneously dramatizes the Lacanian sense of women's marginalization to the symbolic order and artistically refutes it. For that reason it may seem that this final extract from Hélène Cixous, whose work will be discussed in chapter 5, offers a more accurate account of women's anguished relation to language:

Every woman has known the torment of getting up to speak. Her heart racing, at times entirely lost for words, ground and language slipping away – that's how daring a feat, how great a transgression it is for a woman to speak – even just open her mouth – in public. A double distress, for even if she transgresses, her words fall almost always upon the deaf male ear, which hears in language only that which speaks in the masculine.[22]

Summary of Main Points

1 Biological accounts of gender tie women's destiny to their bodies, whereas psychoanalytic theories offer the most powerful explanation presently available of gender as socially constructed, not inborn.

2 Freud's important discovery: we are born bisexual; 'masculinity' and 'femininity' are constructed with difficulty and are never secure. The first intense love of both sexes is the mother, who is perceived as part of a bodily continuum, not as a separate being.

3 Separation from the mother is necessary to achieve self-identity. Fears of castration cause boys to repress incestuous desire and to identify with the father. This 'resolution' of the Oedipal conflict constructs the boy's 'normal' active masculine identity.

4 The little girl 'discovers' that she has been 'castrated', blames her mother and turns instead to her father as love-object. This constructs the 'normal' passive feminine identity.

5 Freud's other key discovery is the unconscious. Incestuous desire and libidinal drives are repressed at the Oedipal stage, but they evade conscious censorship by processes of 'displacement' and 'condensation'. These unconscious energies ensure that our social gender identity is always precarious and unstable.

6 Lacan rereads Freud in the light of structural linguistics which sees language as a grid of meaning (a structure of differences) imposed on the continuum of experience.

7 Lacan theorizes a 'mirror' stage to initiate separation from the mother: this projects a narcissistic fantasy image of self. Separation is completed at the Oedipal stage when the child acquires language, seeking a desired 'self' in the social ideals that the meaning system offers.

8 Language signifies the paternal (phallic) authority which forbids incestuous desire for the mother. So women can never identify with its authority and are always alienated from its order of meaning – the symbolic order.

9 Separation from the mother constructs the unconscious which 'inhabits' language. Words are 'doubled': they name acceptable social goals but also 'speak' our desire. 'I' is a social self which (mis)names a desiring unconscious.

Suggestions for Further Reading

Sigmund Freud

Juliet Mitchell, *Psychoanalysis and Feminism*, pt. 1, pp. 5–119.
Elizabeth Wright, *Psychoanalytic Criticism*, pp. 9–36.

Jacques Lacan

Elizabeth Grosz, *Jacques Lacan: A Feminist Introduction*. A very detailed account of Lacanian theory, divided into separate topics under clear headings, with helpful summaries.

John Sturrock (ed.), *Structuralism and Since*. Contains a chapter on Lacan (pp. 116–53).

Notes

1 Stevenson, 'Writing as a Woman', in Jacobus (ed.), *Women Writing and Writing about Women*, p. 174. Stevenson continues, 'For better or worse, women and men writers in the West, in the later twentieth century, share a common consciousness. Their language is a reflection, or even a definition, of that consciousness.'

2 An influential account combining sociology and psychoanalysis to explain gender identity in terms of women's mothering role as opposed to a merely reproductive role is Chodorow, *The Reproduction of Mothering*. Chodorow claims that gender identities may be changeable if men as well as women take on 'mothering'.

3 Mitchell, *Psychoanalysis and Feminism*, p. xv.

4 For accounts of the various feminist groupings in France in the 1970s, including 'Psych et Po', see Marks and de Courtivron (eds), *New French Feminisms*, pp. 28–38; Jouve, *White Woman Speaks with Forked Tongue*, pp. 61–90.

5 It probably stems from an over-simplification of Moi's argument in her influential *Sexual/Textual Politics*.

6 Mitchell, *Psychoanalysis and Feminism*, p. 17.

7 Sigmund Freud, 'Some Psychological Consequences of the Anatomical Distinction between the Sexes' [1925], in *On Sexuality*, p. 336. This volume contains most of Freud's key texts on the subject of sexuality.

8 Ibid. p. 337.

9 Ibid. p. 142.

10 Blake, *The Complete Poems*, pp. 216–17.

11 Grosz, *Jacques Lacan*, p. 9.

12 Ferdinand de Saussure, *Cours de linguistique generale* (Paris, 1916), (1974) tr. W. Baskin, as *Course in General Linguistics*. For helpful introductions to Saussure see Hawkes, *Structuralism and Semiotics*; Jefferson and Robey (eds), *Modern Literary Theory*; Selden, *A Reader's Guide to Contemporary Literary Theory*.

13 Angelou, *And Still I Rise*, p. 72.

14 Lacan, 'The Mirror Stage as Formative of the Function of the I', in *Ecrits*, pp. 1–7.
15 *To the Lighthouse*, p. 5.
16 Ibid., p. 6.
17 Ibid., pp. 37–8.
18 Ibid., p. 211.
19 Ibid.
20 Ibid., p. 231.
21 Plath, *Collected Poems*, p. 129.
22 Cixous, 'The Laugh of the Medusa', in Marks and de Courtivron (eds), *New French Feminisms*, p. 251.

5

Writing as a Woman: Hélène Cixous, Luce Irigaray and *Ecriture Féminine*

In the previous chapter we saw that while Freud and Lacan cut the essentialist knot joining gender identity to biological sex, what they thus seemed to offer women with one hand they took back with the other. Identity may be a precarious social construction – for Lacan any sense of self as coherent and unitary is illusionary – but precarious and fractured though it be, the process that produces a social gendered identity is perceived as irrevocably enacting the structural subordination of women. As women enter language, learn to name themselves, so they are put in their place within the social order of meaning.

Given these views, why do feminists bother with male psychoanalytic theory? There are good reasons, I think, in that feminists' engagement with psychoanalysis has produced some powerful and original ways of thinking about language and the construction of a feminine identity. Feminists have confronted and questioned Lacan's thinking on two central and related areas: his negative account of feminine subjectivity and his conception of language as a totalizing and determining order of meaning – the symbolic order. It is especially the centrality of language in the debate that makes it important to feminist literary criticism. In attempting to rethink patriarchy, feminists working within this framework focus their attention on the intense pre-Oedipal attachment of the child to its mother instead of concentrating, as Freud and Lacan do, on the Oedipal relationship with the prohibiting father. Feminists have sought to establish a basis for an opposing order of language in the primary love experience with the mother, thereby challenging what they see as the phallocentricity of Freud and Lacan's account of the symbolic order.

I have been writing of 'feminists' here but the three theorists whose response to male psychoanalytic theory I shall discuss in this and the following chapter have all been wary of the term. Moreover, reaction to psychoanalytic theory even just within France has been diverse so that to select out the work of Luce Irigaray, Hélène Cixous and Julia Kristeva is inevitably to simplify that diversity.[1]

Deconstructing the Symbolic Order: Irigaray and Cixous

Luce Irigaray's radical challenge to psychoanalysis has a twofold purpose: to reveal the masculine ideology inscribed throughout our meaning system (the symbolic order) and to construct a feminine order of meaning with which to produce a positive sexual identity for women. In pursuing the first of these aims, Irigaray draws attention to what she calls the 'logic of sameness' operating within all dominant forms of language. By the 'logic of sameness' she means that a social reality containing two gender specificities (man and woman) is persistently collapsed into one and the same: 'Man is [made] the measure of all things.' Psychoanalytic theory is simply one example of this, but it is a useful one for her purpose since it expresses phallocentricism or the 'logic of the same' in a very explicit manner. In her major work *The Speculum of the Other Woman* (1974), she demonstrates with detailed, often wickedly ironic, commentary on Freud's writing, how his theory of sexuality is constructed, in effect, on just one sex. There is masculinity and there is its absence:

> The 'feminine' is always described in terms of deficiency or atrophy [the clitoris is seen by Freud as an atrophied penis], as the other side of the sex that alone holds a monopoly on value: the male sex. Hence the all too well-known 'penis-envy'. How can we accept the idea that woman's entire sexual development is governed by her lack of, and thus by her longing for . . . the male organ? Does this mean that women's sexual evolution can never be characterized with reference to the female sex itself? All Freud's statements describing feminine sexuality overlook the fact that the female sex might possibly have its own 'specificity'.[2]

She points out that Freud never questions the effects of breast atrophy in the male. His thinking on sex is entirely framed by masculine perceptions: a logic of the same. 'As a card-carrying member of an 'ideology' that he never questions, he insists that the sexual pleasure known as masculine is the paradigm of all sexual pleasure.'³ Thus his theorizing of femininity constructs a model of women's sexuality which functions only to affirm the primacy of masculinity. In effect, his concept of femininity becomes an empty mirror which reflects back masculine sexuality as presence. Because the first stage of infancy is bisexual, Freud describes the pre-Oedipal girl as a 'little man'; he does not, of course, think of describing the pre-Oedipal boy as a 'little woman'. The girl's active sexuality at that stage is termed 'masculine'; in other words, sexuality is *a priori* masculine for Freud. Women's 'discovery' of 'lack' functions within psychoanalytic discourse to confirm and valorize masculinity as the fullness of phallic possession and power. Within this logic of the same, a woman is denied any representation as presence, she is only a non-man: 'the little man that the little girl is, must become a man minus certain attributes.'⁴ Irigaray acknowledges that Freud is disarmingly open in the way he elaborates this and that his explicitness allows us to recognize a logic which structures not just psychoanalytic discourse but a great deal of western thought.

In *The Speculum of the Other Woman* she traces this pervasive logic of sameness back to a tradition of philosophical speculation beginning with Plato. This logic continually collapses two gender specificities (man and woman) into one and its negative (man and not man) as in the form A and not A (or A−), rather than the logic of two different but autonomous terms such as A and B. In the former pair only the first term has a positive value attached, the second term (A−) can have only an amorphous meaning as what A is not.⁵ This is very similar to de Beauvoir's claims in *The Second Sex* that 'man' is always the positive term (the norm) and 'woman' the 'other' to that positive male as absolute subject.⁶ Because of the ubiquity of this logic of sameness in traditions of western thought, Irigaray calls our culture homosexual, based on an exclusive privileging of the male as norm: 'This domination of the philosophical logos stems in large from its power to *reduce all others to the economy of the Same* . . . from its power to *eradicate the difference between the sexes* in systems that are self-representative of a "masculine subject".'⁷ From this perspective, the symbolic order can be conceived as a flat, reflecting surface mirroring back to men the presence and fullness of male identity. This is rather how the functioning of love poetry was analyged in chapter 1. The ostensible object of the love, the woman, does not exist in the poem as a positive presence; what the language constructs is an externalized representation of the male poet's own subjective sensibility.

The logic of sameness operating within the symbolic order makes it impossible for women to represent themselves. Within dominant discourse they are always 'off-stage, off-side, beyond representation, beyond selfhood'.[8] Irigaray's critique of the phallocentricism within dominant forms of discourse – particularly philosophy and psychoanalysis – aims at undermining the claims of that language to disinterestedness, to the status of self-evident knowledge and truth. She points to a suspicious similarity of form between the valorization of a single male organ, the phallus, in representations of masculinity and the privileging within patriarchal language of a unitary notion of truth. This privileging of singularity does not correspond to the plural forms of the female body.

If Irigaray's negative project is seen as the deconstruction of patriarchal logic, her positive quest is for a way of theorizing and representing the specificity of 'femininity' – of women's sexual identity in positive terms. She wants to articulate sexual difference autonomously as A and B, rather than as A and A−. She wants to construct what has so far been only an absence in psychoanalytic discourse: an account of a feminine *imaginary* and a feminine *symbolic* so that women can begin to represent themselves. I shall return to this quest for a feminine language in the next section.

Irigaray's critique of psychoanalytic and philosophical discourse shows the important influence on French feminists of the philosopher Jacques Derrida and his methods of deconstruction.[9] The significance of Derrida's work, as of Lacan's, lies in its radical rethinking of language and identity. His work can be seen as opening out and exploiting the most radical implications of structuralist linguistics which originated in the work of the Swiss linguist Ferdinand de Saussure in the early twentieth century.[10] Saussure demonstrated that there exists a gap between words and the world; meaning is an effect produced by language, and language produces meaning only as a system of difference. According to Derrida, however, western thought has always operated on the opposite supposition: that meaning depends on what he calls 'a metaphysics of presence'. He uses this term to point to our persistent impulse to believe or assume that there is an inherent, immanent meaning or truth underlying the contingency of existence. Derrida's deconstructive readings of the tradition of philosophcal thinking since Plato shows how our conceptual system utilizes a series of binary oppositions (oppositional terms) one of which is inevitably valued above the other. The privileging of one term over its opposite functions to sustain a belief in presence. One of his key examples is the opposition between speaking and writing. Derrida points out how persistently speech has been perceived as more 'genuine' than writing because the presence of a speaker is felt to guarantee a definite, that is unitary, intention or meaning to the words. In turn, the invisible thought held to be immanent 'behind' or 'within' the words is believed to be yet more 'true' to an originating, intending presence than the material words themseives: mind is hierarchized over body. Even Saussure seemed to privilege content or thought (signifieds) over the words or form (signifiers). 'In the beginning was the Word' but behind the word, we want to believe, there is the presence of God, or the author, or some unique originating 'I' guaranteeing an intentional meaning or truth.

Derrida calls this belief in intentional unitary meaning, which underlies western conceptual thought, logocentricism. His strategy of deconstruction aims to undo the hierarchies of binary opposition by revealing how the privileged term actually depends on its subordinated opposite term. So, for example, the concept of good, as originating in God, appears prior to the notion of evil. However, what could have constituted a notion of 'goodness' in the unified existence of being prior to Lucifer's originating sin? We could argue that it is the act of evil which makes possible the concept of goodness, just as it takes a caged bird to sing of freedom. Derrida's aim is not, of course, to stabilize this reversal of the binary hierarchy; that would simply substitute an alternative originating presence. His aim is to foreground his motion of *differance* (a word he coins to produce a fusion of *differer* – deferral or delay – with the idea of difference) to suggest the unfixed, unstable nature of meaning – its lack of any unitary defining fixity. Putting binary oppositions into a perpetual play of reversal enacts the continual deferral of any one privileged meaning. There are obvious points of contact here with Lacan's denial of fixed meaning to the signifier 'I'. Subjective identity, according to Lacan, has no authenticating point of origin in a 'real', unitary self; it begins in a fantasy or mirage. Self is simply a continuous deferral of identity enacted by the displacement of desire from one social ideal to another. The Cartesian 'I think therefore I am' has been replaced by Lacan with the notion 'I think I am where I am not'.

Irigaray shows how phallocentricity shadows 'logocentricity'. The presence of the phallus has functioned to guarantee a unitary notion of masculine identity which is inextricably intertwined in western systems of thinking with unitary notions of truth and origins (logocentricity). However, phallic presence depends on its subordinated binary other; it acquires meaning as fullness only by defining femininity as absence or lack. Masculinity as wholeness erects itself on femininity as hole.

Hélène Cixous, like Luce Irigaray, has a two-dimensional project: also influenced by Derrida. She launches a deconstructive critique of the phallocentricism of the symbolic order and advocates the positive agenda of discovering an *écriture féminine* – a feminine practice of writing. Cixous's own writing, however, is more varied in its modes than that of Irigaray. Although first known in Britain by her theoretical texts, she is predominantly a creative writer, a literary critic, novelist and now a dramatist. In an early essay, 'Sorties', in *The Newly Born Woman* (1975) she swings into a typically zestful attack on the working of binary oppositions to uphold masculinity as origin and source of creativity. Everywhere within discourse, Cixous claims, the ordering by binary hierarchy persists. What is more, the coupling is always a relationship of violence; language is 'a universal battlefield . . . Death is always at work.'[11] It is inevitably the feminine term that is killed or erased in the deadly pairing. Because logocentricism founds origins in the phallus, Cixous maintains, life and creative power are constructed as male. 'Intention: desire, authority – examine them and you are led right back . . . to the father. It is even possible not to notice that there is no place whatsoever for woman in the calculations.'[12] We saw in earlier chapters how this logic of exclusion or sameness works to deny women any role in creativity: Christian mythology offers a reading of procreation as a male God creating man; Harold Bloom mythologizes literary history as an exclusive fathering of sons.

In Cixous's writing autobiographical experience is used as a way of relating her theorizing to political realities. In 'Sorties' she relates her sense of the violence of binary oppositions to her early life in Algeria as a French colony: 'So I am three or four years old and the first thing I see in the streets is that the world is divided in half, organized hierarchically, and that it maintains this distribution through violence.'[13] What her personal experience showed her was the working practice of 'the mechanism of the death struggle' involved in binary oppositions. For this system of logic to work, 'There has to be some "other" – no master without a slave, no economico-political power without exploitation, no dominant class without cattle under the yoke, no "Frenchmen" without wogs, no Nazis without Jews, no property without exclusion.'[14] Cixous associates phallocentric language with a cultural order based on possession and property. Within such an order exchange is part of the system of power; nothing can be freely given. Patriarchy is maintained by the exchange of women as possessions from fathers to husbands always so as to control or gain something. In such an economy, she argues, 'what *he* wants . . . is that he gain more masculinity: plus-value of virility, authority, power, money or pleasure, all of which reenforce his phallocentric narcissism at the same time. Moreover that is what society is made for – how it is made; . . . Masculine profit is almost always mixed up with a success that is socially defined.'[15] In contrast to the 'masculine' libidinal economy of 'property', a 'feminine' libidinal economy is that of the 'gift': 'She doesn't try to "recover her expenses". She is able not to return to herself, never settling down, pouring out, going everywhere to the other. . . . If there is a self proper to woman, paradoxically it is her capacity to depropriate herself without self-interest: endless body, without "end".'[16]

Constructing a Feminine Writing: Cixous and Irigaray

From the above quotations of Cixous's writing you will have perceived that her own style of writing conveys a sense of outflow, of waves of energy. She has said that 'it is impossible to *define* a feminine practice of writing, and this is an impossibility that will remain, for this practice can never be theorized, enclosed, coded – which doesn't mean that it doesn't exist'.[17] In her own practice Cixous aims to embody a feminine form of writing and to encourage other women to do the same. Again, personal experience is important to her here. She has written movingly of her search for a sense of self as a way out, an exit, a *sortie*, from an enclosing social identity she was born into as an Algerian French girl who was also a Jew: 'There has to be somewhere else, I tell myself . . . Everyone knows that a place exists which is not economically or politically indebted to all the vileness and compromise. That is not obliged to reproduce the system. That is writing. If there is somewhere else that can escape the infernal repetition, it lies in that direction.'[18]

'The Laugh of the Medusa' (1975) is Cixous's most impassioned appeal to women to follow her example and discover a positive feminine identity through writing. It shares and expresses the excitement and empowerment felt by many women in France and America during the 1970s and into the 1980s. More than any other text, it is the manifesto of feminine writing. Obviously, for Cixous a women's practice of writing has to be based on a very different order of meaning to that of the phallocentric symbolic order. It would have to embody the libidinal economy of the 'gift', not of 'property'. Here, then, are some typical passages from 'Medusa'. Bearing in mind the difficulties of translation as well as Cixous's warning that *écriture féminine* can never be theorized, can we recognize qualities of style, language, tone, syntax and values which embody and advocate a feminine practice of writing?

> We the precocious, we the repressed of culture, our lovely mouths gagged with pollen, our wind knocked out of us, we the labyrinths, the ladders, the trampled spaces, the bevies – we are black and we are beautiful.
>
> We're stormy, and that which is ours breaks loose from us without our fearing any debilitation. Our glances, our smiles, are spent; laughs exude from all our mouths; our blood flows and we extend ourselves without ever reaching an end; we never hold back our thoughts, our signs, our writing; and we're not afraid of lacking.
>
> In women's speech, as in their writing, that element which never stops resonating, which, once we've been permeated by it, profoundly and imperceptibly touched by it, retains the power of moving us – that element is the song: first music from the first voice of love which is alive in every woman. Why this privileged relationship with the voice? . . . a woman is never far from 'mother' . . . There is always within her at least a little of that good mother's milk. She writes in white ink.
>
> Flying is woman's gesture – flying in language and making it fly. We have all learned the art of flying and its numerous techniques; for centuries we've been able to possess anything only by flying; we've lived in flight, stealing away.

A feminine text cannot fail to be more than subversive. It is volcanic; as it is written it brings about an upheaval of the old property crust, carrier of masculine investments; there's no other way. There's no room for her if she's not a he. If she's a her-she, it's in order to smash everything, to shatter the framework of institutions, to blow up the law, to break up the 'truth' with laughter.[19]

The easiest aspect to identify is the tone of these passages, which is celebratory and confident. Clearly, Cixous's aim is to construct a joyful sense of feminine identity to counteract what she sees as centuries of deadly brain-washing in which women have been taught to hate themselves. The insistent use of 'We the' in the first passage affirms a positive collective presence. I think we can see her language and her syntax as attempting to embody this collective feminine identity as spacious, generous and beneficent. Her diction ranges extravagantly from the poetic ('our lovely mouths gagged with pollen') to the theoretic ('carrier of masculine investments') to the colloquial ('There's no room for her if she's not a he. If she's a her-she'). She plays continually on the relation of sound and meaning, implying the presence of a speaking voice. She seeks out puns, finds associative echoes between words and often coins her own terms. A notable example here is her brilliant play on the two meanings of the French verb 'voler': to fly and to steal. Women simultaneously make words fly – soar free from old repressive moorings – and steal them away. But women have flown, too, in men's fears as witches, creatures possessed of magical power. Thus her language is intensely metaphoric, its meaning pluralized, heterogeneous. These stylistic qualities make translation of her work very difficult, of course.

In these passages Cixous's syntax stays fairly orderly. However, questions, exclamations and declaratory affirmations are used to convey the immediacy of voice. So do the many sentences beginning with 'And' or 'But'. Such syntax works accumulatively rather than hierarchically. Sentences tend not to be structured and controlled by the grammatical logic of main and subordinate clauses; instead phrases and clauses pile up and spill over into the next idea: 'Our glances, our smiles, are spent; laughs exude from all our mouths; our blood flows and we extend ourselves without ever reaching an end.' The syntax materializes this libidinal expenditure without division. Thus instead of the feminine as lack and absence, Cixous's writing practice in 'Medusa', embodies abundance, creative extravagance, playful excess, the physical materiality of the female body.

Cixous's association of language with voice is not just a matter of style; it has deeper significance. Both Freud's and Lacan's theories of sexuality depend heavily on the sense of sight for the registering of lack. As Freud says of the little girl: 'She has seen it and knows that she is without it and wants to have it.'[20] In linking language to voice Cixous is moving back beyond the Oedipal stage to the pre-Oedipal relation between mother and child, a time dominated by the tactile and by sound and rhythm far more than by the visual. It is a phase of imaginary abundance, when there seems no end to bodily extension or pleasures, no division of self and m/other so that a child is able 'to love herself and return in love the body that was "born" to her. Touch me, caress me, you the living no-name, give me my self as myself.'[21] This for Cixous is the 'song' of the unconscious, giving access to desire, to a repressed memory of first sensuous knowledge of the body as erotic delight, to language as rhythm, sound pattern and intimate presence. It is this song coded into the body's materiality that must inform and shape a feminine practice of writing.

'The Laugh of the Medusa' is usually classed as part of Cixous' theoretical writing, but obviously she is not easily categorized. Her stylistic excess deliberately spills over the boundaries that usually divide what we would term 'creative' writing from the academic. Unfortunately, not much of her fiction or drama is so far available in English translation. Here is a brief passage from the beginning of her novel *Angst*. Can it too be read as exemplifying Cixous's notion of feminine writing?

> Suddenly you know all is lost. Everthing. Suddenly all is known. No more scene, yet no end. Cut. You say I. And I bleed. I am outside. Bleeding. Yet formless, helpless, almost bodiless. In and out of my body. In pain. Here, I no longer have what I once had; you no longer know what you once knew. You're not there any more. Outside, frozen. Motionless. Deported. Displaced. I still want to have; I still want to be able. Attacked. I want to be on the way to love. To death. To hold on to what is going to disappear. Still losing. Not dead, worse. The body, here. Separate. Flesh; separation.[22]

Obviously, this is not celebratory; what is articulated, it seems, is the physical terror and pain of loss. But loss of what and to whom? The syntax here is far more dislocated than in the 'Medusa' passages. There, the overspill of sentence structure seemed to embody the extensive, unboundaried quality Cixous was claiming for a feminine identity. Here the syntactic fragmentation enacts the rupture and tearing apart that is being expressed. In neither case, though, is the syntax governed by logic or rational order; the sentence structure in both seems to derive from the strong underlying pulse of feeling. What makes the *Angst* passage difficult to pin down is the slide of the pronouns between 'I' and 'You'; are one person or two involved here? It is impossible to be sure. Cixous always writes in the present tense. It is largely this which gives her writing its sense of energy and spontaneity, but it can also be used, as here, to deny the linear ordering of temporal sequence. We are gripped by the simultaneous immediacy of each phrase and cannot arrange it into a meaningful before and after. A similar disorientation is produced in spatial terms as 'inside' and 'outside', 'here' and 'there' slide through each other. While the writing seems intensely subjective, it refuses to settle into a coherent unitary 'I' as character or narrator. It is tempting to read the passage as dramatizing the pain of the child's separation from the mother at the moment of birth, but it can suggest other experiences of bereavement and loss. The refusal of unitary meaning or of single identity, the attempt to bring language close to the bodily materiality of emotion and to capture in syntax the rhythm of libinal drive would all be seen by Cixous, I think, as part of a feminine writing practice.

In 'The Laugh of the Medusa' Cixous associates a feminine text with subversiveness: 'It is volcanic', she says. How could the qualities recognized above be seen as a threat to or as undermining the status quo of existing power structures, particularly that of patriarchy?

I think the threat resides in the challenge such a writing practice asserts to the determining power of Lacan's sense of the symbolic order. For Lacan the language system is the totalizing order of culture and it is an order enacting the repressive Law of the Father: phallocentricism as Cixous terms it. Entry into this order for all human beings is enforced by loss (of the mother) and a denial of their experience of bisexual unboundaried being. For women there is no compensatory identification with paternal authority; their subject position is always one of marginality to the patriarchal order.

A feminine practice of writing is offered by Cixous as a means of resistance; the word-play, metaphors and punning exemplified in her style challenges (explodes it with laughter) any insistence on unitary meaning, the logic of the same, asserting instead that 'nothing is simply one thing'. Her syntax attempts to track the libidinal pulse of repressed desire; rhythm and sound patterns convey a sensuous tactile immediacy rather than rational mastery of what is other and separate. Identity slips free of a unified 'I' into a polyvalent play of the multiple possibilities of self: 'I' and 'you' not 'I' or 'you'. Such heterogeneity mocks any authoritative or dominant language which must always insist on its version of 'truth', 'identity' and 'knowledge' as single and unquestionable. The subversiveness of a feminine practice of writing, then, is aiming to undermine the underlying logic, the very perception of reality on which the present structure of cultural order rests. For this reason Cixous likes the metaphor of women as moles tunnelling out of the darkness imposed on them: 'We are living in an age where the conceptual foundation of an ancient culture is in the process of being undermined by millions of a species of mole. When the process is successful, 'all the stories would be there to retell differently, the future would be incalculable'.[23]

The general project of constructing a woman's language or writing, and Cixous's advocacy of it in particular, have been criticized as utopian and ahistorical. If the symbolic order is perceived as a totalizing system of meaning which wholly determines our perception of reality, then any opposing 'language' would have to exist outside the social and cultural. It would have to occupy some ideologically pure realm beyond the paternal law, but in so doing it would be beyond historical reality as well. It is difficult to see how such a language could ever make contact with the symbolic so as to contest it in a materially effective way. In fact, Lacan's own conceptualizing of the symbolic order as universal repressive law inevitably constructs just such an oppositional linguistic space for its asocial 'other'. In that respect Cixous could be seen as still caught up in his patriarchal logic, falling into the very practice of binary hierarchizing she labels 'death-dealing'. She simply elevates the asocial, libinal 'other' language against a repressive social law.

A related criticism levelled at Cixous's notion of *écriture féminine* is that in urging a woman to 'write herself' by returning to the libidinal drives of the body she is inevitably falling into a form of biologism or essentialism. The lyrical advocacy of the return to the mother, of writing in 'white ink', would seem to confirm this suspicion. Moreover, the effect of emotional spontaneity, the rejection of syntactic order in her own writing could be seen as affirming as 'feminine' the kinds of qualities – emotionalism, irrationality, disorder – that men have been only too pleased to characterize as women's identity and writing.

Cixous is aware of both dangers. One reason why she insists that a feminine practice of writing cannot be defined is to prevent it being slotted into place as a binary opposition to the symbolic. Part of her deconstructive critique of the symbolic order focuses on the construction of woman as 'nature' in the binary pairing 'culture/nature' so as to erase women from history. It therefore seems unlikely that she would propose a feminine form of writing that would effect the same erasure. In trying to look towards a new order of meaning, she can, of course, resort only to the old words which carry with them the traditional freight of cultural meaning: 'men and women are caught up in a network of millenial cultural determinations of a complexity that is practically unanalyzable: we can no more talk about "woman" than about "man" without getting caught up in an ideological theatre where the multiplication of representations, images, reflections, myths, identifications constantly transforms, deforms, alters each person's imaginary order and in advance, renders all conceptualization null and void.'[24]

Throughout her work Cixous persistently links writing and theory with political realities. For all these reasons her advocacy of a feminine writing practice is probably best seen as strategic. She is waging a guerilla campaign within the 'ideological theatre' of phallocentricism, hoping thereby to reform the deformed term 'woman'. Her use of the word 'Mother' is, she says, a metaphor;[25] it is part of the positive project of refiguring the feminine as plenitude. Moreover, the aim to discover a form of writing that will effect a *'sortie'* from the controlling domain of the symbolic order to the repressed pre-Oedipal relationship with the mother is, for Cixous, a way out from an imposed unitary sexual identity towards the release of each person's potential bisexuality. Female and male children experience the pre-Oedipal alike; both sexes can therefore draw on its libidinal energies to construct a feminine practice of writing. At the present time, for historico-cultural reasons, Cixous sees women more than men as 'opening up to and benefitting from this vatic bisexuality which doesn't annul differences but stirs them up, pursues them, increases their number'.[26] However, she cites Jean Genêt as one male writer who is open to the anarchic force of bisexual desire and hence to pursuing a feminine writing practice.

This brings us to another criticism of Cixous and of other French feminists: that they are elitist. The kind of writing they advocate is frequently difficult and the literary texts they admire are invariably those of avant-garde writers like Genet and James Joyce, for instance. Insisting on heterogeneity of meaning, syntactic dislocation and a pluralizing of identity do not make for easy reading, and the revolutionary potential of such texts is questionable. The impact of the extract from *Angst* is undeniable, but is it accessible to as many women as a text like Agnes Smedley's *Woman of Earth*, (see chapter 3), for example? Eyebrows have also been raised at Cixous's claim in 'Medusa' that 'we are black'. Although she comes originally from Algeria, can she really speak thus for black women? There are grounds for unease and criticism here, which I shall return to on chapter 7.

However, Cixous's ideas may provide us with useful insights into a wider range of writing than she herself demonstrates. For example, D. H. Lawrence is a troubling writer. His fiction, and even more so his non-fiction, appears to advocate feminine submission to and submergence in the phallic power of masculinity as the only 'naturally' fulfilling and balanced relationship between the sexes. Both Kate Millett and Simone de Beauvoir singled out Lawrence for his phallocentric views. However, consider the following passage from his short story 'The Fox'. The emotional and sexual control of the heroine, March, has been disturbed first by an encounter with a wild fox and then by the sudden appearance of a young man, Henry, who reminds her in some uncanny way of the fox. Is it possible to make a link here with any quality or image Cixous associates with a feminine unconscious?

> That night March dreamed vividly. She dreamed she heard a singing outside which she could not understand, a singing that roamed round the house, in the fields, and in the darkness. It moved her so that she felt she must weep. She went out, and suddenly she knew it was the fox singing. He was very yellow and bright, like corn.[27]

Lawrence's syntax is rhythmical and his language metaphoric. What I am struck by, though, is that Lawrence represents March's unconscious here primarily through the image of a song, a music originating outside the social order of the house. The sound seems to affect her like a nostalgia for something lost; hearing the song 'she felt she must weep'. Later in the text in a 'sort of semi-dream' March again seems to hear the fox singing 'wildly and sweetly and like a madness'.[28] In the text this singing is left unconnected to the boy Henry or the fox itself. In these passages the dream fox and dream song are associated only with March's unconscious, suggesting an unboundaried, ambiguously passive and active realm of sexuality. This imagery of singing has always puzzled me. It remains marginalized, even at odds with the main projection of the narrative in which March is pursued as Henry's quarry and made captive to his masculine hunter's will. Could it be that Lawrence allowed a momentary opening (a *sortie*) here to an opposing sensibility, an access to the libidinal economy of the 'gift', unboundaried and excessive, instead of the libido of possession and mastery? Perhaps this 'opening up to and benefitting from' his own bisexuality was so disturbing for Lawrence that it accounts for what in narrative logic is the unnecessary killing of the fox by Henry. It is necessary only to bring a potentially transgressive sexuality that irrupts into the text back under control. When March sees the dead fox there is no longer the slightest ambiguity about its masculine identity or the fundamental difference of that identity to herself as female. The binary division threatened by a wild song is firmly redrawn:

> March stood there bemused, with the head of the fox in her hand. She was wondering, wondering, wondering over his long fine muzzle. For some reason it reminded her of a spoon or a spatula. She felt she could not understand it. The beast was a strange beast to her, incomprehensible, out of her range. Wonderful silver whiskers he had like ice-threads. And pricked ears with hair inside. But that long, long, slender spoon of a nose! – and the marvellous white teeth beneath! It was to thrust forward and bite with, deep, deep, deep into the living prey, to bite and bite the blood.[29]

Luce Irigaray, like Cixous, wants a feminine writing practice with which to challenge a repressive and determining symbolic order. She, too, believes that only in a different order of meaning will it be possible to construct a positive representation of feminine identity. Like Cixous, she attempts to embody in her own style a sense of what such a practice would entail. For this reason, summarizing her arguments as I did at the beginning of this chapter not only simplifies what she is saying; it actually erases the main site of its provocation: her linguistic playfulness and, at times, her lyricism. Like Cixous, she is wary of making utopian claims for any immediate or easy construction of a completely alternative woman's language in opposition to phallocentric discourse, although she has been accused of this at times. She is aware that this would simply replace one logic of the same by another: 'What is important is to disconcert the staging of representation according to *exclusively* "masculine" parameters, that is, according to a phallocratic order. It is not a matter of toppling that order so as to replace it – that amounts to the same thing in the end – but of disrupting it and modifying it, starting from an "outside" that is exempt in part, from phallocratic law.'[30]

Her strategy for a disruptive feminine writing practice has much in common with that of Cixous: a dispersal of any unitary subjective 'I', punning and word-play, and syntactic disjunction. In contrast to the mirror effect of the symbolic order which projects a self-reflective image of the fullness and presence of masculine identity, Irigaray envisages a feminine practice of writing as going through the looking-glass, like Alice (A-Luce), into a wonderland of women's self-representation:

> Alice's eyes are blue. And red. She opened them while going through the mirror . . . She only goes out to play her role as mistress. Schoolmistress, naturally. Where unalterable facts are written down whatever the weather. In white and black, or black and white, depending on whether they're put on the blackboard or in the notebook. Without colour changes in any case. Those are saved for the times when Alice is alone. *Behind the screen of representation*. In the house or garden.[31]

In opposition to language as the mirror of masculine presence, Irigaray associates the metaphor of a speculum with a feminine form of representation. Its curved surface produces a deforming image which reverses the narcissistic reflections of phallocentric discourse. Perhaps then 'the specular surface which sustains discourse [will be] found not the void of nothingness but the dazzle of multifaceted speleology [literally the study of caves; here of interiors, concavities]. A scintillating and incandescent concavity.'[32] Moreover, this curved shape of the speculum accords with the inner specificity of the female body, figuring a mode of a self-representation founded on the intimacy of touch, not a distancing projected mirror image.

Irigaray, even more than Cixous, criticizes the priority given to sight in Freudian and Lacanian constructions of sexuality. She, too, returns to the intimacy of the mother–child pre-Oedipal phase where knowledge and experience are first and foremost based on touch. Touching, she points out, cannot lead to any sense of feminine sexuality as lacking. In contrast to the primacy given to the phallus within a unitary masculine identity based on the privileging of sight, a woman's body is not lacking but multiple. Scorning the Freudian contention that women are forced to choose at puberty between clitoral and vaginal orgasm, she writes, 'Why has the woman been expected to choose between the two, being labelled "masculine" if she stays with the former, "feminine" if she renounces the former and limits herself to the latter? . . . In fact, a woman's erogenous zones are not the clitoris or the vagina, but the clitoris and the vagina, and the vulva, and the mouth of the uterus, and the uterus itself, and the breasts . . . what might have been, ought to have been, astonishing is the multiplicity of genital erogenous zones (assuming the qualifier "genital" is still required) in female sexuality.'[33]

Thus Irigaray's writing practice foregrounds multiplicity, fluidity and the erotic intimacy of touching as a way of metaphorically representing a feminine identity, of figuring the colourful 'garden' of the female imaginary behind 'the screen of [masculine] representation'. Her concern with the pre-Oedipal phase is also gender specific. She is not concerned with bisexuality; it is the mother–daughter relationship she wants to reconceptualize. This is because she sees women's inability to represent their identity in positive terms as caused, in large part, by the deformation of the mother–daughter bond within the symbolic order. Within the present patriarchal culture 'motherhood' is allowed only a diminished meaning. It is denied any social or economic status, but equally its meaning is kept rigidly separate from the procreative moment – from any notion of sexuality. Creativity is thus preserved as a godlike and male domain, and motherhood is reduced to the function of nurture and care. Because of this diminished value of the meaning of the term 'mother', there is a risk for women of a compensating over-investment in 'self'-denial, in non-being, or in an over-possessive maternity.

A daughter must separate from maternal nurture to gain identity. Within the restricted meaning allotted to the term 'mother' this entails a total loss, since no other identity is allowed but that of nurturing. Thus, Irigaray argues, the Oedipal crisis exiles girls from their first history and identity, rendering them unknown and unknowable to themselves. What is needed is a new language which can represent the mother as also woman, which can construct a maternal identity that includes sexuality as fullness. Such a language would allow both mother and daughter a separate identity while maintaining the loving unity of the maternal bond. It would be a relationship of one and other at the same time. Irigaray seeks to figure such a relationship in her lyrical essay 'When Our Lips Speak Together'. In this extract notice the qualities the writing shares with Cixous's celebratory construction of feminine identity and language and consider also the kind of criticisms that might be made about it.

> I love you: our two lips cannot separate to let just *one* word pass. A single word that would say 'you' or 'me.' Or 'equals'; she who loves, she who is loved. Closed and open, neither ever excluding the other, they say they both love each other. Together . . .
>
> Open your lips; don't open them simply. I don't open them simply. We – you/I – are neither open nor closed. We never separate simply: *a single word* cannot be pronounced, produced, uttered by our mouths. Between our lips, yours and mine, several voices, several ways of speaking resound endlessly, back and forth. One is never separable from the other. You/I: we are always several at once . . .
>
> Kiss me. Two lips kissing two lips: openness is ours again. Our 'world.' And the passage from the inside out, from the outside in, the passage between us is limitless. Without end. No knot, no loop, no mouth ever stops our exchanges. Between us the house has no wall . . . When you kiss me the world grows so large that the horizon itself disappears.[34]

This particular piece of writing by Irigaray is more sensuously erotic than the passages from 'Medusa', but it expresses a similar affirmation of feminine identity and sexuality as open, flowing, abundant, multiple, as opposed to the masculine valorization of a single organ. Irigaray uses the image of women's lips to suggest the plurality of their sexuality; women's genitals are naturally self-caressing, she says, and this figures the desired loving unity within separation which should be possible for mother and daughter, woman and woman. Does the affirmation of a language and identity based on the physical sensuality of the female body leave Irigaray open to the criticisms of proposing a utopian escape from the social and of essentialism? In relation to the first of these charges, Elizabeth Grosz has argued that 'the "two lips" is not meant as a truthful image of female anatomy but as a new emblem by which female sexuality can be positively *represented* . . . Irigaray's project can be interpreted as a contestation of patriarchal representations *at the level of cultural representation itself.* The two lips is a manoeuvre to develop a different image or model of female sexuality.'[35] The two lips function as a metaphor of the multiplicity of women's eroticism and for the potential of a woman's language to speak that polymorphous excess. This is a convincing argument, and it is clear that Irigaray consistently regards the human body as always already coded within a network of cultural meaning. There is no way of figuring the female body outside the symbolic order; there is no other language available.

Nevertheless, Irigaray's aim is to theorize the separate sexual specificity of a feminine self; she is not concerned with the notion of pre-Oedipal bisexuality. It is difficult to see how this specifically feminine identity can ever be conceptualized without involving some form of essentialism. However, we should remember that Irigaray's conception of sexual difference takes the form of A and B, rather than of A and A−. Perhaps, as some feminists are beginning to argue, this form of difference not founded on the denigration of the subordinated term could produce an essentialism which no longer poses a threat to women's positive identity.[36]

However, this might point towards another problem: the danger that sexuality becomes wholly synonymous with subjectivity. Is there not more to feminine identity than being able to represent the specificity of feminine sexuality, important though this is? The relationship of sexuality and identity to social and historical reality will form the theme of chapters 6 and 7. So finally, here is a poem by Grace Nichols celebrating the specificity of the female body. To what extent does the sexual identity the poem constructs articulate an opposing order of meaning outside or beyond the symbolic order? How far does it remain within that order, contesting it?

My Black Triangle

My black triangle
sandwiched between the geography of my thighs

is a bermuda
of tiny atoms
forever seizing
and releasing
the world

My black triangle
is so rich
that it flows over
on to the dry crotch
of the world

My black triangle
is black light
sitting on the threshold of the world
overlooking
all my deep probabilities

And though
it spares a thought for history
my black triangle
has spread beyond his story
beyond the dry fears of parch-ri-archy

Spreading and growing
trusting and flowing
my black triangle
carries the seal of approval
of my deepest self.[37]

Summary of Main Points:

1 A feminist critique of male psychoanalytic theory focuses on its negative constructions of feminine identity within a repressive patriarchal system of language: feminist theorists emphasize the pre-Oedipal mother-child relationship to propose alternative accounts.

2 Irigaray attacks the 'logic of the same' in western thought whereby two genders (female and male) are collapsed into a male norm, so that women remain unrepresented within our meaning system. Freud's 'penis-envy' makes this most explicit: feminine identity is defined only as a lack.

3 Irigaray points to a suspicious similarity between male valorization of a single sexual organ and the privileging of a unitary notion of truth.

4 Deconstructionist theory demonstrates that any privileged term depends on

its subordinated opposing term. (The concept 'truth' gains meaning only in relation to the term 'false'.) Irigaray insists that masculinity as phallic presence depends on defining femininity as lack.

5   Cixous links the political violence produced by such binary oppositional thinking with a male libidinal economy based on possession and property: there can be no ownership without exclusions.

6   Women's libidinal economy is based on the 'gift' – giving without calculating return – and this is the foundation of a woman's practice of writing which Cixous advocates as a means of discovering a feminine identity.

7   Cixous claims that feminine writing can never be defined; her own practice foregrounds excess as opposed to lack. It emphasizes pre-Oedipal qualities of voice, rhythm, touch, when child and mother were one. It pluralizes meaning to construct feminine identity as multiple in opposition to the claim of patriarchal language to unitary truth.

8   Irigaray theorizes a very similar pluralized woman's language, but while Cixous believes that men share pre-Oedipal bisexuality and so can produce 'feminine' writing, Irigaray's concern is gender-specific. She celebrates the multiple forms of the female sexual body and the loving identity of the mother–daughter bond.

Suggestions for Further Reading

Luce Irigaray

You may like to read some of Irigaray's own writing. Marks and de Courtivron (eds), *New French Feminisms*, contains two extracts from her work (pp. 99–110).

Elizabeth Grosz, *Sexual Subversions*, contains a detailed chapter on Irigaray (pp. 100–83). Grosz also provides a shorter but useful section on Irigaray in *Jacques Lacan*, pp. 167–83.

Sara Mills et al., *Feminist Readings/Feminists Reading*, provides a reading of Angela Carter's *The Magic Toyshop* using Irigaray's ideas (pp. 170–86).

Hélène Cixous

Marks and de Courtivron (eds), *New French Feminisms*, contains the whole of 'The Laugh of the Medusa' and an extract from 'Sorties' (pp. 90–8, 245–64). Extracts of Cixous's writing are also included in Belsey and Moore (eds), *The Feminist Reader*, pp. 101–16, and in dialogue with Catherine Clément in Mary Eagleton (ed.), *Feminist Literary Criticism*, pp. 110–34.

Morag Shiach, *Hélène Cixous*. A helpful introduction to her work generally.
Nicole Ward Jouve, *White Woman Speaks with Forked Tongue*, pp. 91–100,
provides a spirited personal defence of Cixous's work against her critics.

Notes

1   Writing by many other French feminists is represented in Marks and de
    Courtivron (eds), *New French Feminisms*. See also Moi (ed.), *French Feminist
    Thought*.
2   Irigaray, *This Sex which is not One*, p. 69.
3   *The Speculum of the Other Woman*, p. 28.
4   Ibid. p. 27.
5   My discussion here is indebted to Grosz, 'Luce Irigaray and Sexual Dif-
    ference', in *Sexual Subversions*, pp. 104–7.
6   De Beauvoir, *The Second Sex*, p. 16.
7   Irigaray, *This Sex which is not One*, p. 74.
8   *The Speculum of the Other Woman*, p. 22.
9   The key texts in which Derrida elaborates these ideas are *Of Grammatology*
    and *Writing and Difference*. For an intoduction to Derrida's work see
    Norris, *Derrida*.
10 There is an outline of Saussure's ideas in ch. 4.
11 Cixous, 'Sorties: Out and Out: Attacks/Ways Out/Forays', in Cixous and
    Clément, *The Newly Born Woman*, p. 63.
12 Ibid., p. 64.
13 Ibid., p. 70.
14 Ibid., p. 71.
15 Ibid., p. 87.
16 Ibid.
17 Cixous, 'The Laugh of the Medusa', in Marks and de Courtivron (eds),
    New French Feminisms, p. 253.
18 Cixous and Clément, *The Newly Born Woman*, p. 72.
19 Cixous, 'The Laugh of the Medusa', pp. 248, 251, 258.
20 'Some Psychical Consequences of the Anatomical Distinction between the
    Sexes', in *On Sexuality*, p. 336.
21 Cixous, 'The Laugh of the Medusa', p. 252.
22 Cixous, *Angst* p. 7.
23 Cixous and Clément, *The Newly Born Woman*, p. 65.
24 Ibid., p. 83.
25 Cixous, 'The Laugh of the Medusa', p. 252.
26 Ibid., p. 254.

27 *The Ladybird*, pp. 99–100.
28 Ibid., p. 110.
29 Ibid., p. 124.
30 Irigaray, *This Sex which is not One*, p. 68.
31 Ibid., p. 9.
32 Irigaray, *The Speculum of the Other Woman*, p. 143.
33 Irigaray, *This Sex which is not One*, pp. 63–4.
34 Ibid., pp. 208, 209, 210.
35 Grosz, *Sexual Subversions*, p. 116.
36 Margaret Whitford, 'Rereading Irigaray', in Brennan (ed.), *Between Feminism and Psychoanalysis*, pp. 106–26, also defends Irigaray against the charge of essentialism.
37 Nichols, *Lazy Thoughts of a Lazy Woman*, p. 25.

6

Identities in Process: Poststructuralism, Julia Kristeva and Intertextuality

The ideas outlined in chapters 4 and 5 form part of a large-scale questioning in western societies, since the end of the nineteenth century, of the two most central aspects of our reality: the way we perceive the human individual and language.[1] As always with major changes in frameworks of thinking, there are multiple interacting causes and effects. The scale and horror of the First World War destroyed any easy reliance on established beliefs, social and spiritual. Also in the early twentieth century, Freud and Einstein propounded radical new theories of human nature and of our relation to the universe. At the same time, writers, visual artists and musicians produced what then seemed strange, disturbing works that dismantled traditional forms and challenged existing values and assumptions. This iconoclastic movement in the arts in the early decades of the twentieth century is known as Modernism largely because of its claims to 'make new' all the old forms of expression and perception. In many ways the theories we discussed in earlier chapters can be seen as the conceptualization and development of the explosion of new ideas and ways of perceiving at the beginning of the century. At the centre of this thinking and questioning are some of our long-held 'common-sense' assumptions about the individual and language.

The long tradition of western humanist individualism is so-called because it places the human individual at the centre of its conception of reality. Our belief in the possibility of truth, knowledge and freedom is based, ultimately, in our belief in a sovereign individual who is the intentional author of her or his own words, thoughts, deeds and will. Our notion of a coherent inner consciousness – subjectivity – is central to our sense of individual existence. Human beings, we believe, can reflect on their experience – can know it – and can then express it truthfully. To be able to do so, we feel, is the guarantee of human freedom. This set of assumptions is succinctly expressed for us in Descartes's famous dictum 'I think therefore I am'. However, the belief in individual consciousness as guaranteeing the possibility of meaning and truth to human existence is fundamentally challenged by Freud's theory of the unconscious.[2] An individual's conscious intention and knowledge cannot provide the basis for a self-certain and sovereign identity when the self is perceived as fractured, the unconscious as an unknowable 'other scene' of some its most powerful desires, fantasies and self-projections. In Lacan's elaboration of Freudian theory instead of a unitary, coherent self, identity is perceived as plural, indeterminate, even illusionary.

The common-sense view that language can unproblematically express the truth of human experience has also been wholly undermined. Modernist writers refused to confirm the sense, offered in earlier writing, that their words were expressing their personal thoughts and feelings or offering objective reflections of reality. Instead, they made readers focus on language itself and think consciously about the relationship of words to experience. This questioning of language by writers was taken further by structuralist linguistics, which points out that there is always a gap between language and the world, that our sense of 'reality' is produced by the grid of meaning we impose on the continuity of experience. Words do not reflect, they construct our sense of self and the world. Deconstruction has developed this insight to reveal the complicity of language with power structures. Language – the symbolic order – imposes its grid of meaning in the form of a system of conceptual differences or oppositions: masculine and feminine, self and other, good and evil. By this means it continually reproduces 'reality' as a hierarchy of values which sustains the interests of dominant power. Language is the means by which these hierarchical values seem to us natural and true. It is in the interest of power to impose this ideological perception of reality as the only possible one, the unitary 'Truth'. However, deconstructive theories of language also show us that unitary closed definition is actually impossible. Even the most privileged concept has to depend on its despised opposite for its meaning. 'Good' needs 'evil' to acquire its sense, 'masculinity' is dependent on 'femininity'. The unconscious, too, disrupts attempts to control social meaning. Repressed feeling is *condensed* and *displaced* in language, pluralizing words, making them ambiguous and heterogeneous. What we ask for is rarely all that we desire.

Within this poststructuralist framework the conventional idea of the author is also deconstructed.[3] Instead of thinking of a literary text as originating in the conscious intentions of a rational, gendered individual, shaping and controlling every aspect of the work to produce her or his own unique meaning, poststructuralist critics see literary texts as sites of multiple meanings and intentions. Instead of 'author', the term 'writing subject' is preferred to suggest that conscious intention is only one impulse among many determining meaning; unconscious desire also 'speaks' through the words, but equally the words are saturated with cultural implications. No writer comes to words or literary forms that are newly minted; multiple previous uses and meanings remain active to some extent within each new arrangement. For this reason the term 'intertextuality' has become current to suggest that many 'texts' or voices (conscious authorial intention, unconscious desire, current and past social implications) meet in every apparently discrete individual work. The conscious intended meaning of the author determines only a small part of this complex intertextuality. As Julia Kristeva argues, 'Writing is upheld not by the subject of understanding, but by a divided subject, even a pluralized subject, that occupies . . . permutable, multiple and even mobile places.'[4] We saw, in chapter 5, that the writer as a 'mobile' subject can be conceived as occupying the 'permutable' place of bisexuality.

Poststructuralist theory suggests there is a continuous contestation within meaning and within individual identity between repressive social control on the one hand and disruptive excess on the other. Language is the means of imposing unitary definition on things and people, denying the continuum and multiple potential of actuality. So, too, our socially gendered identity is constructed and fixed as we are 'put into our place' within the conceptual order. However, as well as this repressive function, language also contains the excess of meaning that constantly threatens to disrupt the boundaries of these defined identities and expose the fiction of any imposed 'truth'. It is easy to see why these ideas have been so attractive to feminists and why feminists have made such substantial contributions to poststructuralist theory. It offers the most powerful explanation currently available for the intransigency of patriarchal structures of power. What is more, as Irigaray argues, the imposed binary gender oppositions are the keystone of the whole conceptual order.

Within feminist literary criticism, poststructuralist ideas have been influential since the early 1980s. In general, this theoretical orientation has not been sympathetic to earlier feminist approaches which affirmed the authority and truth of women's writing on the basis of the author's own subjective identity as a woman. Any simple identification of author and meaning seems to ignore the pluralized identity of the writing subject and the intertextuality of texts. In the same way, realist forms of women's writing, valued by feminists operating within a humanist framework for offering positive images of female experience, find less favour with poststructuralist critics. The depiction of characters as 'real' and the implicit claims to offer 'life as it is', can seem complicit with a humanist account of truth as guaranteed by individual consciousness and reflected in language. In Cixous's terms such texts are not 'mole-like': they do not undermine the very foundations of our conceptual order. For example, even though a realist text like *Daughter of Earth* offers a searing account of women's suffering, it may still seem to confirm a restricted unitary sense of individual identity and the binary opposition of male and female categories. As such it does not break apart the gender ideology which sustains a patriarchal order as natural. I shall return to the debate between realism and poststructuralism at the end of the chapter.

Poststructuralist critics acclaim pluralized texts which exceed stable systems of meaning. A reading practice has been developed which aims to decode the repressive ideology of the text and its complicity with dominant power. But equally it aims to bring into full play the text's own 'revolutionary' excess, the places where language turns against itself, refusing to settle into a unitary meaning. As an example of this we could take Shakespeare's play, *Cymbeline*, which we considered in chapter 1. You will remember that the heroine, Imogen, is constructed according to the stereotypical 'good woman': she is loyal, chaste, loving and forgiving. In stark contrast, her stepmother is false, murderous and vengeful. This provides a typical example of the repressive binary ordering of identity within dominant discourse: women are either good or evil, true or false. The play offers no explanation for each woman's personality; their virtue or vice is simply the essential innate attribute of their character. This sense of identity or 'nature' as inborn (natural) is important elsewhere in the play in relation to kingly and royal class identity. Imogen's brothers, the young princes, are stolen from the court as babies and brought up in a cave in Wales. Despite their rude upbringing, they spontaneously develop the 'royal' qualities of courage and leadership, which are presented as the essential attributes of kingly blood.

There are, however, moments of 'excess' in the text which subvert the conservative essentialist ideology of gender and class identity as innate nature, unalterable by any external, social circumstances. In her despair at her husband's, condemnation of her as unfaithful, Imogen is persuaded by her servant to disguise herself as a man. 'You must forget to be a woman', he says, and as Imogen seizes eagerly on the idea she affirms, 'I see into thy end, and am almost / A man already.'[5] Simply by putting on male clothing Imogen passes as a man, unremarked by any other character despite the play's ideological insistence on identity as innate and inborn. When, unknown to any of them, Imogen meets up with her two lost brothers, blood instinctively recognizes blood and strong impulses of affection spring up between them, but there is no such intuitive recognition of her actual gender identity. Within Shakespeare's texts generally the representation of female characters confirms essentialist definitions of woman, but equally they suggest, in the frequent cross-dressings and disguised identities, a plural and unboundaried quality to sexuality.[6]

French feminists associate such excess of meaning with a subversive feminine libidinal energy which is ultimately uncontainable within the binary gender identities imposed by the symbolic order. However, women should be cautious, perhaps, of assuming too readily that discovering their denied sexuality is always and necessarily a route (a *sortie*) to freedom; that its articulation is invariably the language of subversion and excess in opposition to the order of control. The work of Michel Foucault, especially his *History of Sexuality* (1976), offers a sober warning of the way even seemingly 'progressive' language can be an effect of repressive power. Foucault shows how, since the eighteenth century, specialisms of 'knowledge' have proliferated (medicine, psychology, criminology, education) which position the human body within a network of observational, disciplinary and training structures. In *The*

History of Sexuality he produces a persuasive argument against the optimism that the twentieth century has seen the beginning of a liberation from the sexual repressions of the past. He suggests that we have merely seen a change in methods of control from external force to internalized coercion. He begins by noting how gratifying we find the sense of daring to speak openly on a subject considered to be taboo: 'If sex is repressed, that is condemned to prohibition, nonexistence and silence, then the mere fact that one is speaking about it has the appearance of a deliberate transgression . . . we are conscious of defying established power, our tone of voice shows that we know we are being subversive.'[7]

He then demonstrates that the gratification in subversive freedom of speech is actually a coerced effect of 'an apparatus for producing an ever greater quantity of discourse about sex'.[8] This 'discursive apparatus' was brought into being by an increasingly personalized and detailed concern with sexual behaviour on the part of authority from the eighteenth century onwards. In effect, the 'apparatus' consists of a network of discourses and practices which acquire their authority from the traditional and newly developing professions and disciplines of religion, law, medicine, psychiatry, criminology and education. 'Sex was driven out of hiding and constrained to lead a discursive life . . . Surely no other type of society has ever accumulated – and in such a relatively short span of time – a similar quantity of discourses concerned with sex.'[9] Foucault also points out that the proliferation of 'discourses of knowledge' on sexual behaviour focused particularly upon those social groups it was felt necessary to control for the maintenance of social order: children, the working class and women. The effect of the discursive scrutiny is that 'sex was constituted as a problem of truth' and that western society has 'become a singularly confessing society'.[10] The internalized compulsion to discover and articulate sexuality as a problem is confused by us for a newly found freedom to speak the 'truth'.

> The obligation to confess is now relayed through so many different points, is so deeply ingrained in us, that we no longer perceive it as the effect of a power that constrains us; on the contrary, it seems to us that truth, lodged in our most secret nature, 'demands' only to surface.[11]

The transformation of fiction during the nineteenth century from narratives of external adventures to explorations of the hidden 'inner' nature of the characters is seen by Foucault as another feature of the western confessional compulsion. Foucault's work is suggestive in relation to the predisposition of many women writers towards the 'confessional' forms of autobiography and first-person narration, types of writing that foreground identity. Women, more than any other group, have been the object of the most intense and elaborated discourses aimed at producing female sexuality as a 'problem' to be minutely observed, pathologized and articulated. Could this perhaps have produced in women a particularly intense compulsion towards confession? This might make us pause before we celebrate all such writing as a liberating form of self-expression. What Foucault's work on discourses as historically situated practices has consistently demonstrated is that the will to discipline and control frequently operates covertly in those forms of language we might associate with progressive thinking. We can only recognize this will to control if we situate language as specific historical practice. It is for this reason that the term 'discourse' has come into use to indicate a linguistic system or practice specific to a particular social group or historical time. 'Language', in contrast, tends to imply a universal, overarching structure of meaning encompassing an entire culture. [12]

There is a further danger involved in the tendency to equate sexuality with a liberation of self: it can easily function to shift attention from the public and historical to the private and individual. 'The personal is the political' easily slides into a slogan for depoliticization. In some radical feminist discourse sexuality seems to become synonomous with subjectivity – synonomous even with 'freedom'. Foucault remarks that it is 'as if it were essential for us to be able to draw from that little piece of ourselves not only pleasure but knowledge . . . Whenever it is a question of knowing who we are, it is this logic that henceforth serves as our master key.'[13] The novel *Open the Door* (1920), by Catherine Carswell, can be used to illustrate the point. It is set in Glasgow and London in the first two decades of the twentieth century and, as the title suggests, traces the heroine Joanna Bannerman's attempts to escape the confinement of her middle-class Calvinistic upbringing and find a more meaningful identity than that of her mother's self-denying conception of womanhood. In the early pages of the book, as a little girl, Joanna experiences a visionary moment as the train she is on crosses the Jamaica Bridge over the Clyde as a great liner makes its way seaward. This picture is framed and cut by the interposing black metal trellis of the bridge: 'The sunshine on that outgoing vessel and the great, glistening current of brown water filled her with painful yet exquisite longings.'[14]

For the rest of the narrative Joanna fights against the grids of convention and social expectations in order to reach that glimpsed wider world. She insists on going to art school, wins a scholarship and begins to develop the capacity to earn money from her work so as to be financially independent. The early parts of the novel evoke a specific sense of a precise historical moment and social group in Glasgow at the beginning of the century. However, as the narrative progresses the cultural specificity of the writing fades just the heroine's struggle for the right to work, to earn a living, falls away. More and more the need to 'open the door' (to find a *sortie*) becomes a search solely for sexual fulfilment. In the final section, amid much Lawrencian symbolism, the heroine at last reaches 'living knowledge'; 'It was life that she ran for now.'[15] What she is actually running towards are the arms of the only man who can offer her sexual realization, who can offer her her self. In narrative time this culmination takes place just as the First World War begins; moreover, Joanna's quest for personal space and freedom coincides with the suffragists' struggles which in Glasgow centred on the activities of students and teachers at the College of Art. Her search for her 'self', however, becomes wholly identified with her sexuality.

It would be unfair to say that either Cixous or Irigaray seeks to divert the political into the narrowly individual, but at times their ahistorical emphasis on sexuality as excess and their identification of it with a universal feminine subjectivity tends towards this danger. In this respect, Foucault's work on the production of discourses at specific moments of history and his analysis of their functioning as material practices of control and discipline (medicine, education, sexology) provides a useful counterbalance to the depolitical and ahistorical tendency within poststructuralism at times.

Julia Kristeva

Of the three French feminist theorists whose work has been most influential in the English-speaking world, Julia Kristeva is the most cautious in her claims. Although her early major work, her doctoral thesis, is entitled *Revolution in Poetic Language* (1974), her theories of language and the construction of subject identity are less affirmatively optimistic than those of Cixous or Irigaray. Kristeva is like Cixous and Irigaray in basing language on the pre-Oedipal relationship between child and mother and in shifting the emphasis away from Freudian and Lacanian concern with the Oedipal father. Indeed, Kristeva's work draws considerably on the psychoanalyst Melanie Klein's study of the early mother–child relationship. Kristeva uses the term 'semiotic' for the first pre-Oedipal phase of life to suggest that it is at this stage that the first traces of what will become the signifying process of verbal language are established. In the preverbal semiotic phase the child has acquired no sense of separate identity; its physical experience is part of a continuum with the maternal body. The sensations that construct its physical existence are the rhythms of heartbeat and pulse, dark and light, hot and cold, the regular intaking and outgiving of breath and food and faeces. It is the gradual ordering and patterning of these physical drives and impulses that provides the necessary basis of possibility for the process of signification – the production of meaning. 'Voice, hearing, and sight are the archaic dispositions where the earliest forms of discreteness emerge. The breast given and withdrawn; lamplight capturing the gaze; intermittent sound of voice or music . . . At that point, breast, light, and sound become a *there*: a place, a spot, a marker.'[16] Without this initial ordering of the continuous flux of physical sensation and libidinal drives washing over the child and the resulting simultaneous beginnings of separate identity, language would be impossible, Kristeva argues. These rhythmic semiotic traces provide and remain the foundation of all language.

Hence she argues that language, once it is acquired with the child's entry into the symbolic order by means of the Oedipal crisis, always contains within it two dispositions or 'modalities': 'We shall call the first *"the semiotic"* and the second *"the symbolic"*. These two modalities are inseparable within the signifying process that constitutes language, and the dialectic between them determines the type of discourse (narrative, metalanguage, theory, poetry, etc.) involved.'[17] What Kristeva calls the *symbolic* modality is the aspect of language that the child directs towards the object world of other people and things. As such, its disposition is towards fixed and unitary definition in order to provide the basis of shared meaning which enables interpersonal communication to take place.

However, the *symbolic* disposition is also driven by an urge to master and control, through the act of defining, what is other and therefore potentially threatening to the self. On the other hand, the origins of the *semiotic* modality lie in the non-gendered libidinal drives of the pre-Oedipal phase so that its disposition is towards meaning as a continuum, with identification rather than separation from what is other. Hence Kristeva's sense of language is of a dialectical relationship between its two modalities to produce discursive practice (language as actually spoken or written) *as a process*, not a static structure or order of meaning. The symbolic disposition imposes the necessary uniformity of meaning and syntactic structure to allow for social communication, while the semiotic continually destabilizes that urge for fixity, producing a 'revolution' in the controlling force of the symbolic so as to ensure the generative potential for new meaning.

Thus Kristeva, unlike Cixous or Irigardy, does not put forward a separate 'other' language of excess in opposition to the repressive force of the symbolic order; rather she theorizes an alternative view of language as constituting both order and disruption within itself *as a process*. Forms of discourse can then be characterized according to which disposition predominates; scientific language and mathematics, for example, allow little irruption of the semiotic and aim at closely defined fixed meanings. Language that allows maximum opening to the semiotic is termed 'poetic language' by Kristeva and is characterized by rhythmic qualities, a heightening of sound patterning, disruption of syntax and heterogeneity. The examples Kristeva analyses are almost invariably literary texts, and she repeatedly insists that even in its most intense manifestations the semiotic must always retain the ordering presence of the symbolic. Without this control, such language is completely overwhelmed by the force of unconscious drives and becomes psychotic utterance. For this reason she is sceptical of claims for a woman's language derived from a feminine libidinal body or economy.

A key concept throughout Kristeva's work has been that of a 'boundary' or 'threshold', especially the permutable boundary between the conscious and unconscious. It is on this threshold site that the social and the psychic interact in a dialogue or dialectic which produces communicative utterance. Kristeva describes this as a dialogue between unconscious desire ('I say what I like') and the social ('I say for you, for us, so that we can understand each other').[18] This 'intertext' or dialogic (in dialogue) interaction between the unconscious and social forms produces language as utterance always 'in process', as Kristeva puts it. Meaning remains shareable but always in a state of generative instability. Similarly, identity is constructed on this intertextuality or boundary between the unconscious drives and the social; self is thus a dialogic interaction of these two dispositions and produces a subject also 'in process' – a pluralized identity never fixed and finished. Crucially for Kristeva, it is a self that remains within the social order; to opt out of the symbolic order altogether is, for her, to opt out of history. Disengaged from the symbolic modality, the 'revolutionary' potential of the semiotic disposition explodes into non-sense or madness.

Like Cixous, Kristeva associates the maternal pre-Oedipal stage with non-gendered sexuality and perceives men as having the same access as women to the creative force of the semiotic. Indeed, most of the texts Kristeva has based her work on have been written by avant-garde male writers, and her work, too, is open to the charge of elitism (see chapter 5). What about women, though, in Kristeva's scheme of things? In *About Chinese Women* (1974), she writes of 'the importance of pre-Oedipal phases . . . in the subsequent development of both boy and girl. The child is bound to the mother's body without the latter being, as yet, a "separate object". Instead, the mother's body acts with the child's as a sort of socio-natural continuum.'[19] Kristeva considers the consequences for girls of this intense mother–child attachment and sets out three positions they can assume at the Oedipal stage as they enter the social order.

In her essay 'Women's Time' (1979), she associates the three positions with the historical development of the women's movement in the twentieth century. She argues that different stages of the movement's development have been characterized by the predominance of one or other of these three positions or modalities. In order to become social beings at all women must identify with the symbolic order, and this involves accepting the system of meanings and values which embodies patriarchy. Kristeva argues that the very difficulty that girls, as opposed to boys, have in detaching themselves from the pre-Oedipal mother can intensify their subsequent identification with patriarchal values as a kind of safeguard against the maternal. In adopting this position a woman may either internalize 'masculine' ideals of competition, aggressiveness, power, thereby seeking success and recognition as if a man, or she may conform eagerly to the 'feminine' ideals men value in women. Either of these moves aligns her with the paternal or symbolic modality. In their struggle to reject an apparently all-powerful pre-Oedipal mother, women may over-invest emotionally in the paternal position.

In 'Women's Time' Kristeva characterizes the first stage of the women's movement, up to 1968, with its egalitarian demands for equal wages and social and political rights as operating predominantly from this position. She is not critical of it as such, but points out that up to now women's success in these aims have left the existing power structures unshaken. There is always the danger for women of over-investing in the patriarchal values these systems ultimately validate: 'The difficulty presented by this logic of integrating the second sex into a value-system experienced as foreign . . . [is] how to detach women from it and how then to proceed, through their critical, differential and autonomous interventions, to render decision-making institutions more flexible.'[20]

In contradistinction to paternal 'symbolic' identification, women can retain their attachment to the maternal, the 'semiotic'. However, Kristeva criticizes those feminists who build what she sees as utopian hopes on this second position. A desire to return to the maternal will always entail a more seductive and dangerous impulse for women, since for them the social order is inevitably more 'frustrating, mutilating, sacrifical' than it is for men.[21] Kristeva associates the second women's generation (post-1968) with a predominance of the maternal modality. She sees it as a reaction to women's sense of disenchantment, at that time, with the egalitarian political aims of the first generation. Instead of demanding equality with men, the second generation of the 1970s insists on a feminine difference and affirms the maternal as the foundation of a counter-society 'imagined as harmonious, without prohibitions, free and fulfilling' – all that the social order is not.[22] This construction of an idealized myth of maternal femininity, universal and timeless, is sought as a refuge to a historical reality which denies women even an adequate language to articulate 'their relationships with the nature of their own bodies . . . [with a] child, another woman, or a man'.[23] However, Kristeva argues that this maternal dream is always utopian. By espousing this form of mythic ideal, feminism risks opting out of the historical struggle. This form of radical feminist separatism, which characterized much of the women's movement in France and America during the 1970s, easily evolves into a substitute for religious belief, Kristeva claims, its discourse rejoining that of 'marginal groups of spiritual and mystical inspiration'.[24]

Kristeva believes that the desire to return to an imagined semiotic order is a dangerous position for an individual woman, as well as for feminism as a movement. By rejecting the symbolic order which sustains social identity a woman leaves herself unprotected and open to the full force of unconscious desire, of which the most powerful is always the death drive. A desire to return to the mother can become a desire for loss of identity, for a dissolution of self in m/other – for death. Since poetic language is the form of discourse most open to the semiotic drive, constructing itself on the threshold of the unconscious with the social, creative aesthetic activity is seen by Kristeva as more risky for women writers than for male writers. There is always a greater chance that they will be overwhelmed by the repressed unconscious forces they release: 'I think of Virginia Woolf, who sank wordlessly into the river . . . Haunted by voices, waves, lights, in love with colours – blue green . . . Or I think of the dark corner of the deserted farmhouse in the Russian countryside where, a few months later in that same year of 1941, Maria Tsvetaeva, fleeing the war, hanged herself, the most rhythmic of Russian poets.'[25] At times like this in her writing Kristeva is open to the criticism that in austerly refusing a consolatory myth of a nurturing utopian pre-Oedipal mother she falls for the opposing myth of an engulfing, annihilating mother, an image we are familiar with in many male-authored texts.

This is perhaps a little unfair, since what she is concerned with is not real mothers but with the fantasy mother the child constructs during the pre-Oedipal phase and which remains a repressed but potent image in the unconscious. Obviously, a child's fantasies encompass both maternal images – of plenitude and annihilation. It is the former that Kristeva perceives as offering the delusory temptation for women, given what she terms the sacrificial demands made on them within the social order. Before going on to the third position available to women, let's consider how the following passages from Kate Chopin's *The Awakening* (1899), one of the first 'rediscovered' women's texts, could be read thematically and stylistically within the framework of Kristeva's ideas. The heroine Edna Pontellier gradually comes to see her comfortable and conventional social identity as wife and mother as alienating and imposed. This 'awakening' takes place during the family's long summer vacation by the sea at

Grand Isle, when she becomes romantically attracted to the son of a neighbour.

> Edna Pontellier could not have told why, wishing to go to the beach with Robert, she should in the first place have declined, and in the second place have followed in obedience to one of the two contradictory impulses which impelled her.
>
> A certain light was beginning to dawn dimly within her – the light which, showing the way, forbids it . . .
>
> In short, Mrs Pontellier was beginning to realize her position in the universe as a human being, and to recognize her relations as an individual to the world within and about her. This may seem like a ponderous weight of wisdom to descend upon the soul of a young woman of twenty-eight – perhaps more wisdom than the Holy Ghost is usually pleased to vouchsafe to any woman . . .
>
> The voice of the sea is seductive; never ceasing, whispering, clamoring, murmuring, inviting the soul to wander for a spell in abysses of solitude; to lose itself in mazes of inward contemplation.
>
> The voice of the sea speaks to the soul. The touch of the sea is sensuous, enfolding the body in its soft, close embrace.[26]

After this passage it is no surprise to discover that Edna's most sensuous experience of freedom comes not in the arms of Robert, but when she learns to swim. Gradually she rejects all the conventional ways of behaving expected of women in her situation and class; she even gives up the care of her children to their grandmother. Her husband offers surprisingly little resistance, allowing her to follow her own inclinations in the hope that she will eventually see sense. This is not a story of a woman forcibly required to conform to a repressive social code. The climax of her rejection of her previous conventional identity is symbolized by her in a farewell dinner she gives before leaving her former marital home:

> But as she sat there among her guests, she felt the old ennui overtaking her, the hopelessness which so often assailed her, which came upon her like an obsession, like some extraneous, independent volition. It was something which announced itself; a chill breath that seemed to issue from some vast cavern wherein discords wailed. There came over her the acute longing which always summoned into her spiritual vision the presence of the beloved one, overpowering her at once with a sense of the unobtainable.[27]

Ultimately, under the force of this 'chill' impulse Edna returns to the sea at Grand Isle:

> Despondency had come over her there in the wakeful night, and had never lifted. There was no one thing in the world that she desired. There was no human being she wanted near her except Robert; and she even realized that the day would come when he, too, and the thought of him would melt out of her existence, leaving her alone . . .
>
> The water of the Gulf stretched out before her, gleaming with the million lights of the sun. The voice of the sea is seductive, never ceasing, whispering, clamoring, inviting the soul to wander in abysses of solitude . . .
>
> The foamy wavelets curled up to her white feet, and coiled like serpents about her ankles. She walked out. The water was chill, but she walked on. The water was deep, but she lifted her white body and reached out with a long sweeping stroke. The touch of the sea is sensuous, enfolding the body in its soft, close embrace.[28]

What is represented here is a process in which rejection of social identity by the heroine slips into a desire for the total dissolution of self. The narrative sets out as if to chart Edna Pontellier's discovery and expression of her repressed sexuality, rather in the way *Open the Door!* traces its heroine's pursuit of sexual fulfilment. What it actually seems to trace is the working of the death instinct once the barrier of social identity is breached. It is death in the seductive image of a soft, enclosing maternal embrace.

The stylistic features one could pick out as suggesting a strong semiotic impulse within the writing are perhaps almost too obvious. There is the heightening of sound effects with massive use of alliteration ('The voice of the sea is seductive'), rhythmic phrasing and persistent repetition of words and phrases. The repeated lists of present participles – 'never ceasing', 'whispering', 'clamoring', 'murmuring', 'inviting' – and the switch to the present tense in those places produces an effect of hypnotic dream-like timelessness. I think the most interesting feature of the passages quoted here is the sudden and complete change of tone from the brisk, rational, no-nonsense voice of the omniscient narrator in the initial paragraphs of the first quoted passage ('This may seem like a ponderous weight of wisdom to descend upon . . .') to the incantatory poetic intensity of the final two paragraphs in that passage ('The voice of the sea is seductive'). It really does seem as if an unconscious force suddenly makes itself felt in the language.

For Kristeva, repressed desire is not to be identified as an inevitable force for freedom; libidinal energies can equally be invested in an over-zealous conformity with patriarchal values or in a regressive impulse for self-dissolution. The possibility of 'revolution' exists only in language and in subjects operating on the threshold between control and disruption; between the unconscious and the social. This is the third position available to women. Moreover, despite the risks involved for women in operating across this permutable border, Kristeva suggests that women, because they are always marginalized within the social order, are more likely than men to become generating spaces of a new order of meaning. In 'Women's Time' this is the third generation of feminism which Kristeva both advocates and believes may be emerging: 'Are women not already participating in the rapid dismantling that our age is experiencing . . . and which poses the *demand* for a new ethics'?[29] It is perhaps here that she most closely aligns herself with the utopian feminist hopes of the 1970s. In *About Chinese Women*, having called for a rejection of the two extremes of the symbolic and semiotic dispositions, she urges instead the 'impossible dialectic of the two terms; a permanent alternation'. Who, here and now, she asks, is capable of this risky balance of extremes, and answers, 'perhaps, a woman'.[30]

Kristeva uses the term 'intertextuality' to refer to the dialectic interaction of the symbolic and semiotic modalities which constitutes language.[31] Like the 'symbolic', the 'semiotic' is a signifying system producing meaning by those unconscious processes of displacement and condensation (which are outlined in chapter 4). Thus all our utterances can be seen as the meeting-place of at least two texts – of social meaning with unconscious desire – hence an intertextuality.

The poetry of H.D. has been recognized by many readers as operating across boundaries. She described women as having to do 'a tight-rope act' balanced on 'very, very frail wire'.[32] Her first book of poems was called *Sea Garden*, the title itself indicating an intertextuality of two disparate verbal concepts: water and earth. Many poems in the collection celebrate the qualities of flowers that exist on that harsh borderline between sea and land. The 'Sea Rose' 'marred and with a stint of petals' is 'more precious / than a wet rose / single on a stem'.[33] In

'Oread', one of her most anthologized poems, the imagery effects a complete textual fusion of sea wave with pine tree:

> Whirl up, sea – whirl your pointed pines,
> splash your great pines
> on our rocks,
> hurl your green over us,
> cover us with your pools of fir.[34]

What the poem also achieves is the dramatic utterance of a passionate unnamed yearning, displaced and condensed into the images of natural energy. So, as well as the permutable boundary between sea and land, the poem can also be read as an intertextual dialogue between that undefined desire and the social meaning of the poem as an intense evocation of the sea. A later and longer poem directly articulates this dialogism between frustrated desire and social forms of language, dramatizing it as the anguished indecision of the speaker of the poem suspended between the impulse for art (for 'song') and an intensely physical desire for an indifferent lover. In multiple ways it constructs what we could call linguistic thresholds between separate elements: wakeful speaker and sleeping lover, physical love and artistic song, burning breath and snow, stillness and energy, and so on.

Fragment Thirty-six

I know not what to do:
my mind is divided – Sappho.

> I know not what to do,
> my mind is reft:
> is song's gift best?
> is love's gift loveliest?
> I know not what to do,
> now sleep has pressed
> weight on your eyelids.
>
> Shall I break your rest,
> devouring, eager?
> is love's gift best?
> nay, song's the loveliest:
> yet were you lost,
> what rapture

could I take from song?
what song were left?

I know not what to do:
to turn and slake
the rage that burns,
with my breath burn
and trouble your cool breath?
so shall I turn and take
snow in my arms?
(is love's gift best?)
yet flake on flake
of snow were comfortless,
did you lie wondering,
wakened yet unawake.

    .   .   .   .

My mind is quite divided,
my minds hesitate,
so perfect matched,
I know not what to do:
each strives with each
as two white wrestlers
standing for a match,
ready to turn and clutch
yet never shake muscle nor nerve nor tendon:
so my mind waits
to grapple with my mind,
yet I lie quiet,
I would seem at rest.[35]

This poem, like 'Oread' is typical of much of H.D.'s poetry in that it constructs a dramatic persona, the apparent speaker of the poem's utterance. That the self of Fragment Thirty-six is *divided* is also typical; the personae of H.D.'s poem are always yearning for completeness, a desire which is forever frustrated. For this reason 'Fragment' is an apposite title. H.D.'s speakers are, to use Kristeva's term, 'subjects in process', a voice constructing self upon a sense of lack. Since social identity is initiated by the loss of the mother, subjectivity is always for Kristeva the production of self upon that absence. Identity as she sees it is essentially imitative, learning to perform a role, to parody, to adopt a mask. For this reason she praises Mozart's Don Juan as 'an artist with no authenticity other than his ability to change, to live without internality, to put on masks just for fun'.[36]

Although Kristeva has linked women's creativity with the risk of suicide, I find her sense of identity as performance, often with elements of self-parody, a more positive way of thinking about the writing of women like Sylvia Plath and Anne Sexton. Sexton's poetry, like that of Plath's, has been labelled 'confessional', but she insisted rather that she was a story-teller, that her poems were not spontaneous outpourings of personal inner emotion − the 'real' Anne Sexton − but the construction of dramatic voices and situations. She told an interviewer, 'I tend to lie a lot.'[37] Sexton popularized her work by public readings, highly theatrical events in which she performed both her 'self' and the characters of her poems. A poem entitled 'Self in 1958' dramatizes a fracturing of identity into performative self and a wry sceptical observation of that performance. 'What is reality?' the poem's persona asks, 'I am a plaster doll / . . . Am I approximately an I'. The voice goes on to catalogue her 'doll's' reality: 'I have hair / . . . nylon legs, luminous arms / and some advertised clothes. / . . . I live in a doll's house / . . . Someone plays with me, / plants me in the all-electric kitchen, / . . . Someone pretends with me.'[38]

Sexton's poems construct the subjectivities of many women, old and young, mothers, daughters and lovers, even the voice of a young girl sacrificially buried alive with her dead father. In all of them, though, there is this sense of identity as split, of an alert, intelligent, often wry, awareness of a self watching a self perform. Even in poems that seem at one level intensely personal, this 'comic gleam',[39] fracturing self from its own performance − even performance of anguish − is unextinguished. In Sexton's fine poem 'Flee on your donkey', recounting a return to the mental hospital, the balancing act − intertextuality − between the comic and the tragic constructed by the edge of self-parody in the poetic voice maintains an aesthetic control. The title of the poem is taken from a line by the French poet Rimbaud, '*Fuis sur ton ane*'. '*Ane*' is French for donkey and Sexton plays on the association with the name 'Anne' to summon up a self beyond her social performance as mental patient.

> Anne, Anne,
> flee on your donkey,
> flee this sad hotel,

ride out on some hairy beast,
gallop backward pressing
your buttocks to his withers,
sit to his clumsy gait somehow.[40]

The desperation of this injunction to self to discover a liberating libidinal energy ('some hairy beast') is simultaneously heightened and controlled by the wry self-parody of the comic image. The writing of Sexton, Plath and, I think, many other women can be seen to operate across the boundary site where a self constructs self as voice or performance, yet retains a comic cynicism – frequently of black humour – towards that construction of identity. It is this parodic resilience that constitutes the aesthetic control in their work, preventing any emotional excess or slide into a purely confessional discourse.

Kristeva's sense of identity as performative and 'in process' has been much influence by the work of the Russian theorist Mikhail Bakhtin, especially by his notion of the 'carnivalesque'.[41] Carnival during the Middle Ages was a unique time of licence from repressive authority. Its most typical form was parody: parody of all forms of official language – there were parodic masses and sermons for example – and parody of official figures in public performances, carnival masks and comic effigies. Bakhtin's analysis of parody provides us with a further sense of intertextuality, or, as he calls it, dialogism. In a parody two different texts are brought together in an oppositional relationship: the parodied language is suffused with a tone of voice which implies an alternative point of view to the apparent truth of the original. This dialogic construction of two voices interacting within the words of a single utterance produces a crucial effect for Bakhtin: it relativizes language. It constructs a cynical linguistic distance between the two voices or perspectives, causing them to interrogate each other's 'truth', thereby refuting either's claim to unitary, uncontestable 'Truth'. In a similar way, we can see how in Sexton's poetry an element of self-parody within the voice refuses to take the 'truth' of its social identity absolutely seriously. Bakhtin argues that carnivalesque forms invaded late medieval and early Renaissance literature and remain as radicalizing elements in the kind of writing he calls polyphonic: that is within texts that challenge the dominant ideological codes by pluralizing (dialogizing) meaning.

Like the other male theorists whose ideas I have discussed, Bakhtin makes no attempt at a feminist viewpoint. Some feminists have expressed doubt as to whether a feminist literary practice should utilize work by men or even work like that of Kristeva who is strongly influenced by male writers. To do so, they argue, is to re-endorse the authority of masculine discourse and to continue women's submission to their views. My own feeling is that women should appropriate all useful ideas no matter where they come from, trusting to their own creative capacity to transform them for their own purposes. It does, however, remain a contested issue within feminist criticism.

Appropriation is a key concept for Bakhtin. He sees individual words as well as whole texts as sites of dialogic or intertextual conflict, where various social sections – classes, genders, age, ethnic and professional groups – struggle to inscribe their way of seeing things, their meaning, on language. Words therefore can have no unitary definition; each is a microcosmic dialogue of all the sectional voices echoing within it. This notion of intertextuality/dialogism is a useful way of perceiving women's relation to canonical texts. As we saw in chapter 3, women writers, rather than being intimidated, frequently appropriate male-authored forms, language and myths to contest and reinvent their meanings, as Eudora Welty does, for example, in *The Golden Apples*.

One of the most triumphant examples of a woman writer's dialogic engagement with male literary language is Angela Carter's *Nights at the Circus*, a brilliant tapestry of parodied snatches from every conceivable form of novel: Dickensian eccentricity and comedy, Zolaesque realism, hard-boiled American detective fiction, travel narrative, popular sentiment and romance. Her heroine is the narrator of her own story, thereby constructing her identity from this absurd mixture of already used language. In the process she points out what we must all do to produce an identity. 'Self' is always an intertextual patchwork of all the second-hand language that has constructed us. 'Freedom' is perhaps just a comic recognition that this is so. Throughout the novel, identity is foregrounded as a carnival process of masking and clowning. When Walser 'first put on his make-up . . . he felt the beginnings of a vertiginous sense of freedom . . . he experienced the freedom that lies behind the mask, within dissimulation, the freedom to juggle with being, and, indeed, with the language which is vital to our being, that lies at the heart of burlesque'.[42]

However, it is the heroine, Fevvers, who most fully embodies the vertiginous freedom of self-making: she spreads wings, defies the law of gravity, as well as feminine decorum, and flies. In constructing this self-burlesquing heroine, Carter also enters into a brilliant dialogic exchange with Rabelais's novel, *Gargantua*, seen by Bakhtin as the supreme example of carnivalesque literary form. Fevvers is larger than life in every way; her gestures are huge, in size she is a 'giantess', she gorges and stuffs herself with 'gargantuan enthusiasm'.[43] However, unlike Rabelais's work, praised by Bakhtin because it brings birth and death into an organic relationship to each other − an organicism founded on the female body of course − Fevvers rejects birth as the beginning of her narrative:

> 'I never docked via what you might call *normal channels*, sir, oh, dear me, no; but just like Helen of Troy, was *hatched*'.
> 'Hatched out of a bloody great egg while Bow bells rang, as ever is'.
> The blonde guffawed uproariously, slapping the marbly thigh on which her wrap fell open and flashed a pair of vast, blue, indecorous eyes at the young reporter . . . as if to dare him: 'Believe it or not!' Then she spun round on her swivelling dressing-stool . . . and confronted herself with a grin in the mirror as she ripped six inches of false lash from her left eyelid.[44]

Due to the lack of personal and familial pre-history, Fevvers, as her stepmother, Lizzie, tells her, 'never existed before. There's nobody to say what you should do or how to do it . . . You haven't any history and there are no expectations of you except the ones you yourself create.'[45] Given this plotless space in which to play with the fictions of being, Fevvers incorporates into her burlesque of identity the feminine and the masculine, mother and daughter, whore and saint, fraud and freak, self-interested rationalism and big-hearted sentimentality, and her story-telling language continually reverses and parodies them all. Fevvers is pre-eminently the pluralized subject 'in process'. Seen from a distance, Fevvers with her minute stepmother, Lizzie, 'looked like a blonde, heroic mother taking her little daughter home . . . their ages obscured, their relationship inverted'.[46] To be a mother, as opposed to giving birth, is not linked to nature or biology, it is to perform a role, to step into a position. Lizzie teaches herself how to be the mother Fevver needs: 'though flightless herself, my Lizzie took it upon herself the role of bird-mother.'[47]

In *The Sadeian Woman* Carter claims that the 'theory of maternal superiority is one of the most damaging of all consolatory fictions . . . It puts those women who wholeheartedly subscribe to it in voluntary exile from the historical world, this world, in its historic time.'[48] Elsewhere in the book she declares that women who turn for consolation for their lack of access to material and intellectual horizons to 'hypothetical great goddesses, are simply flattering themselves into submission . . . All the mythic versions of women are . . . consolatory nonsense . . . Mother goddesses are just as silly a notion as father gods.'[49]

Carter's fiction relentlessly demythicizes the regressive idealization of the mother; mothers in her stories make themselves, invent themselves in the act of loving and caring for children. In Carter's last novel, *Wise Children*, the two aged heroines joyfully take charge of twins, pushing the pram home at midnight to the tune of 'We can't give you anything but love, babies'.[50] Love is not missing from these performances of mothering, but the characters avoid falling into the narcissistic trap of the Mother myth by retaining in their performance an edge of burlesque or self-parody, the comic gleam that recognizes all identity as performance.

Only by rejecting 'the bankrupt enchantments of the womb', Carter argues, will 'we learn to live in this world, to take it with sufficient seriousness, because it is the only world we will ever know'.[51] Kristeva writes from the same perception in 'Women's Time'. The term 'Woman' as it is used in much feminist discourse has been helpful for its political effect in activating women to struggle for a common cause. However, it also has a reductive universalizing, ahistoricizing effect, effacing the important differences in women's actual lives: 'Indeed the time has perhaps come to emphasize the multiplicity of female expressions and preoccupations.'[52] Kristeva too believes that the concept 'Woman' needs transforming back into 'women' and into 'history'.

Poststructuralism has shattered the traditional concept of individual identity as the authenticating origin of meaning and truth: of individuals as conscious agents of their own history and as authors of their own stories. Humanist individualism has been shown to rest ultimately on a restricting conceptual system of differences: male *or* female, man *or* woman. Within this binary ordering, throughout long centuries of western history and thought, 'man' has been imposed as the human subject, the norm; woman has been the subordinated term, whatever is 'other' to the norm. This ideology of the unitary (male) subject has been promoted alongside the valorization of 'truth' as unitary meaning. If we stay within this humanist conceptual order we can only struggle to reverse the hierarchies: women instead of men, my 'truth' instead of your 'truth'. Individualism is founded on difference and competition. Poststructuralism aims to undo this thinking: especially it aims to deconstruct the notion of the unified, gendered sovereign subject.

In opposition to an ideology of individualism and singleness of 'Truth', poststructuralist thinking asserts the always plural nature of identity and the indeterminacy of meaning. This is held to accord more closely with what is termed our 'postmodern condition', in which 'presentation' is identified with truth and 'personality' has become a cult of endless imitations of imitations. However, as theory, poststructuralist thinking runs into problems of its own; for all its intellectual radicalism, there is within it an ahistoricizing tendency. In their writing post-structuralist theorists make frequent use of terms like 'language', 'excess', 'power', 'repression', 'sexuality', 'woman', in a universalizing way which slides them out of any historical or political specificity. Psychoanalytic theory, which underlies much of this thinking, utilizes the Oedipal myth, taken from classical western cultures, to provide a universal narrative of gender construction for the whole of the human species and for the whole of history.

For feminist literary critics who share the political agenda of feminism to change existing political realities, poststructuralism offers both hope and difficulty. Its deconstruction of the patriarchal logic at the centre of the meaning system is exhilarating; the possibility of escaping a restrictive defining identity even more so. However, it is precisely here in this key issue of identity that the difficulty resides. If the notions of self and individual agency are replaced by a concept of the 'subject in process', the site of bisexual libidinal drives, how is political identity and struggle to be articulated? In the name of what are we fighting and for whom? Is language, and above all avant-garde literary writing by men or women, really the primary site of revolutionary struggle as French feminists often seem to imply? Or do such texts by their very difficulty serve an elitist function, preserving 'literature' for a privileged educated class and acting as an intimidating, disempowering force on others? It has been important for many women to find their experiences, suffering and needs given meaning in literary texts and thereby recognized and authenticated. What happens if we insist that the writing subject and meaning are always plural and indeterminate? Can we argue for more women writers in the canon and yet deny any stability to the terms 'author', 'identity' and 'woman'?

The dynamic trajectory of feminist literary criticism in the relatively short time since the late 1960s has brought us to these questions. Probably the most important challenge presently facing feminist theory is the need to find a way of thinking of identity so as to retain a sense of the subject as agent of history and meaning, while avoiding the traps of individualism, essentialism and the ahistoricism of some versions of postmodernism. Within the feminist movement this challenge has been most sharply posed and articulated in relation to three groups of women, all of whom occupy a threshold position to mainstream culture: lesbian, black and working-class women.

Summary of Main Points

1 Poststructuralists have overturned the notion of the sovereign individual (as author of meaning) for a sense of identity as plural and indeterminate. The literary term 'author' has been replaced by the 'writing subject' to acknowledge that conscious intent determines only a small part of any text.

2 A perpetual struggle takes place within language and identity between repression and disruptive desire/excess. Poststructural critical reading aims to recognize both in texts.

3 French feminists associate linguistic disruption and excess with a feminine libidinal writing, but Michel Foucault's study of historically specific discourses demonstrates that control and repression can masquerade as desire. There is also a risk of depoliticization in the identification of sexuality with identity and freedom.

4 Julia Kristeva analyses two 'dispositions' in language: the 'semiotic' deriving from rhythmic, libidinal pre-Oedipal experience, and the social forms of the 'symbolic'. The 'dialogic' (in dialogue) interaction between these two produces language as a generative process, not as a static fixed structure of meaning.

5 At the Oedipal stage Kristeva sees three positions available to girls: identification with the paternal order, or with a maternal order, or a third, co-existing between these two extremes.

6 She sees each position as predominating during a different stage of the women's movement. The second post-1968 maternal stage of separatist feminism is criticized as utopian. For individual women over-identification

with the pre-Oedipal maternal force is also risky; it can lead towards suicide.

7   Kristeva advocates the third 'threshold' phase as an 'intertextual' dialogue of unconscious 'semiotic' desire with social 'symbolic' meaning. This permits the construction of social identity as a process, as not fixed.

8   Mikhail Bakhtin's notion of carnival as masking and parody has influenced Kristeva's sense of identity as a performance. His sense of 'dialogism' or 'intertextuality' also provides insight into women's appropriating and parodic relationship to male writing. They produce writing as intertextuality: a dialogue of texts.

9   Angela Carter's sense of parodic identity deconstructs the Mother myth: to be a mother is to act the part. Myths keep women out of history. Poststructuralism also produces problems of ahistoricism for feminists.

Suggestions for Further Reading

Julia Kristeva, 'Women's Time', in *The Kristeva Reader*, pp. 187–213. Kristeva is not easy reading, but this piece is worth struggling with.

Sara Mills et al., *Feminist Readings/Feminists Reading*, pp. 162–70, has a Kristevan reading of *Wuthering Heights*.

Toril Moi, *Sexual/Textual Politics*, pp. 150–73, offers a positive and clear account of Kristeva's thinking. Moi, 'Feminist Literary Criticism', in Jefferson and Robey (eds), *Modern Literary Theory*, pp. 204–21, also provides a useful overview of many of the topics in this chapter.

Notes

1   There are many books on various aspects of this. For useful introductions see Weedon, *Feminist Practice and Poststructualist Theory*; Belsey, *Critical Practice*; Nicholson, *Feminism/Postmodernism*; Waugh, *Practising Postmodernism/Reading Modernism*.

2   As well as Freud the two other names usually associated in this assault on humanist thinking are Nietzsche and Marx.

3   The seminal text asserting 'The Death of the Author' is by Barthes, in *Image-Music-Text*. See also Belsey, *Critical Practice*, for a helpful introduction to a poststructuralist approach to literature.

4   Kristeva, *Desire in Language*, p. 111.

5   *Cymbeline*, III. iv. 156, 168–9.

6   For a more detailed discussion see Belsey, 'Disrupting Sexual Difference:

Meaning and Gender in the Comedies' in Drakakis (ed.), *Alternative Shakespeares*, pp. 166–90.

7   Foucault, *The History of Sexuality*, vol. 1, p. 6.
8   Ibid., p. 23.
9   Ibid., p. 33.
10 Ibid., pp. 56, 59.
11 Ibid., p. 60.
12 For example, we speak of 'medical discourse' and 'seventeenth-century dissenting discourse', but of the English language.
13 Ibid., pp. 77, 78.
14 Carswell, *Open the Door!*, p. 19.
15 Ibid., pp. 394, 395. Lawrence read Carswell's manuscript of the novel, making many suggestions for extensive alterations, but allowing that it was '*marvellously good*' (ibid., p. xi).
16 Kristeva, *Desire in Language*, p. 283.
17 Kristeva, 'Revolution in Poetic Language', in *The Kristeva Reader*, p. 92. Where possible I have used quotations from this edition, for it offers a good range of Kristeva's writing in one easily available volume and has helpful introductory notes.
18 Kristeva, 'Psychoanalysis and the Polis', in *The Kristeva Reader*, p. 316.
19 Kristeva, 'About Chinese Women', ibid., p. 148.
20 Kristeva, 'Women's Time', ibid., p. 202.
21 Ibid., p. 202.
22 Ibid.
23 Ibid., p. 199.
24 Ibid., p. 192. American feminist separatism in the 1970s will be discussed in more detail in chapter 7.
25 Kristeva, 'About Chinese Women', p. 157.
26 Chopin, *The Awakening*, p. 25.
27 Ibid., p. 148.
28 Ibid., pp. 188–9.
29 Kristeva, 'Women's Time', p. 211.
30 Kristeva, 'About Chinese Women', p. 156.
31 For a systematic reading of Woolf's major novels using Kristeva's concept of a semiotic/symbolic dialectic see Minow-Pinkney, *Virginia Woolf and the Problem of the Subject*.
32 *H.D.: Collected Poems 1912–1944*, p. xi.
33 Ibid., p. 5.
34 Ibid., p. 55.
35 Ibid., p. 165. My reading of H.D.'s poetry is much indebted to Buck, *H.D. and Freud*.

36 Kristeva, *Tales of Love*, p. 199.
37 *The Selected Poems of Anne Sexton*, p. xiii.
38 Ibid., p. 106.
39 Kristeva, *Powers of Horror*, p. 209.
40 *The Selected Poems of Anne Sexton*, p. 75.
41 The main text on carnival is Bakhtin, *Rabelais and his World*. Bakhtin, *The Dialogic Imagination*, pp. 259–422, provides the fullest account of his sense of language as dialogic.
42 Carter, *Nights at the Circus*, p. 103.
43 Ibid., p. 22.
44 Ibid., p. 7.
45 Ibid., p. 198.
46 Ibid., p. 89.
47 Ibid., p. 32.
48 Carter, *The Sadeian Woman*, p. 106.
49 Ibid., p. 5.
50 Carter, *Wise Children*, p. 231.
51 Carter, *The Sadeian Woman*, p. 109, 110.
52 Kristeva, 'Women's Time', p. 193.

7

A Return to Women in History: Lesbian, Black and Class Criticism

This final chapter is not a conclusion, for, happily, the history of feminist literary criticism shows no sign of coming to an end. If you look back over the range of writing, ideas, approaches and theories we have covered in just this one book, it is easy to see why feminist literary criticism and theory has been the most productive, radical and far-reaching body of work in literary studies in the second half of the twentieth century. The main reason for this continuously self-renewing vitality is that, from the start, feminist criticism has been inherently dialogic in nature. It has always engaged in a critical debate or dialogue with itself as well as with various patriarchal institutions.

The first discussions arose over the relative priority of rereading male-authored texts or affirming a woman's literary tradition (gynocriticism). The very success of the second enterprise provoked the first radical questioning by lesbian, black and working-class women of the universalizing implications of the term 'woman'. Was not the construction of this 'woman's' tradition of writing actually producing a literary history of exclusively western, white, middle-class, heterosexual women? The questioning of canon construction leads to further complex problems of how to establish criteria of selection and evaluation, indeed, to the question of whether such a project is inevitably elitist and exclusive?

Questions of politico-aesthetic evaluation also arise in the engagement between a humanist individualist feminism associated with American tradition and French-derived poststructural feminism. In *Sexual/Textual Politics* (1985) Toril Moi recognizes that the divergences between American and French approaches is a rearticulation of early twentieth-century literary-political debates over the relative merits of realist writing and avant-garde texts.[1] Given that feminist literary criticism is not just woman-centred criticism, that its interest is not just in texts that foreground women's experiences, but in actually bringing about social change, what kind of writing should be viewed as most progressive? Moi's book is now part of the history of feminist criticism. It speaks – as all texts do – from its moment of production, from Moi's sense, in the early 1980s, of the need to incorporate French theoretical rigour into the feminist literary agenda. One can now see that in her critique of realism as a conservative form which works to naturalize the existing social order Moi tended to underestimate an aspect of realism which can assume a politically progressive function. She pays little attention to the urgency with which many women have turned to literary texts as a means of finding a positive identity in opposition to demeaning cultural images. In denying the theoretical value of the work of American black and lesbian feminist critics while it remains within a humanist tradition, she fails to ask what challenge *their* perspective might bring to the European poststructuralism she prefers. What questions an Afro-American woman submerged in an underclass of urban poverty and violence, whose name, even, derives from a white slaveowner, might pose for an aesthetics of excess, celebrating identity as multiple and mobile – a playful assumption of masks?

In fact, black, lesbian and working-class feminists have articulated the current debates within feminism over identity, canon construction and the politics of aesthetics in their most urgent forms. If the creative productivity of feminist literary criticism derives largely from its dialogic self-questioning, then the writing from these groups of women seems likely to provide some of the crucial new insights and directions of feminist literary aesthetics and theory. However, I have encountered problems in the writing of this chapter which relate to the issues of identity and authority. A central feature of lesbian and black feminists' critique of mainstream feminism has been its assumption that it speaks for all women. Mainstream feminism, until fairly recently, has tended to articulate the viewpoint of white, heterosexual women as *the* woman's view. In writing this chapter I am, therefore, uncomfortably aware that I am neither lesbian or black, and that my present life-style is undeniably privileged, culturally, economically and professionally. Furthermore, within the allotted space of one chapter it is impossible to represent adequately the diversity and achievements of lesbian, or Afro-American, or postcolonial or Marxist feminist criticism, let alone attempt to convey a sense of them all. My aim here is to focus on their productive engagement with what seem to me the most pressing and interesting issues facing feminism: the interlocking debates over identity/essentialism and realism/experimental form. However, I will also try to provide a brief overview of the historical development of these different traditions within feminist criticism.

For the purpose of clarity I shall discuss first lesbian, then black and finally Marxist or class-based feminist criticism, but the separation can be misleading and is not wholly possible since some of the most important critics and creative writers work across these boundaries. Afro-American writers like Alice Walker, Toni Morrison and Audre Lorde celebrate the love of women for women as an empowering force within a disabling nexus of poverty, racism and misogyny. Gayatri Chakravorty Spivak, a Marxist feminist American academic, trained in literary deconstruction, was born in India, and thus writes at the intersection of cultural and intellectual tensions. Monique Wittig is a French Marxist lesbian, a critic and novelist, and sceptical of some French feminist theory. Jeanette Winterson, author of the immensely successful lesbian novel *Oranges are not the Only Fruit*, set that story in, and herself comes from an English working-class culture. All such writers work 'out on the borderlands, [have] lives for which the central interpretive devices of culture don't quite work'.[2]

Lesbian Feminist Criticism

In its early stages lesbian feminist criticism followed a similar pattern to that of mainstream feminist literary criticism. If feminism starts from the recognition that previously perceived 'universal' truths about men and women are very frequently masculine views, then lesbian critical consciousness begins with awareness of the prevailing heterosexual assumptions which claim universality, and of the inherent heterosexism and homophobia implicit in many of those assumptions. Sadly, lesbian critics have found it necessary to point out that negative representation of lesbians, marginalization of their literary presence, and silence about their achievements and concerns as writers occur not only in the work of male critics and reviewers; much feminist criticism has reproduced these heterosexist prejudices. Many lesbians were active supporters of the rising women's movement in America from the early days of the 1960s, but discovered that not every heterosexual sister welcomed their participation. There was a fairly widespread fear that lesbianism would give the movement a bad name. Betty Friedan, author of *The Feminine Mystique* (1963) and often honoured as the pioneer of women's liberation in America, conducted what was almost a witch-hunt against lesbians in the National Organizartion of Women.[3]

The pervasive fear of and hostility towards lesbianism is a central concern within the history and theory of lesbian feminist criticism. Given this context of homophobia, it is not surprising that one of the first projects of lesbian feminist criticism was to establish a tradition of lesbian writers who could be expected to project a positive lesbian identity to counteract the 'sin and sickness' images prevailing almost everywhere else. However, this was by no means the straightforward task that producing a women's canon had been for feminist critics like Elaine Showalter. From the outset, lesbian criticism was faced with complex questions of identity and definition. What constitutes 'lesbianism'? How is a 'lesbian' text to be recognized given the circumspection many women may have felt about admitting to feelings universally stigmatized as perverted and diseased? Claiming and proclaiming a lesbian identity, therefore, has been a primary issue for lesbian literary criticism in a way that identity has never been within mainstream feminism.

In 1975 Jane Rule produced a pioneering text of lesbian literary history, *Lesbian Images*. As the title implies, her aim is to 'discover what images of lesbians women writers have projected in fiction, biography, and autobiography'.[4] Her women writers are chosen either as identified lesbians or for showing a predominant concern with women-centred relationships in their work. Rule's approach is realist and biographical. She praises her writers for truthful and positive images of women's relations with women. However, her main concern is to demonstrate that the long tradition of religious condemnation of homosexuality as a heinous sin, followed in the late nineteenth and early twentieth centuries by the medical diagnoses of sexual 'inversion' as sickness or congenital abnormality, constructed versions of lesbianism which many lesbians internalized and which then haunted their writing. For Rule the classic case of this internalization was Radclyffe Hall. Her renowned but contentious lesbian novel, *The Well of Loneliness* (1928), was intended to gain public sympathy and acceptance for lesbians, but it did so by representing them as 'inverts' – unable to alter an inborn inversion of 'normal' sexuality and therefore the tragic victims of an affronted and punishing society.

Although Rule is thus concerned with the damaging internalization of socially constructed images of lesbianism, the implicit assumption of her writing is that there does exist an innate lesbian identity, even though some women may have felt it necessary to deny their own 'nature'. In *Surpassing the Love of Men* (1981) Lillian Faderman begins to move towards a consideration of lesbian identity in terms of social construction. She opens her scholarly and persuasive book with the problem of definition: what are the defining aspects of a lesbian relationship? Do these remain constant throughout history? In her survey of the representation of love between women in women's writing from the sixteenth century to the nineteenth century it became clear to her that women's love-relationships were seldom defined in explicitly sexual terms. Only in male fantasy and pornographic literature did female love figure as primarily genital. Throughout this long period, women writers felt uninhibited about expressing romantic feelings for each other in terms that were explixcitly those of love-relationships in every sense but the sexual. Faderman suggests that women's own perception of their passionate attachments to other women as non-sexual and the apparent male tolerance of these friendships was due to the general belief that women were naturally asexual. Empathetic sharing of emotion, professions of tenderness and lasting attachment were taken by both sexes as manifestations of women's greater spirituality and sensibility and as such worthy of admiration and emulation. Faderman's many quotations of women's passionate declarations to each other support her contention that these were deeply felt love-relationships:

> Women who were romantic friends were everything to each other. They lived to be together. They thought of each other constantly. They made each other deliriously happy or horribly miserable . . . . They were jealous . . . They embraced and kissed and walked hand in hand and some even held each other all night in sleep.[5]

Faderman's thesis is that when women began to demand social and political equality at the end of the nineteenth century social tolerance for romantic friendship between women came to an end. Men began to perceive the revolutionary potential of women's attachment to women. The incipient growth of male suspicion and hostility coincided with the emergence of lesbianism as a topical concern in medicine and science.

Sexologists like Krafft-Ebing in Germany and Havelock Ellis in England constructed what became a popularized medical 'knowledge' of sexuality in terms of inherited degeneracy and abnormality. Faderman comments, 'it was primarily through Krafft-Ebing and Ellis's writings that the twentieth century received its stereotypes of lesbian morbidity.'[6] The effect of their work, and of popular accounts deriving from it, was to change the perception, and hence the reality, of relationships between women. Even though lesbians since the 1970s have actively rejected and counteracted those morbid images, the word 'lesbian' is now part of a shared linguistic landscape. The whole range of women's interactions with women cannot take place, as did those of earlier centuries, in the absence of that term, which, like all words, can function to universalize actual differences and to impose unitary definitions on what is indeterminate. Faderman's historical approach implicitly suggests that we need to consider lesbian identity as socially constructed across a range of specific historical discourses rather than as an unchanging inborn 'nature'. Although she left the implication undeveloped, her study has been influential on the next generation of lesbian critics.

However, for many feminist lesbians in the 1970s the goal was to affirm a positive radical lesbian separatism, not to question lesbian identity.[7] Heterosexuality was perceived as the keystone of male power and by withdrawing from it altogether women could effectively bring patriarchy to an end. Instead of 'sin and sickness', a lesbian identity could be affirmed in terms of heroic social terrorism. However, for many radical separatists this political goal was less important than the positive cultural one of establishing an all-female community based on what were perceived as 'female' values of co-operation, non-aggression, nurture, creativity and an intuitive affinity with the ecologic welfare of the planet.

Inevitably there is much that is visionary in this dream, but it inspired some powerfully imaginative writing in women. A typical text was Sally Miller Gearhart's best-seller *The Wanderground: Stories of the Hill Women* (1978), which presents a harmonious community of women who have withdrawn from male violence and the destructiveness of urban life to the natural world of an earth which has itself revolted against the threat men present to the survival of life on the planet. In the story the earth figures metaphorically as Earth-Mother; birth, necessarily left vague, takes place deep underground in warm womb-shaped cells. A common theme in separatist writing of this time is the desire to return to the maternal, to reconnect to the intimate lost knowledge of the body and love of the mother. Visions of a separatist lesbian identity and culture based on these maternal, female qualities are, almost invariably, essentialist. From this perspective all women can be seen as inherently lesbian; heterosexual women remain the unwitting victims of the system that oppresses them. Thus, in 1980, Adrienne Rich proposed a 'lesbian continuum' defined as 'woman-identified experience' ranging throughout each individual woman's life and throughout history within the social order of prescribed and compulsory heterosexuality.[8]

Her collection of poems entitled *Dream of a Common Language* (1978) stems from this particular moment and vision within the lesbian movement. The poem 'Transcendental Etude' from the collection offers a clear and powerful figuring of that vision.[9] It begins with an intense evocation of natural beauty, life, fruitfulness as felt by the poem's female speaker on an August evening driving home 'over backroads fringed with queen anne's lace'. The stubborn persistence of this fragile and vulnerable natural world is placed against the violence and brutality with which human beings invade and desecrate it: 'triggers fingered by drunken men' leaving shattered animals 'stunned in . . . blood', 'raw' new roads 'bulldozed through a quiet village', children 'conceived in apathy' their lives twisted by 'rotgut violence' and poverty.

The sense that it would take a life-time's study and more to apprehend all the multiple forms 'so dense with life' leads the speaker to the realization that with life we are given no opportunity of gradually growing into knowledge. We cannot as when learning music start from simple scales and exercises, 'we're forced to begin in the midst of the hardest movement, / the one already sounding as we are born'. At best we enjoy only a short initial pause in which we can hear 'the simple line / of a woman's voice singing'. Too soon we are wrenched away from this mother's song and heartbeat, heard thereafter like a distant persistent note of loss and homesickness. We are thrust into a different music, a different counterpoint, 'trying to sightread what our fingers can't keep up with, learn by heart / what we can't even read'. It is a world of competitive virtuoso performance.

This meditation has led the speaker of the poem to a sense of women's alienation entailed in the loss of their first love:

> Birth stripped our birthright from us,
> tore us from a woman, from women, from ourselves

The subsequent social chorus buzzing in women's ears denies them knowledge of origins, falsifies as unnatural the first 'acute joy' in which 'we lay, flesh against flesh, / eyes steady on the face of love'. For a woman to apprehend and recall this experience is to be reborn into a new kind of life, to a sense of 'how I can love myself – / as only a woman can love me. / . . . a whole new poetry beginning here'.

There is no difficulty in recognizing the importance Rich is attaching here to the first sensuous maternal love in shaping a woman's future identity and desire. Her imagery, too, derives from the maternal (the shared language); new thought is like 'the tiny, orbed, endangered / egg-sac of a new-world'. This imagery, especially the word 'endangered', associates with the sense of women's ecological affinities and the idea is developed in the loving enumeration of preserved natural objects which concludes the poem: 'small rainbow-coloured shells', 'skeins of milk-weed', 'the dark blue petal of the petunia', 'the finch's yellow feather'. These too are a shared language, to be touched, remembered and given among women. This nurturing, loving order of meaning is affirmed against a conflictual language of 'argument and jargon' from which the woman speaker in a separatist movement walks away into a vision of a new life.

Monique Wittig is also a radical lesbian separatist, but as a Marxist influenced by French poststructuralism her views diverge sharply from those of American lesbian separatists like Rich, and provide a critique of the latter. In 'One is not Born a Woman' (1981) and other related essays Wittig sets out her total opposition to essentialism; she sees it as an illusion fostered to further male interests. Heterosexual discourse functions to produce sexual categories as if they are natural and biological, always prior to the social, she claims. This naturalizing language is used to disguise 'the brutal political fact of the domination of women'.[10] It constructs an identity for 'woman' as reproductive being; woman is mythicized as 'mother' in order to impose on women 'the rigid obligation of the reproduction of the "species", that is of heterosexual society'.[11] Wittig calls the dominant order of meaning which naturalizes gender into biological categories the 'straight mind'.

The most urgent task, as Wittig sees it, is to deconstruct the logic of the 'straight mind' to reveal that 'woman' and 'man' are not natural categories but two social classes produced by culture and within history, not biology. The class 'woman' is constructed and has meaning only in its oppositional relation to the class 'man'. For this reason Wittig is critical of French feminists like Cixous and Irigaray, and American feminists like Rich, who advocate 'feminine writing', drawing on notions of a lost maternal realm. This, she argues, colludes with the straight mind's naturalizing of 'woman'; it makes woman's writing seem like a biological process rather than work as material production. It amounts 'to saying women do not belong to history'.[12] In her own experimental fiction, one of the main ways Wittig attempts to undermine the logic of the straight mind is by deconstructing the binarism of pronouns. This is much more powerful in a gendered language like French, of course.[13] However, Wittig claims that the most potent subversive agency for undoing the whole repressive order of heterosexism is the lesbian identity. 'Lesbianisn is the only concept I know of which is beyond the categories of sex (woman and man), because the designated subject (lesbian) is *not* a woman, either economically, or politically, or ideologically.'[14] As escapees from the class 'women' which is constituted as identity only in its relation to the class 'men', lesbians explode the biologist myth and reveal the socially constructed nature of gender. 'Thus being a lesbian, standing at the outposts of the human (of humankind) represents historically and paradoxically the most human point of view.'[15]

It is paradoxical that in rigorously rejecting the essentialist myth of the maternal which traps women within a restrictively biological, non-social category, Wittig then constructs a subversive lesbian identity which in turn slides out of history.[16] By claiming 'lesbians are not women', she seems to construct an acultural, totalizing, even mythic, lesbian identity which cannot account for the real differences of race, class, politics and so on existing among actual lesbians. Wittig's writing thus provides a graphic illustration of the identity dilemma facing any non-dominant group.

Constructing a positive identity is necessary to contest the internalization of degrading images prevalent in the mainstream culture and to produce political group consciousness and activism. However, identity based on any form of essentialism risks erasing actual differences and of sliding into myth and out of history. This, we saw in chapter 6, was a danger that Julia Kristeva perceived to be particularly risky for women because of their marginalized and 'sacrificial' position within the social order. However, a deconstructionist espousal of identity as plural and contingent brings its own anxieties. Can marginalized and oppressed groups afford the luxury of perceiving 'self' as multiple and 'in process'? This, in turn, relates to the realism/experimentalism debate. Canon formation had as its major aims the identification of a body of texts which offered positive images of lesbians (or black women) and affirmed the literary value of a tradition of lesbian (or black) writers. If the notion of identity is deconstructed what happens to the carefully constructed canon?

Following the heroic 'women's decade' of the 1970s, and with the advent of poststructuralist ideas from France, lesbian critics since the mid 1980s have been facing up to these questions. A recent collection of lesbian critical essays influenced by poststructuralist thinking, *New Lesbian Criticism* (1992), sees the 'desire for a unified and heroic self-image [as] one of the central dilemmas of contemporary lesbian cultural politics'.[17] In the same edition Bonnie Zimmerman describes her earlier assumption of an innate lesbian identity as 'naive', recognizing that all the basic concepts for such assurance have been undermined: 'Experience, authenticity, voice, writer, even lesbianism itself – all have been scrutinized, qualified, and sometimes abandoned by theorists trained in deconstructive and poststructuralist modes of analysis.'[18] Despite this, Zimmerman recognizes her continuing 'desire to affirm a historical lesbian collective identity', and goes on to suggest that perhaps it may be possible to rethink the present conceptual cleavage between essentialism and constructionism.[19] An empowering notion of a shared and knowable identity *is* necessary to activate political struggle against homophobia. However, she argues, this could be a notional lesbian identity based on a firmly historical perception of 'self' as always 'a shifting matrix of behaviours, choices, subjectivities, textualities, and self-representations'.[20]

The sense of shifting textuality and self-representation provides a helpful way of thinking about some recent lesbian writing, where style seems to shift constantly across the borderlands of historically situated realism and autobiographical writing and experimental or avant-garde forms. By producing itself across these textual boundaries, such writing constructs positive character identities and images while foregrounding fictionality and the play of verbal excess. A good example of this is Jeanette Winterson's *Oranges are not the Only Fruit*, with its precise cultural setting and use of first-person narrative to facilitate reader identification with the heroine's positive self-representation. Yet this realist verisimilitude is persistently undercut by stylistic movement towards a comic gothicism or carnivalesque which achieves its most intense pitch in the ludic representation of Elsie's funeral tea. In addition to this stylistic doubling of voice, the almost realist narrative is intersected continually with fairy-tales which may or may not be read as part of the heroine's subjectivity, conscious or unconscious. In *Zamie: A New Spelling of My Name* Audre Lorde achieves a similar effect: first-person narrative form constructs an empathetic reader relationship with the powerful narrator/heroine. The 'authenticity' of this autobiographical construction of identity is heightened by precise social representation: the climate of fear engendered among the gay community by the McCarthyism of the United States in the 1950s. However, operating against this realist mode is a constant shifting of stylistic register, narrative silences and dislocations to produce a many-layered textuality which undermines any sense of unitary and coherent subjectivity. A positive identity is constructed in these texts but as readers we remain at some level aware that it is 'notional', to use Zimmerman's term.

Black and Postcolonial Feminist Criticism

The inadequacy of the term 'black' to speak collectively of the feminist literary criticism produced by Afro-American and 'third-world' women is only part of a larger problem. While the word foregrounds the common interests and conflicts these critics work with and within, it also functions (just as 'lesbian' or 'woman' can) to impose a totalizing identity which erases the enormous cultural, economic, national and individual differences between them. Awareness that for centuries western imperialist and capitalist power has imposed its language, names and terminology on the rest of the world makes my unease over my own act of naming only a minor aspect of my wider sense of discomfort and even of illegitimacy. My inevitably western-orientated critical discourse can itself be regarded as a colonizing and expansionist language, appropriating the writing of 'black' women for my own academic purposes. To construct black feminist writing as the object of my 'knowledge' would be to engage in one of the most typical forms of colonial linguistic oppression. The prevalence of imperialist or colonialist metaphors in many of the critical accounts of 'newly discovered' 'third-world' writing has been pointed out; it is frequently referred to as an 'important area of development', as a 'source of new material', and so on. [21] In addition to these dubious critical activities, Gayatri Spivak has pointed to the immense distance separating privileged 'first-world' feminists and the great majority of women in the 'third-world'. She asks: 'How, then, can one learn from and speak to the millions of illiterate rural and urban Indian women who live "in the pores of" capitalism, inaccessible to the capitalist dynamics that allow us our shared channels of communication, the definition of common enemies?' [22] I cannot resolve these difficulties. I will, however, try to keep them visible in the discussion of 'black feminist criticism' which follows.

In 1981 the Afro-American critic Houston Baker produced an influential essay, 'Generational Shifts and the Recent Criticism of Afro-American Literature', in which he argued that between the 1950s and the early 1980s Afro-American writing and criticism moved through three plases or generations. [23] The 1950s and early 1960s were 'Integrationist', with black writers believing entry into the mainstream of American culture to be both desirable and possible. The next generation was dominated by a 'Black Aesthetic' closely associated with the Black Power movement and its political affirmation of a unique black identity and culture in opposition to the ingrained racism of white America and its demeaning stereotypes of black people. Black Art celebrated the authenticity of all forms of black aesthetic activity, especially those in which the links to African culture remained vibrant and recognizable. Black Aesthetics lasted through the 1960s and 1970s giving way to

'Reconstructionism' at the end of the 1970s and into the 1980s. Reconstructionists are critics influenced by European poststructuralist ideas and therefore wary of any notion of essential identity and of totalizing definitions. For 'reconstructionists' the task of the critic is not to use literature to affirm a black identity or to reflect the 'truth' of black experience. For such critics 'black' is simply a concept to be deconstructed in its binary relationship to 'white'. However, for other Afro-American writers these views heralded the whole identity-politics dilemma: to reject 'black' as the essential or 'given' basis of identity is to reject Blackness as source of consciousness and pride.

Where do women writers figure in the forty-year history of Afro-American literary criticism? Until the most recent stage they have not figured at all. It is a history of male criticism and writing, which, like white male canonical constructions, erases the presence of women. In a landmark essay written in 1977, 'Toward a Black Feminist Criticism', Barbara Smith wrote, 'I do not know where to begin . . . All segments of the literary world – whether establishment, progressive, black, female, or lesbian – do not know, or at least act as if they do not know, that black women writers and black lesbian writers exist . . . It seems overwhelming to break such a massive silence.'[24] Afro-American women writers and critics have been trapped in the double oppressions of racism and sexism – to be lesbian as well adds a third circle of intense prejudice to contend against. Afro-American male culture, especially during the Black Aesthetic period in the 1960s and 1970s, represented black manhood in terms of power and sexuality as a means of rejecting the disempowerment experienced by black men within a violently racist society. Black women who expressed any criticism of this male literary chauvinism or who were reluctant to perform a secondary and nurturing role to writing men were vulnerable to accusations of betrayal of black values and solidarity. 'Uppity' black women could be charged with trying to be white.

Since the 1980s Afro-American women writers have been asserting a powerful literary presence. A long tradition of almost forgotten black women writers has been established; writing by current Afro-American women tops the best-seller lists; and black feminist critics have made powerful contributions to the current debate with poststructuralism.[25] However, it is not surprising, given their experience of the double denials of racism and sexism, that black women writers and critics have been more wary than men of fully embracing a sense of identity as contingent, constructed and performative.[26] Toni Morrison, for example, contends that racism must be seen as a pathology rather than a discourse to be deconstructed. She sees the total dislocation and loss of identity wrought by slavery as *the* example of postmodern fragmentation, but there is nothing celebratory in her concept of it: 'in terms of confronting where the world is now, black women had to deal with "post-modern" problems in the nineteenth century and earlier . . . Certain kinds of dissolution, the loss and the need to reconstruct certain kinds of stability'.[27] For Morrison 'identity' is not a concept black women can afford to abandon, and her fiction can be seen as an intense concern with loss and reconstruction of identity and history. However, her sense of identity is grounded in a sense of community, not individualism. She argues that autobiographical form has been important in black writing because it unites individual and group identity; the individual life is 'like the lives of the tribe'.[28] In her fiction she attempts to evoke this sense of community by drawing on the oral story-telling tradition of black American and African culture. In this sense she does not perceive the identity of the writer as unitary, but as a 'we', and this 'is disturbing to people and critics who view the artist as the surpreme individual'.[29] For Morrison identity is always ultimately political in that it is always based on the community, the social group.

'Third-world' women writers also suffer from the double mechanism of racial and sexual oppression. The most influential theoretical analyses of colonization emphasize it as a process of cultural expansionism and appropriation; western history, literature, aesthetics, education, religion and law were imposed on colonized peoples, erasing their own identity, social formations and patterns of living. For this reason nationalist writing assumed a central place in most of the liberation struggles and continues to play an important role in the reconstruction of national identity and history. Despite the cultural focus of postcolonial theory, however, its two most influential writers, Frantz Fanon and Edward Said almost wholly ignored the experience and role of women as colonized people.[30] Neither was women's writing perceived as central to the nationalist movements. Moreover, in many of the postcolonial male nationalist literary texts aimed at reconstructing a sense of national history and identity, women are represented in exceedingly stereotypical ways.

However, in the postcolonial context it is very difficult for African, Indian, Caribbean, Egyptian or any 'third-world' woman to criticize such writing without being accused of (and indeed herself feeling) a lack of identification with national values and traditions. Even the position 'feminist' is a difficult one for 'third-world' women since it is so closely associated with American and European women. The anxiety and tension felt by many 'third-world' women writers caused by their need to articulate criticism and solidarity simultaneously is precisely caught in Ama Ata Aidoo's novel *Our Sister Killjoy*. In the section expressly entitled 'A Love Letter' the heroine Sissie attempts to communicate to an unnamed lover her sense that language and perceptions divide them, even while she admits that the need to argue with him is what has driven him away. The tone Aidoo constructs is skilfully loving, warm, self-deprecating but ultimately insistent: 'My Darling: it seems as if so much of the softness and meekness you and all the brothers expect of me and all the sisters is that which is really western. Some kind of hashed-up Victorian notions hm? Allah, me and my big mouth!!'[31] Despite the loving supplications throughout – 'My Beloved', 'My Lost Heart' – Sissie finally decides not to send the love-letter to her male lover. She can come home to Africa as a woman on her own terms.

Although *Our Sister Killjoy* is experimental in form, it is, like *Oranges are not the Only Fruit*, deceptively simple and not in the least difficult or intimidating to read. In fact, Aidoo has constructed the novel across many textual boundaries – it is multiply intertextual. Like much post-colonial literature, it returns to traditional African oral and cultural forms of story-telling and poetry, but it is also in dialogic relation (a dialogue between texts) with European fiction. In one of the most well-known colonial novels, Joseph Conrad's *Heart of Darkness*, the white male narrator travels into the 'black' heart of the Congo and towards some unspeakable barbaric atrocity. In *Our Sister Killjoy* Sissie the African narrator travels to the cultivated affluence of German Bavaria, but where forests may cover over the historical European atrocity of Nazi death-camps.[32] In contesting the male chauvinism operating within her national culture, Aidoo equally stakes her claim to speak from a position of national postcolonial identification.

The interconnection of gender identity with national identity and history is made more complicated and contradictory for black women by the emotive use of notions of 'Motherland' and 'Mothertongue' in many of the colonial liberation struggles. Some African male writers associate even the shape of Africa with a full-bellied maternal homeland. This liberation rhetoric draws on many earlier national traditions and religions which sanctify and celebrate the image of maternal fertility and nurture. Inevitably these exert their own powerful imaginative and emotional influence on women as writers. In an essay on this subject Elleke Boehmer points out that while nationalist ideals are projected in metaphors of a naturalized femininity, in political reality women have often been excluded from full participation in national public life and debate: 'Mother Africa may have been declared free, but the mothers of Africa remained manifestly oppressed.'[33] Postcolonial women writers are, therefore, faced with the painful necessity of simultaneously rejecting these essentialist national metaphors of feminine identity while constructing positive narratives of a collective national identity for women.

Gayatri Spivak includes in her collection of essays *In Other Worlds* her translation of two short fictions by Bengali writer Mahasweta Devi. One of them is the story 'Draupadi', which is about a freedom fighter in the peasant rebellion in the Naxalbari region of West Bengal, which in 1971 was stamped out with extreme severity by the central Indian government. Mahasweta Devi's narrative seems very simple, but operates on multiple levels. Although Draupadi, or Dopdi, has long been sought by the military authorities, they remain confused as to her correct name. The latter is a tribal, peasant form, whereas the former derives from the name of the heroine of one of India's great national dynastic epics, *The Mahabharata*. In the epic Draupadi is married to five royal sons. The eldest of these loses her in a game of dice as part of his property. Since she belongs to many husbands she is deemed little better than a prostitute, and the enemy chief who wins her at dice begins to pull off her sari. Draupadi prays to Krishna and the more the sari is pulled the longer it becomes. The divine Krishna has saved Draupadi's honour.

In Mahasweta Devi's story Dopdi/Draupadi remains faithful to the memory of her peasant husband who was killed by the Indian forces. The success of the national army in destroying the 'rebels' begins when they enlist the help of a Bengali army officer, Senanayak, who specializes in knowledge of extreme left-wing politics. Senanayak prides himself on knowing the 'other side' better than they know themselves: '*If you want to destroy the enemy become one.*'[34] So Dopdi is tracked and captured, but before she can be seized she ululates a tribal song into the forest whose words make no sense to her captors. After an hour's unproductive questioning, Senanayak leaves her with the soldiers: 'Make her. *Do the needful*.'[35] Throughout the story Mahasweta Devi's use of language combines colloquial and regional Bengali dialect with a variety of English words and phrases (here italicized) to indicate the westernized language of war and fighting. Dopdi uses the word '*counter*' an abbreviated form for the official 'killed by the police in an encounter', which is code for death by police torture. Dopdi is tortured as a woman – she is multiply raped and mutilated. But in the morning following the endless night, she behaves 'incomprehensively', refusing to put on her cloth, walking out naked into the bright sunlight towards Senanayak:

> Draupadi's black body comes even closer. Draupadi shakes with indomitable laughter that Senanayak simply cannot understand. Her ravaged lips bleed as she begins laughing. Draupadi wipes the blood on her palm and says in a voice that is as terrifying, sky splitting, and sharp as her ululation, What's the use of clothes? You can strip me, but how can you clothe me again? Are you a man?
>
> She looks around and chooses the front of Senanayak's white bush shirt to spit a bloody gob at and says. There isn't a man here that I should be ashamed. I will not let you put my clothes on me. What more can you do? Come on, *counter* me – come on, *counter* me –?
>
> Draupadi pushes Senanayak with her two mangled breasts, and for the first time Senanayak is afraid to stand before an unarmed *target*, terribly afraid.[36]

This is undeniably powerful, shocking writing. Could it be read as a feminist dialogic engagement with the great patriarchal traditions of Indian national culture and religion, as embodied in The Mahabharata, for example? What kind of identity is constructed for the fictional woman 'Dopdi' or 'Draupadi'? In Mahasweta Devi's story no powerful male god intervenes to save Dopdi/Draupadi. Power is male and women always 'encounter' that power in sexual terms. In the national epic Draupadi's sari is the occasion for Krishna's intervention, but it is an intervention that functions to construct and glorify male dynastic expansionism as divine narrative. Draupadi is as much an object of that patriarchal narrative as she is perceived to be an object by the men within the narrative. Krishna's miracle in fact confirms the sexual terms in which women are perceived as objects – losing her 'honour', Draupadi would have dishonoured male lineage. Mahasweta Devi's story unveils what actually happens to women when they are so perceived. Her heroine Dopdi refuses to clothe the brutal consequence of rendering women sexual objects for use or possession. She presents her mangled body to Senanayak as 'The object of your search'. She insists on the materiality of what women are for men; literally a *target* on which they can practise their power.

As well as entering into polemical debate with sacred patriarchal national texts, Mahasweta's narrative can also be read as challenging current male accounts of nationalism and history by constructing a female identity for an activist within a political struggle. However, there is nothing mythic in the representation of Dopdi as terrorist. The narrative is set in a precisely researched historical and social context. In parts the writing adopts realist conventions in presenting details about Dopdi/Draupadi as if from official documents. Thus the character is constructed in traditional fictional terms as a believable identity. At the end of the story Dopdi/Draupadi becomes the active author of her own meaning. She refuses to remain the object of a male narrative and insists on the truth of her own presence. Becoming woman as presence, she produces a meaning which 'Senanayak simply cannot understand'. She becomes that which resists – 'counters' – male knowledge, mastery, power, hence he is 'terribly afraid'.

Thus Mahasweta resolves the dilemma of identity by that double textual move. She uses techniques derived from realist forms of writing to construct character as a positive female image – a woman as subject of her own narrative. The precise historical content of the narrative conveys Dopdi as a fully realized tribal-community identity. However, the writing, like the unresolved movement between Dopdi/Draupadi, implies that there is an excess to this identity that will always resist final definition or restricted social meaning. Spivak has usefully suggested that we think of this kind of construction of identity which serves a 'scrupulously visible political interest' as *strategic*.[37] The lesbian critic Bonnie Zimmerman also commends this notion of identity, arguing for the need to move beyond the 'cleavage' of essentialism and constructionism while retaining a political sense of identity. I shall come back to the concept of strategic identity towards the end of the chapter.

Finally, how does this story reflect upon the position of the western feminist reader? In her own commentary on 'Draupadi', Spivak suggests that the character Senanayak, who prides himself on knowing the other side better than they know themselves, offers uncomfortable parallels with 'first-world' feminist readers as literary investigators of the 'third world': 'We congratulate ourselves on our specialists' knowledge of them.'[38] We enjoy the sense of interrogating and mastering the texts they offer us as the 'unknown', penetrating them as objects other to us. The result of this uncritical critical activity is almost invariably the loss or destruction of the 'object of our search'. Western feminists tend either to apply an essentializing definition to 'third-world' writing, subsuming it as 'woman's writing' and thereby denying its cultural specificity, or to perceive it in terms of a totalizing ethnic or national identity – 'black writing' or 'African writing'. A deconstructionist reading dissolves identity altogether: a playfulness possible only within the privileged security of western culture perhaps.

Marxist and Class-Based Feminist Criticism

The contention over the 'political correctness' of realist or Modernist (avant-garde) writing is part of the early twentieth-century history of Marxist literary criticism.[39] Realism was favoured over experimentation as more accurately 'reflecting' the material and economic conditions of existence and the resulting structural inequality of class relations between capitalism and labour. These economic conditions – termed the material base – were perceived as the determining factors in constructing a class-based identity. Early Marxists attempted to provide an anti-essentialist explanation of the subordination of women by relating it to class divisions. The labour of reproduction, especially during the harsh conditions of the nineteenth century, inevitably put women at a disadvantage to working men in the labour market. Hence women were confined to the sphere of reproduction and domesticity or to the lowest-paid work. This 'separate sphere' arrangement suits the interests of both capitalists and working-class men and so continues to be imposed. There are various inadequacies in this kind of account – women's inequality long predates capitalist modes of production, for example – and theorizing a satisfactory relation between class and gender in terms of determining material and economic conditions remains an unresolved problem for Marxism.[40]

However, in the 1970s ideas from Marxist poststructuralists in France began to make an impact on British Marxist theory and literary criticism. The emphasis shifted from analysing the economic conditions determining class identity to a concern with the production of self-identity by means of language. Of crucial importance was the 'translation' of Lacan's psychoanalytic theory into a Marxist account of the 'ideological construction of the subject' by the Marxist philosopher Louis Althusser. 'Self', Lacan tells us, begins with loss, the separation from the mother which impels us into a social world. Bereft of our first and only known security, how can we find our self? Language, Althusser suggests, calls us into being − it 'interpellates' us − offering us in the approved positions of our culture a self which will be again secure, loved and accepted. So we actively comply with the demands of constructing and recognizing our self as 'good mother', 'achieving man', 'brave boy', 'loyal worker'. As Althusser says, we 'willingly' subject ourselves to subjection.[41] In this way, ideology functions to reproduce the kinds of human beings of varied skills and degrees of initiative needed to reproduce a capitalist mode of production. As a result, we live in an imaginary or fantasy relation to our real relations of existence; we believe ourselves to be freely choosing in the very act of subjecting ourselves to conformity.

The recognition that language, as well as the material conditions of existence, plays a large role in determining 'reality' as we perceive it freed Marxist criticism from its traditional realist approach to literature. The Marxist critic Pierre Macherey suggested that texts should be read 'symptomatically': what cannot be said may well reveal more than the explicit content.[42] Gaps and silences and dislocations of form will speak of what has to be repressed so that the imaginary or fantasy nature in which we live out our real relations of existence can be maintained. Thus a 'symptomatic' reading of texts is rather analogous to the way in which a psychoanalyst may decode unconscious repressions in the silences and slippages of speech. By reading the text's unconscious − what it cannot say − we reveal the repressions at work to sustain as 'truth' the illusions of dominant ideology. It was this kind of theoretical framework that informed the rereading practice of male-authored texts utilized in chapter 1.

The centrality of psychoanalytic theory to these new directions within Marxism was, clearly, conducive to the development of gender-orientated

Marxist criticism. Between 1976 and 1979 these ideas became the focus of critical discussion and practice among a group of women meeting in London as the Marxist-Feminist Collective.[43] They produced innovative readings of the work of the Brontës and Barrett Browning using symptomatic interpretative approaches to reveal the tensions in these texts between incipient feminist radicalism and class-based conservatism. What the texts could not say – the knowledge they repressed of an underlying identity between the political demands of middle-class women and the working class – produced gaps and disturbances in the writing. This form of poststructuralist approach is still the predominant mode of much Marxist feminist criticism.

However, as with the history of the lesbian and black movements, the espousal of theory has given rise to debate and anxiety. As usual, this centres on the issues of identity and the authentic site for revolutionary struggle. In *Women's Oppression Today* (1980) the Marxist feminist Michèle Barrett expressed a deep reservation about the tendency to claim language as the privileged location of political engagement. This view is both flattering and exciting for intellectuals and literary critics, but, she insists, 'a distinction must be retained between this form of struggle and the more terrestrial kind. Are we really to see the Peterloo massacre, the storming of the Winter Palace in Petrograd, the Long March, the Grunwick picket – as the struggle of discourses?'[44] Her second objection is also one expressed by both lesbian and black feminists: the problem of sustaining a political agenda when identity is perceived as indeterminate. 'It is unclear that the project to deconstruct the category of woman could ever provide a basis for a feminist politics. If there are no "women" to be oppressed then on what criteria do we struggle, and against what?'[45]

However, despite this apparent symmetry between the engagement of lesbian, black and Marxist feminist criticism with poststructuralism, there is, I think, a significant difference in Barrett's articulation. Whereas lesbian and black feminists are concerned with the identity dilemma as it effects a specific oppressed social group Barrett makes use of the most general term 'woman'. There is nothing wrong with Barrett's formulation; the identity problem certainly arises for women generally in their need for collective struggle against male domination. Nevertheless, given Barrett's Marxist orientation, it seems a little odd that she leaves out any notion of class in her concern for women's struggle in the sentence quoted. In particular, it is strange that as a Marxist she does not draw attention to the dilemma of identity sited in the working-class woman as subject of history. In an influential essay Judith Newton and Deborah Rosenfelt call on Marxist feminist critics to espouse historical specificity so as to avoid the 'tragic essentialism' of much American feminist criticism, which, they claim, depicts women as always and everywhere the tragic victims of a monolithic patriarchy.[46] This historicizing approach has produced some excellent feminist criticism, bringing to light the complex ever-shifting relation of middle-class women to the dominant power structures. Nowhere, though, is there any sustained study of a working-class woman; she remains historically unconstituted, still a vague mythic figure of essential victimization. This omission in Marxist feminist literary criticism is surprising and seems to require a symptomatic reading itself as that which cannot be said – the repressed – in the work of feminist literary academics.

The most obvious – self-evident even – reason for this omission is the lack of either working-class women writers or texts that foreground the experience of working-class women. However, the absence may itself be worth thinking about. How might these untold stories of poor women relate to the dominant plots we have for interpreting women's experience? It is striking that some of the most powerful literary representations of the interconnection of gender, class and poverty have been made by Afro-American women writers. Toni Morrison, Alice Walker and Maya Angelou have used a variety of narrative forms to explore the precarious nature of subject construction for a woman who is both poor and black. This is not too surprising; a black woman in the United States is not inevitably poor, but is likely to be so. What is worth considering, though, is whether being black somehow offers the basis for a positive self-interpellation (a calling of self into being) which being working class does not so easily provide for a woman.

Britain, like the United States is a multiracial culture and there are positive indications of a vibrant movement of black women writers and artists emerging. 'Black women writing in Britain at this moment share a commitment and a need to leave a legacy, an investment for all those young Black people whose only experience of life is in Britain.' 'We are writing to tell our own particular histories; to speak our mothers' silences; to share among our isolated sisters, our experiences, and our joys; to stand out for each other like poppies in a wheatfield.'[47] (Why is it difficult to imagine a movement of white working-class women writers with such consciously shared voices?) In Britain, as in the United States, to be black is often to be trapped in poverty as well as in the double oppressions of racial and sexual injustice. In a recent book of writings by black and 'third-world' women in Britain the majority of the contributors define their identity in terms of the threefold determining pressures of class, race and gender.[48] Many of the women write of their sense of isolation from the perspectives and aims of white middle-class women activists. However, nowhere in the book is there any speculation about the experience and lives of white working-class women.

This is not a criticism. Despite their evident concern with class as an oppressive structure, there are many obvious and good reasons why these black women do not summon up any image of a white working woman. One of these is her absence within cultural representation. There is no collective working-class woman's identity. A working-class identity has been constructed as male. By relegating women to the separate sphere of reproduction and domesticity, Marxist theorists denied them a historical and social identity, performing that now familiar trick of sliding them into a purely biological realm. Male historians of the working class, male working-class writers and male working-class autobiographies have consolidated the effect: collective working-class identity as source of pride and self-recognition has been constructed as male.[49] Within this male writing a mythicized female figure does present itself, usually known as 'our mam'. It is an image of self-sacrifing epic motherhood.

What kind of stories do working-class daughters have to tell? What questions might the extracts below pose to dominant cultural stories of motherhood? What do they suggest of problems facing working-class girls in constructing a positive sense of self?

Our Mum was also very cruel and spiteful towards us, especially to me, and I could never make out why until I was old enough to be told . . . Many a time we felt the flat of her hand, Liza, Frankie and me. We never knew what for at times, but down would come the cane from its place on the wall. If we tried to run away then we really had it. Neither our parents nor the neighbours had the time to give us any love or affection and they didn't listen to our troubles. [Later her elder sister tells her] Mum didn't want Dad to love her and to have any more babies. She's had thirteen which is what's called a 'baker's dozen' and you being the thirteenth, Mum calls you the 'scraping of the pot'.[50]

She had a mysterious attitude towards the begetting of children; it wasn't that she couldn't do it, more that she didn't want to do it. She was very bitter about the Virgin Mary getting there first. So she did the next best thing and arranged for a foundling. That was me.[51]

My mother's anger humiliates me; her words chafe my cheeks, and I am crying. I do not know that she is not angry at me, but at my sickness. I believe she despises my weakness for letting the sickness 'take holt.' By and by I will not get sick; I will refuse to.[52]

Such writing challenges any cultural idealizations and generalizations of the maternal. Motherhood is not a universal condition. It is constructed socially and materialized within a specific set of economic and material conditions which interlock and interact with equally specific expectations and values associated with the role.[53] To talk of the maternal in the absence of historical and social specificity is meaningless. On the other hand, the writing, by black and white women, does suggest that poverty may shape common stories of women's identity that cut across racial boundaries. The extracts clearly indicate the supreme difficulty for the working-class girl of recognizing a possibly acceptable self. She lives the painful contradiction of knowing herself as an unwanted burden and she sees mirrored in that pain her future self as burdened, undesiring mother.

In one of the few critical studies of a working-class woman as subject, Carolyn Steedman recounts her mother reiterating 'Never have children, dear . . . they ruin your life.'[54] Her mother's story, like the stories she told to her daughters, was a narrative of unfulfilment, of the princess who never found prince or kingdom. 'They were stories designed to show me the terrible unfairness of things, the subterranean culture of longing for that which one can never have.'[55] The precarious, isolated, consumer-based identity her mother constructed for herself was an attempted answer to this longing. Steedman suggests that this may be the hidden narrative of many working-class women: 'The faces of the women in the queues are the faces of unfulfilled desire; if we look, there are many women driven mad in this way, as my mother was.'[56]

I am struck by the parallels between the story of Steedman's mother and the fictional narrative of Pecola Breedlove and her mother in Toni Morrison's *The Bluest Eye*. Pecola's mother rejects her for the little blonde daughter of her white employers, and Pecola dreams of a fairy-tale transformation which will make her beautiful and lovable. She prays for blue eyes like Shirley Temple's. For Pecola, too, fairy-tales fail. What she needed to discover was that 'black is beautiful', not blue eyes; a self-interpellation made possible by a constructed political identity. But what narrative is available for the construction of a positive self-image as 'not-ugly' for the desiring women referred to by Steadman: women haunted by poverty, exiled characters from a consumerist fairy-tale in which they have never figured? Except perhaps, to feel not-ugly because they are not black? This suggests the need for what Spivak calls a sense of a strategic identity when it is 'serving a scrupulously visible political interest'. How are the stories that could construct such an identity to be produced? Is some sense of 'I', even if only strategic (perhaps best of all when know as strategic, as a fiction) necessary to assume a voice at all? Jeanette Winterson writes, 'When you have found your voice, you can be heard', but she also records the positive effect of her evangelical childhood: 'I belonged to God and had been chosen by God, and because God was empowering me, I could do anything.'[57] This provides a stark contrast to those working-class daughters who are aware of themselves only as burdens.

Their stories are important, if only because their absence distorts the way we interpret other narratives. The issue of identity is at the centre of a network of urgent feminist debates. We need a theory of the subject which can account for the possibility of political agency and for the production of a voice – for texts. The most promising way of conceiving this seems to be a notional strategic identity: a process of self-narrating in response to specific historical, cultural and sexual demands. Another way of seeing this might be as a necessary fiction, as when characters in Angela Carter's novels take upon themselves the necessary role of mothers, but perform that identity with a love that is always comically aware of the fiction. As always, writing is ahead of theory. Much current women's work moves continually across the boundaries of autobiography, realism, experimentalism and earlier traditional forms of fairy-tale and rhyme. Winterson writes, 'Oranges is an experimental novel: its interests are anti-linear. It offers a complicated narrative structure disguised as a simple one, it employs a large vocabulary and a beguilingly straightforward syntax . . . Is *Oranges* an autobiographical novel? No not at all and yes of course.'[58]

I am not suggesting that we value most highly the kinds of texts that seem able to combine the strengths of innovation and tradition and thereby transcend the sterile opposition between realism and avant-garde writing. This would simply be to construct another aesthetic hierarchy. Reading practices should aim to respond adequately to the multiple forms of writing that empower women. Clearly, the question of literary value remains another major area of challenge for feminist literary critics and it has always been closely involved with the politics of identity. Feminist criticism began with demands for more women-authored texts in the canon, to counteract misrepresentation in male works; lesbian, Afro-American and postcolonial women in turn insisted on canonical representation. However, it would be quite inadequate to continue to couch such demands in terms of equal representation. Women's writing is far too good for that; it demands inclusion because it is too powerful, innovative and accomplished to be kept out. This is not to fall back on specious claims for purely aesthetic literary qualities. Judgements are always made from an ideological position, but to acknowledge that is not to sweep away the sense and need we have to evaluate literary work. Not all writing by women is equally good, although it is usually interesting. What do I mean by 'good'? There is no easy or presently available answer, but that is not to say that feminist critics should dodge the issue. We can begin to consider this, now, from a position of strength – from writing by women. Feminist criticism is inherently self-questioning, in all senses – fortunately – for out of its debates comes the next move forward. Women's writing – literary and critical – is a dialectical record of the achievements produced by the struggle to overcome obstacles.

Summary of Main Points

1 Feminist criticism is self-interrogating and hence self-renewing. The current debates (arising from the spread of poststructuralist theory since the 1980s) on canon formation, the identity dilemma and the politics of experimental form versus realism are articulated most urgently by lesbian, black and working-class women.

2 Lesbian feminist criticism began with the need to proclaim a positive lesbian identity to counteract prevailing association of lesbianism with sin and sickness. A lesbian canon was constructed to promote this positive tradition. In the United States in the 1970s lesbian writing advocated an

essentialist radical separatism based on a perceived 'lesbian continuum' within all women's experience.

3 By the mid 1980s poststructuralist theory had deconstructed essentialist views of self, giving rise to a dilemma of identity for lesbian critics: how is a canonical tradition to be sustained as part of a collective political agenda to resist homophobia if identity is perceived as pluralized and indeterminate?

4 Some lesbian creative writing seems to overcome this problem by combining realist and experimental techniques to construct positive lesbian 'characters' for reader identification while simultaneously indicating their fictionality.

5 Black women writers experience the double oppressions of race and gender; the Black Consciousness movement of the 1970s was often chauvinistic in its celebration of black manhood. Since the 1980s black women writers have established their own tradition and are more reluctant than black male writers to embrace deconstruction of Blackness as a source of identity.

6 'Third-world' women writers are also trapped by the double oppressions of race and gender. National liberation struggles gave an important place to literature as means of reconstructing a national identity to oppose degrading imperialist images.

7 However, much of this literature represents women in very stereotypical ways. Nationalist rhetoric utilizes idealized metaphors of 'Motherland' and 'Mothertongue' but these mythicize Woman, while women are marginalized from actual public life.

8 'Third-world' women who dissent can be accused of being 'Westernized'. Hence 'third-world' women writers have to deconstruct essentialist national womanhood while constructing a positive national identity for women. To do this they, too, write at the intersection of realism and experimentalism and return to oral traditions.

9 French Marxist poststructuralism freed Marxist literary criticism from its attachment to realism. The attention shifted from the economic and material determinants of class identity to the importance of ideology and language (discourses) in constructing subjects.

10 Literary texts could be read 'symptomatically' to reveal the ideology which produced them. The centrality of psychoanalytic theory within this approach made it a useful one for developing a Marxist feminist gender-orientated criticism.

11 However, there has been no recognition of an identity problem situated in the working-class woman's need to construct a 'self'. Working-class tradition is a story of collective identity as male. In contrast to black writers, working-class women in Britain rarely seem to find a literary voice.

12   The need to construct a 'strategic' theory of identity remains an important issue on the feminist agenda. Related to this is the need for a feminist aesthetics which can adequately recognize all empowering forms of women's writing.

Suggestions for Further Reading

Lesbian criticism

Bonnie Zimmerman, 'What Has Never Been: An Overview of Lesbian Feminist Criticism', in Showalter (ed.), *The New Feminist Criticism*, pp. 200–24.

Bonnie Zimmerman, 'Lesbians Like This and That: Some Notes on Lesbian Criticism for the Nineties', in Munt (end.), *New Lesbian Criticism*, pp. 1–15.

Barbara Smith, 'The Truth that Never Hurts: Black Lesbian Fiction in the 1980s', in Warhol and Herndl (eds), *Feminisms*, pp. 690–712.

Black and postcolonial criticism

Barbara Smith, 'Toward a Black Feminist Criticism', in Showalter (ed.), *The New Feminist Criticism*, pp. 168–85.

Valerie Smith, 'Gender and Afro-Americanist Literary Theory and Criticism', in Showalter (ed.), *Speaking of Gender*, pp. 56–70.

Alice Walker, *In Search of our Mothers' Gardens*, esp. pp. 231–331.

Gayatri Chakravorty Spivak, 'French Feminism in an International Frame', in *In Other Worlds*, pp. 134–53. The essay is reprinted in Belsey and Moore (eds), *The Feminist Reader*, pp. 175–95, and Mary Eagleton (ed.), *Feminist Literary Criticism*, pp. 83–109. Not an easy piece but it has been influential, as its reprinting indicates.

Marxist feminist criticism

Judith Newton and Deborah Rosenfelt, 'Introduction: Toward a Material Feminist Criticism', in Newton and Rosenfelt (eds), *Feminist Criticism and Social Change*, pp. xv–xxxix.

Sara Mills et al., *Feminist Readings/Feminists Reading*, pp. 187–226, provides a Marxist-feminist' reading.

Notes

1   This was a debate within European Marxism. The official Soviet position, as practised and advocated by the distinguished Marxist critic Georg

Lukács, criticized the experimental Modernist writing produced at the beginning of the century as subjective and individualistic. Socialist art demanded realist forms which represented individuals in relation to the social world. The opposite view was argued by Theodor Adorno who claimed that Modernist art was more progressive, because it radically challenged conventional perceptions. For the most important expressions of this debate see Robert Taylor (ed.), *Aesthetics and Politics*.

2   Steedman, *Landscape for a Good Woman*, p. 5.

3   Rule, *Lesbian Images*, pp. 197–209, gives a brief outline of the history. See also Kate Adams, 'Making the World Safe for the Missionary Position: Images of the Lesbian in Post-War II America', in Jay and Glasgow (eds), *Lesbian Texts and Contexts*, pp. 255–74.

4   Rule, *Lesbian Images*, p. 3.

5   Faderman, *Surpassing the Love of Men*, p. 84.

6   Ibid., p. 241.

7   For a personal account of 1970s separatism see Sonya Andermahr, 'The Politics of Separatism and Lesbian Utopian Fiction', in Munt (ed.), *New Lesbian Criticism*, pp. 133–52.

8   Rich, 'Compulsory Heterosexuality and Lesbian Existence', *Signs*, 5(4) (1980), pp. 631–60, reprinted in Snitow, Stansell and Thompson (eds), *Powers of Desire*, pp. 212–41.

9   Rich, *The Fact of a Doorframe*, p. 264.

10   Wittig, *The Straight Mind and Other Essays*, p. 59.

11   Ibid., p. 6.

12   Ibid., p. 60. You may recall the extract from Robert Lowell in ch. 2 which constructs Sylvia Plath's poetry very much in this way, obscuring its production as work. Male critics typically think of women's writing inseparably from the female body.

13   See Wittig's own discussion of this in *The Straight Mind and Other Essays*, pp. 76–89.

14   Ibid., p. 20.

15   Ibid., p. 46.

16   For a more detailed discussion of this see Diana Fuss, 'Monique Wittig's Anti-essentialist Materialism', in *Essentially Speaking*, pp. 39–53.

17   Reina Lewis, 'The Death of the Author and the Resurrection of the Dyke', in Munt (ed.), *New Lesbian Criticism*, p. 19.

18   Bonnie Zimmerman 'Lesbians Like This and That: Some Notes on Lesbian Criticism for the Nineties', ibid., p. 2. Zimmerman's earlier essay, one of the founding pieces of lesbian criticism, 'What Has Never Been: An Overview of Lesbian Criticism' (1981), is reprinted in Showalter (ed.), *The New Feminist Criticism*, pp. 200–24.

19 Zimmerman, 'Lesbians Like This and That', p. 8.

20 Ibid., p. 9.

21 See e.g. Caroline Rooney, 'Dangerous Knowledge', in Nasta (ed.), *Mother-lands*, pp. 101–3; Gayatri Chakravorty Spivak, *In Other Worlds*, p. 135.

22 Ibid., p. 135.

23 For an account of this history in relation to black feminist criticism see Valerie Smith, 'Gender and Afro-Americanist Literary Theory and Criticism', in Showalter (ed.), *Speaking of Gender*, pp. 56–70.

24 Barbara Smith, 'Towards a Black Feminist Criticism', in Showalter (ed.), *The New Feminist Criticism*, p. 168.

25 For a brief account of these developments see Wall, 'Introduction: Taking Positions and Changing Words', in Wall (ed.), *Changing our Own Words*, pp. 1–15. See also Valerie Smith, 'Gender and Afro-Americanist Literary Theory and Criticism'.

26 For an expression of reservation see Barbara Christian, 'But What do We Think We're doing Anyway: The State of Black Feminist Criticism(s) or My Version of a Little Bit of History', in Wall (ed.), *Changing our Own Words*, pp. 58–74.

27 Morrison, 'Living Memory', *City Limits* (31 Mar.–7 Apr. 1988), p. 11.

28 Morrison, 'Rootedness: The Ancestor as Foundation', in Walder (ed.), *Literature in the Modern World*, p. 327.

29 Ibid., p. 330.

30 The most influential texts by these writers are: Fanon, *Black Skin, White Masks* and *The Wretched of the Earth*, Said, *Orientalism*. For a feminist critique of their work as 'masculinist' see Jane Miller, *Seductions*, pp. 108–35.

31 Aidoo, *Our Sister Killjoy*, p. 117.

32 I am indebted to a reading of this novel by Caroline Rooney, ' "Dangerous Knowledge" and the Poetics of Survival: A Reading of *Our Sister Killjoy* and *A Question of Power*', in Nasta (ed.), *Motherlands*, pp. 99–126.

33 Boehmer, 'Stories of Women and Mothers: Gender and Nationalism in the Early Fiction of Flora Nwapa', ibid., p. 7.

34 Mahasweta Devi, 'Draupadi', in Spivak *In Other Worlds*, p. 194.

35 Ibid., p. 195.

36 Ibid., p. 196.

37 Ibid., p. 205.

38 Ibid., p. 179.

39 See n. 1. For a useful account of Marxist literary criticism see Terry Eagleton, *Marxism and Literary Criticism*.

40 *Coward, Patriarchal Precedents*, pp. 163–87, provides an account of 'the woman question' within early Marxism. See also Heidi Hartmann,

'The Unhappy Marriage of Marxism and Feminism', in Sargent (ed.), *The Unhappy Marriage of Marxism and Feminism*, pp. 1–41.

41 Althusser, 'Ideology and Ideological State Apparatuses', in *Essays on Ideology*. The most illuminating demonstration of Althusser's notion of 'interpellation' is found in Williamson, *Decoding Advertisements*, pp. 40–70; Belsey, *Critical Practice*, pp. 56–84, also provides a helpful explanation.

42 Macherey, *A Theory of Literary Production*. Belsey, *Critical Practice*, pp. 103–24, also provides an introduction to Macherey.

43 Cora Kaplan, a member of the collective, provides an account of the excitement of the first introduction to French theory, in 'The Feminist Politics of Literary Theory', in *Sea Changes*, pp. 57–66. A version of Mary Jacobus's essay on *Villette* for the collective is reprinted in Jacobus (ed.), *Women Writing and Writing about Women*, pp. 42–60.

44 Barrett, 'Ideology and the Cultural Production of Gender', reprinted in Newton and Rosenfelt (eds), *Feminist Criticism and Social Change*, p. 72. This essay, extracted from *Women's Oppression Today* by Barrett, gives a succinct account of her main ideas.

45 Ibid.

46 Newton and Rosenfelt, 'Introduction', ibid., pp. xvi–xvii. Newton expands this argument and provides a good example of her own historicizing approach in 'Making – and Remaking – History: Another Look at Patriarchy', in Benstock, *Feminist Issues in Literary Scholarship*, pp. 124–40.

47 Grewal et al. (eds), *Charting the Journey*, p. 99.

48 Ibid.

49 For a discussion of this see Jane Miller, *Seductions*, pp. 38–69.

50 Dayus, *Her People*, pp. 6, 9,

51 Winterson, *Oranges are not the Only Fruit*, pp. 3–4.

52 Morrison, *The Bluest Eye*, p. 15.

53 Another interesting representation of a working-class mother is Olsen, 'I Stand Here Ironing', *in Tell me a Riddle and Yonnondio*, pp. 13–25.

54 Steedman, *Landscape for a Good Woman*, p. 17.

55 Ibid., p. 8.

56 Ibid., p. 22.

57 Interview in the *Guardian* (26 Aug. 1992), p. 29.

58 Winterson, *Oranges are not the Only Fruit*, p. xiv.

Glossary

aesthetics the study of the formal arrangement, qualities, techniques and practice of literary works.

author until recently, the term referred to the individual who wrote the work, the person whose intellectual and aesthetic judgements *author*ized the form and content and hence the *intention*al meaning of the text. This sense of a unitary author has been challenged by poststructuralist critics (especially Roland Barthes and Michel Foucault) who stress the pluralization of language by the unconscious and the situatedness of the author *in* language as a determining system of meanings which constructs social reality. For this reason the term 'writing subject' is used to indicate the writer's *subject*ion to the order of language and lack of *author*ity over the meaning of the text she or he produces. *See also* interpellation.

binary opposition two terms considered to be direct opposites, for example light/dark, culture/nature, good/evil. These largely construct our conceptual system, and one term is usually hierarchized above the other. However, deconstructionist practice shows that the 'higher' term is dependent on the 'lower' for its meaning and vice versa (*see* deconstruction).

biological determinism *see* essentialism.

bisexuality the term derives from Freudian theory of infant sexuality. In the first, pre-Oedipal, phase of infancy, sexuality in female and male children is undifferentiated; it is both active and passive and unconfined to any specific bodily zone.

canon the body of texts culturally perceived as pre-eminent for their aesthetic quality and their imputed 'truth'. Ecclesiastically, it refers to works accepted as having divine authority.

closure this denotes the resolution of problems, mystery, uncertainty, to produce a sense of comprehensively known meaning to the text, to character and to words. *See also* totalizing *and* unitary meaning.

condensation and **displacement**   terms used by Freud in his work on dreams to describe the processes of the unconscious. A single sign (word, sound image, etc.) condenses into itself a whole cluster of consciously forbidden feelings and meaning; repressed desire traverses a chain of associated signs as a displacement of an impulse that is refused fulfilment in social reality. *See also* desire.

deconstruction   a term associated with the work of Jacques Derrida. Deconstructionist reading seeks to 'untie' the logic of binary hierarchies and reveal the working of logocentrism in texts. By this is meant the belief that 'meaning' and 'truth' are guaranteed by an intentional presence outside the words themselves, either as author, as an individual consciousness, or as God. *See also* author.

desire   a term associated with psychoanalytic theory, especially that of Jacques Lacan. To enter the cultural order as a social being, the child must separate from its coextensive unity with the pre-Oedipal mother. Thus self-identity is based on loss or lack of the maternal body. This lack produces unconscious desire which can never regain the maternal plenitude, and displaces itself into a chain of social meanings which can never satisfy it. As opposed to 'want' and 'need', which have specific demandable objects, desire cannot be named since it originates in a loss prior to language.

determinism   *see* essentialism.

dialogism   *see* intertextuality.

discourse   a term often associated with the work of Michel Foucault who associates it with the working of power. It denotes a socially and historically situated use of language – a discursive practice – sustaining shared vocabulary, assumptions, values and interests, for example medical discourse, teenage discourse, the discursive practice of English teachers.

discursive practice   *see* discourse.

displacement   *see* condensation.

écriture féminine   literally 'feminine writing', as advocated by some French feminists. It is perceived as writing that remains in contact with a feminine libidinal energy and hence opposes the repressive phallic order of social meaning: the symbolic order. *See also* phallocentrism.

essentialism   the belief that attributes are inherent and distinctive to an object, for example that certain qualities are universal to women. Often these qualities are held to derive from female biology and hence to be inevitable; this belief is also referred to as biological determinism.

gynocriticism   a term coined by Elaine Showalter to describe the practice of reading and studying texts written by women.

heterogeneity *see* unitary meaning.

ideology a consciously held system of beliefs, or the naturalized perception of self and the world, constructed as the individual enters the social order. This much wider determining sense of ideology is associated with the work of Louis Althusser. *See also* interpellation.

Imaginary a term used by Lacan to refer to the first pre-Oedipal phase of infancy when the child's relation to reality is structured by fantasy and narcissistic desires.

individual *see* interpellation.

intentional meaning *see* author.

interpellation a term used by Louis Althusser to describe the way in which language 'hails' us into an identity as we recognize a self in its system of meaning and take up our expected position in its structure. This thinking radically challenges the concept of the individual as an autonomous, coherent, unified identity, the intentional author of her or his own words, thoughts and actions. To suggest the subjection of the individual to the interpellative process which produces social identity, the term 'subject' is used in preference to 'individual'.

intertextuality a term introduced by Julia Kristeva to replace 'dialogism' (used by Mikhail Bakhtin), which retains largely the same sense. Both terms refer to the interactive meeting (dialogue) of two or more meaning systems or 'texts' within a single, apparently discrete, word, utterance or text. As well as the writer's conscious meaning, there is the 'text' of the unconscious, and other prior usages ('texts') also remain active within the writer's usage – hence all writing and utterances are a dialogic interaction of several voices, an inter-textuality.

lack *see* desire.

Law of the Father a term used by Jacques Lacan to signify the phallic order structuring language. In the Oedipal crisis the child is forced to separate from the mother and enter the social order – that is language – through fear of castration. Thus it is phallic authority that imposes and determines cultural order: the symbolic order.

logocentricism *see* deconstruction.

Marxism a materialist philosophy based on the work of Karl Marx, which insists on the primacy of the material and economic conditions in determining the structures of social and individual life. Recently, ideology has taken on more importance within Marxist theory largely due to the ideas of Antonio Gramsci and Louis Althusser. *See also* interpellation.

Modernism this normally refers to artistic and cultural production, practices and attitudes arising in the first two to three decades of the twentieth century. Modernists proclaimed the innovatory nature of their work and their attack on traditional forms, values and perceptions.

narcissisism   the normal condition during the early pre-Oedipal stage of infancy when the child is totally self-centred and autoerotic, having no perception of anything other to it. In adults this over-investment of libido in self precludes a full sense of others as real existences.

narrative point of view   the position from which a narrative is told, which strongly influences the way we perceive and judge characters and events. In first-person narration the teller uses the pronoun 'I' and is a character within the narrated events. A third-person narrator is wholly outside the narration, refering to all the characters by name or using a third-person pronoun. An omniscient narrator has access into the thoughts and feelings of all the characters.

Oedipal complex   the Freudian term used to describe the process which produces 'normal' masculine and feminine sexuality. A crisis results from the male child's fear of castration; it is resolved when he represses incestuous desire for the mother and learns to identify with the father as source of authority and power. The female child 'discovers' she has been 'castrated', blames her mother and resolves the crisis by turning to her father, desiring a baby as substitute for a penis.

patriarchy   a social order in which male interests and power are privileged and women are subordinated to male authority.

phallocentricism   a term much used by French feminists and associated by them with logocentricism. *Phallocentricism* refers to the implicit logic within most Western thinking that constructs 'man' as the norm and erases the presence of two genders into the singularity of a universal male.

pre-Oedipal mother   the imaginary perception of the mother constructed by the child before the Oedipal crisis and thus before entry into the social order of meaning – the symbolic order. It bears very little relation to the actual mother.

realism   this refers to conventions of representation in literary and visual art which seek to construct the illusion that a work is offering an unmediated version or 'reflection' of reality. In contrast to Modernist or experimental and avant-garde forms, realism seeks to naturalize or efface its status as art.

semiotic   a term used by Julia Kristeva to refer to the first, pre-verbal but already social, ordering of reality during the earliest pre-Oedipal stage of infancy. Thus the semiotic order or 'disposition' is founded on the child's relationship with the mother and is characterized by the predominance of rhythmic patterning and libidinal drives, and by touch and sound as much as sight.

structural linguistics   this originated in the work of Ferdinand de Saussure early in the twentieth century. The central notion is that language does not derive its meaning from its relation to reality but from the internal differential relationship between words: language is a 'structure of differences'. Binary oppositions provide an illustration of the production of meaning by difference; for example 'short' gains meaning only in its opposition to 'long'.

subject *see* interpellation.

symbolic order the order of language and culture which constructs our sense of identity and reality.

totalizing this term is used in current theoretical discourse to suggest an imposed conceptual unity and completeness which ignores or disallows actual existing diversity and non-conclusiveness. Hence a term like 'the woman's struggle' can function in a totalizing way to efface the many different specific forms of women's political activity. *See also* closure.

unitary meaning a belief that words, knowledge and representations can be defined and stabilized in single discrete meanings often perceived as the authorized meaning of an intentional consciousness. Recent deconstructionist views of language and theories of the unconscious insist on the heterogeneity of language, that is its pluralized meaning, its instability and dialogism.

writing subject *see* author.

Bibliography

This contains all the works referred to in the book and selective other texts for readers who wish to follow up more specific areas. The list of literary works also includes a few extra suggestions for further reading. Unless otherwise stated the place of publication is London.

Literary Works

Prose

Aidoo, Ama Ata, *No Sweetness Here* [1970] (Longman, 1988).
—— *Our Sister Killjoy* [1977] (Longman, 1988).
—— *Changes* (Women's Press, 1991).
Angelou, Maya, *I Know Why the Caged Bird Sings* (Virago, 1984).
Austen, Jane, *Persuasion* [1818] (Oxford, Oxford University Press, revised edn, 1990).
Barker, Pat, *Union Street* (Virago, 1982).
—— *The Century's Daughter* (Virago, 1986).
—— *The Man Who Wasn't There* (Virago, 1989).
Barnes, Djuna, *Nightwood* [1936] (Faber, 1963).
Brontë, Charlotte, *Shirley* [1849] (Harmondsworth, Penguin, 1974).
Brown, Rita Mae, *Ruby Fruit Jungle* (Corgi, 1978).
Bruner, Charlotte H. (ed.), *African Women's Writing* (Heinemann, 1993).
Carswell, Catherine, *Open the Door!* [1920] (Virago, 1986).
Carter, Angela, *The Magic Toyshop* (Virago, 1981).
—— *The Passion of the New Eve* (Virago, 1982).
—— *The Bloody Chamber* [1979] (Harmondsworth, Penguin, 1981).
—— *Nights at the Circus* (Pan, 1985).
—— *Wise Children* (Vintage, 1991).

Chopin, Kate, *The Awakening* [1899] (Women's Press, 1978).

Cixous, Hélène, *Angst* [1977], tr. Jo Levy (John Calder, 1985).

—— *Promethea* [1983] tr. Betsy Wing (Lincoln, University of Nebraska Press, 1991).

Dangarembga, Tsitsi, *Nervous Conditions* (Women's Press, 1988).

Dayus, Kathleen, *Her People* (Virago, 1982).

Desai, Anita, *Clear Light of Day* (Harmondsworth, Penguin, 1980).

—— *Games at Twilight* (Harmondsworth, Penguin, 1982).

—— *The Village by the Sea* (Harmondsworth, Penguin, 1987).

Dickens, Charles, *Pickwick Papers* [1836] (Harmondsworth, Penguin, 1972).

—— *Great Expectations* [1860] (Harmondsworth, Penguin, 1965).

Eliot, George, *Middlemarch: A Study of Provincial Life* [1871] (Harmondsworth, Penguin, 1965).

Gilman, Charlotte Perkins, *The Yellow Wallpaper and Other Fiction* (Women's Press, 1981).

—— *Herland* [1915] (Women's Press, 1979).

Hall, Radclyffe, *The Well of Loneliness* [1928] (Virago, 1982).

Head, Bessie, *A Question of Power* (Heinemann, 1968).

—— *When Rain Clouds Gather* (Heinemann, 1968).

—— *Maru* (Heinemann, 1972).

Holmström, Lakshmi (ed.), *The Inner Courtyard: Stories by Indian Women* (Virago, 1990).

Hurston, Zora Neale, *Their Eyes were Watching God* [1937] (Virago, 1986).

James, Henry, *The Portrait of a Lady* [1881] (Harmondsworth, Penguin, 1966).

—— *What Maisie Knew* [1897] (Harmondsworth, Penguin, 1966).

Jouve, Nicole Ward, *Shades of Grey*, tr. Jouve (Virago, 1981).

Kincaid, Jamaica, *Annie John* (Pan, 1985).

Kuzwayo, Ellen, *Call Me Woman: Autobiography* (Women's Press, 1985).

—— *Sit Down and Listen: Stories from South Africa* (Women's Press, 1990).

Lawrence, D. H., *The Ladybird* [1923] (Harmondsworth, Penguin, 1960).

Le Guin, Ursula, *Always Coming Home* (Grafton, 1988).

Lessing, Doris, *The Grass is Singing* [1950] (Grafton, 1980).

—— *The Golden Notebook* (Panther, 1973).

—— *Shikasta* (Granada, 1981).

—— *The Making of the Representative for Planet 8* (Granada, 1983).

—— *The Sentimental Agents in the Volyen Empire* (Granada, 1985).

Lorde, Audre, *Zami: A New Spelling of my Name* (Sheba Feminist Publishers, 1984).

Manguel, Alberto (ed.), *Other Fires: Stories from the Women of Latin America* (Pan, 1986).

Miller, Jill, *Happy as a Dead Cat* (Women's Press, 1983).

Morrison, Toni, *The Bluest Eye* [1970] (Grafton, 1981).

—— *Sula* [1974] (Grafton, 1982).

—— *Song of Solomon* [1978] (Grafton, 1980).

—— *Beloved* (Pan, 1987).

Mukherjee, Bharati, *The Middleman and Other Stories* (Virago, 1990).

—— *Jasmine* (Virago, 1990).

Namjoshi, Suniti, *The Conversations of Cow* (Women's Press, 1985).

Olsen, Tillie, *Tell me a Riddle and Yonnondio* [1960] (Virago, 1980).

Piercy, Marge, *Woman on the Edge of Time* (Women's Press, 1979).

Rhys, Jean, *Wide Sargasso Sea* (Harmondsworth, Penguin, 1966).

El Saadawi, Nawal, *Woman at Point Zero*, tr. Sherif Hetata (Zed, 1983).

—— *The Fall of the Iman*, tr. Sherif Hetata (Minerva, 1989).

Smedley, Agnes, *Daughter of Earth* [1929] (Virago, 1977).

Thompson, Tierl (ed.), *Dear Girl: The Diaries and Letters of Two Workig Women 1897–1917* (Women's Press, 1987).

Walker, Alice, *The Colour Purple* (Women's Press, 1982).

—— *Meridian* (Women's Press, 1983).

—— *The Temple of my Familiar* (Women's Press, 1988).

Welty, Eudora, *The Collected Stories of Eudora Welty* (Harmondsworth, Penguin, 1983).

—— *Delta Wedding* [1945] (Virago, 1982).

—— *The Optimist's Daughter* [1969] (Virago, 1984).

Winterson, Jeanette, *Oranges are not the Only Fruit* (Vintage, 1991).

—— *The Passion* (Harmondsworth, Penguin, 1988).

—— *Sexing the Cherry* (Vintage, 1990).

Wittig, Monique, *Les Guerilleres* [1969], tr. David Le Vay (Boston, Beacon, 1985).

—— *Across the Acheron* [1985], tr. David Le Vay with Margaret Crosland (Women's Press, 1989).

Wolf, Christa, *The Quest for Christa T* [1968], tr. Christopher Middleton (Virago, 1982).

—— *Cassandra: A Novel and Four Essays*, tr. Jan van Heurck (Virago, 1984).

Woolf, Virginia, *To the Lighthouse* [1927] (Harmondsworth, Penguin, 1964).

Poetry

Akhmatova, Anna, *Selected Poems*, tr. Richard McKane (Harmondsworth, Penguin, 1969).

Angelou, Maya, *And Still I Rise* (Virago, 1986).

Chaucer, Geoffrey, *The Complete Works of Geoffrey Chaucer*, ed. F. N. Robinson, second edn (Oxford, Oxford University Press, 1968).

Barrett Browning, Elizabeth, *Her Novel in Verse Aurora Leigh and Other Poems*, intro. Cora Kaplan (Women's Press, 1978).

—— *Selected Poems* (Dent, 1988).

Blake, William, *Complete Poems*, ed. W. H. Stevenson, text by David V. Erdman (Longman, 1971).

Couzyn, Jeni (ed.), *Contemporary Women Poets: Eleven British Writers* (Newcastle upon Tyne, Bloodaxe, 1985).

Doolittle, Hilda, *H. D.: Collected Poems 1912–1944*, ed. Louis L. Martz (New York, New Directions, 1986).

Kay, Jackie, *The Adoption Papers* (Newcastle upon Tyne, Bloodaxe, 1991).

Kerrigan, Catherine (ed.), *An Anthology of Scottish Women Poets* (Edinburgh, Edinburgh University Press, 1991).

Linthwaite, Illona (ed.), *Ain't I a Woman! Poems of Black and White Women* (Virago, 1987).

Lochhead, Liz, *Dreaming Frankenstein and Collected Poems* (Edinburgh, Polygon, 1984).

Lorde, Audre, *Chosen Poems: Old and New* (New York, W. W. Norton, 1982).

MacDiarmid, Hugh, *The Hugh MacDiarmid Anthology: Poems in Scots and English*, ed. Michael Grieve and Alexander Scott (Routledge & Kegan Paul, 1972).

Milton, John, *Poetical Works*, ed. Douglas Bush (Oxford, Oxford University Press, 1966).

Nichols, Grace, *Fat Black Woman's Poems* (Virago, 1984).

—— *Lazy Thoughts of a Lazy Woman and Other Poems* (Virago, 1989).

Plath, Sylvia, *Collected Poems*, ed. Ted Hughes (Faber, 1981).

Rich, Adrienne, *The Fact of a Doorframe: Poems Selected and New 1950–1984* (New York, W. W. Norton, 1984).

Sexton, Anne, *The Selected Poems of Anne Sexton*, ed. Diane Wood Middlebrook and Diana Hume George (Virago, 1991).

Smith, Stevie, *Selected Poems*, ed. James MacGibbon (Harmondsworth, Penguin, 1978).

Spenser, Edmund, *The Faerie Queene*, ed. A. C. Hamilton (Longman, 1977).

Tsvetayeva, Marina, *Selected Poems*, tr. David McDuff (Newcastle upon Tyne, Bloodaxe, 1987).

Wain, John (ed.), *Oxford Anthology of English Poetry*, 2 vols (Oxford: Oxford University Press, 1986).

Wordsworth, William, *William Wordsworth*, ed. Stephen Gill (Oxford, Oxford University Press, 1984).

Yeats, W. B., *Collected Poems* (Macmillan, 1961).

Critical and Theoretical Works

Abel, Elizabeth (ed.), *Writing and Sexual Difference* (Chicago, University of Chicago Press, 1982).

—— Marianne Hirsch and Elizabeth Langland (eds), *The Voyage In: Fictions of Female Development* (Hanover, NH, University Press of New England, 1983).

Althusser, Louis, *Essays on Ideology* (Verso, 1984).

Ashcroft, Bill, Gareth Griffiths and Helen Tiffin, *The Empire Writes Back: Theory and Practice in Post-colonial Literatures* (Routledge, 1989).

Auerbach, Nina, *Communities of Women: An Idea in Fiction* (Cambridge, Mass., Arvard University Press, 1978).

Bakhtin, Mikhail, *The Dialogic Imagination: Four Essays*, ed. Michael Holquist, tr. Caryl Emerson and Michael Holquist (Austin, University of Texas Press, 1981).

—— *Rabelais and his World*, tr. Helene Iswolsky (Bloomington, Indiana University Press, 1984).

Barrett, Michèle, *Women's Oppression Today* [1980], rev. cdn (Verso, 1988).

Barthes, Roland, 'The Death of the Author', in *Image-Music-Text*, tr. Stephen Heath (Fontana, 1977).

Bauer, Dale M., and Susan Jaret McKinstry, *Feminism, Bakhtin, and the Dialogic* (New York, State University of New York Press, 1991).

Beauvoir, Simone de, *The Second Sex* [1949], tr. H. M. Parshley (Harmondsworth, Penguin, 1972).

Beer, Gillian, *Reader, I Married Him: A Study of the Women Characters of Jane Austen, Charlotte Bronte, Elizabeth Gaskell and George Eliot* (Macmillan, 1974).

Belsey, Catherine, *Critical Practice* (Methuen, 1980).

—— and Jane Moore (eds), *The Feminist Reader* (Macmillan, 1989).

Benstock, Shari, *Women of the Left Bank: Paris, 1900–1940* (Austin, University of Texas Press, 1986).

—— (ed.), *Feminist Issues in Literary Scholarship* (Bloomington, Indiana University Press, 1987).

—— (ed.), *The Private Self: The Theory and Practice of Women's Autobiographical Writing* (Routledge, 1988).

Berger, John, *Ways of Seeing* (Harmondsworth, Penguin, 1972).

Bloom, Harold, *The Anxiety of Influence* (Oxford, Oxford University Press, 1973).

Boumelha, Penny, *Thomas Hardy and Women: Sexual Ideology and Narrative Form* (Brighton, Harvester, 1982).

Brennan, Teresa (ed.), *Between Feminism and Psychoanalysis* (Routledge, 1989).

Brownstein, Rachel, *Becoming a Heroine: Reading about Women in Novels* (Harmondsworth, Penguin, 1982).

Buck, Claire, *H. D. and Freud: Bisexuality and a Feminine Discourse* (Hemel Hempstead, Harvester Wheatsheaf, 1991).

Butler, Judith, *Gender Trouble: Feminism and the Subversion of Identity* (Routledge, 1990).

Calder, Jenni, *Women and Marriage in Victorian Fiction* (Thames & Hudson, 1976).

Cameron, Deborah, *Feminism and Linguistic Theory* (Macmillan, 1985).

Carter, Angela, *The Sadeian Woman: An Exercise in Cultural History* (Virago, 1979).

Chodorow, Nancy, *The Reproduction of Mothering: Psychoanalysis and the Sociology of Gender* (Los Angeles, University of California Press, 1978).

Christian, Barbara, *Black Women Novelists: The Development of a Tradition* (Westport, Conn., Greenwood, 1980).

Cixous, Hélène, and Catherine Clément, *The Newly Born Woman* [1975], tr. Betsy Wing, intro. Sandra M. Gilbert (Manchester, Manchester University Press, 1986).

Claytin, Jay, and Eric Rothstein (eds), *Influence and Intertextuality in Literary History* (Madison, University of Wisconsin Press, 1991).

Clément, Catherine, *The Weary Sons of Freud* [1978], tr. Nicole Ball (Verso, 1987).

Conley, Verena Andermatt, *Hélène Cixous: Writing the Feminine* [1984] (Lincoln, University of Nebraska Press, 1991).

Cornillon, Susan Koppelman (ed.), *Images of Women in Fiction: Feminist Perspectives* (Bowling Green, Ohio, Popular Press, 1972).

Coward, Rosalind, *Patriarchal Precedents: Sexuality and Social Relations* (Routledge & Kegan Paul, 1983).

—— *Female Desire: Women's Sexuality Today* (Paladin, 1984).

—— and John Ellis, *Language and Materialism: Developments in Semiology and the Theory of the Subject* (Routledge & Kegan Paul, 1977).

Daly, Mary, *Beyond God the Father: Towards a Philosophy of Women's Liberation* (Boston, Beacon, 1973).

—— *Gyn/Ecology* (Women's Press, 1978).

Derrida, Jacques, *Of Grammatology* [1967], tr. Gayatri Chakravorty Spivak (Baltimore, Johns Hopkins University Press, 1976).

—— *Writing and Difference* [1967], tr. Alan Bass (Chicago, University of Chicago Press, 1978).

Diamond, Arlyn, and Lee R. Edwards (eds), *The Authority of Experience: Essays in Feminist Criticism* (Amherst, University of Massachusetts Press, 1977).

Drakakis, John (ed.), *Alternative Shakespeares* (Methuen, 1985).

Draper, R. P. (ed.), *Hardy: The Tragic Novels: A Casebook* (Macmillan, 1975).

Eagleton, Mary (ed.), *Feminist Literary Criticism* (Longman, 1991).

Eagleton, Terry, *Marxism and Literary Criticism* (Methuen, 1976).

—— *Literary Theory: An Introduction* (Oxford, Blackwell, 1983).

Eisenstein, Hester, and Alice Jardine (eds), *The Future of Difference: The Scholar and the Feminist* (Boston, G. K. Hall, 1980).

Eliot, T. S., *Selected Prose*, ed. Frank Kermode (Faber, 1975).

Ellmann, Mary, *Thinking about Women* (Macmillan, 1968).

Evans, Mari (ed.), *Black Women Writers* (Pluto, 1985).

Faderman, Lillian, *Surpassing the Love of Men: Romantic Friendship and Love between Women from the Renaissance to the Present* [1981] (Women's Press, 1985).

Fanon, Frantz, *Black Skin, White Masks* [1952], tr. Charles Lam Markmann (Paladin, 1970).

—— *The Wretched of the Earth* [1961], tr. Constance Farrington (Harmondsworth, Penguin, 1967).

Felski, Rita, *Beyond Feminist Aesthetics: Feminist Literature and Social Change* (Hutchinson Radius, 1989).

Feminist Review, 'Perverse Politics: Lesbian Issues', 34 (spring 1990).

Fetterley, Judith, *The Resisting Reader: A Feminist Approach to American Fiction* (Bloomington, Indiana University Press, 1978).

Fiedler, Leslie A., and Houston A. Baker Jr (eds), *English Literature: Opening Up the Canon* (Baltimore, Johns Hopkins University Press, 1979).

Firestone, Shulamith, *The Dialectics of Sex: The Case for Feminist Revolution* [1970] (Women's Press, 1979).

Fitton, Christine, 'From Reactive to Self-Referencing Poet: A Study of Twentieth Century British Women's Poetry' (Ph.D. Thesis, Open University, 1992).

Foucault, Michel, *The History of Sexuality: An Introduction* [1976], vol. 1, tr. Robert Hurley (Harmondsworth, Penguin, 1981).

Freud, Sigmund, *On Sexuality*, Pelican Freud Library, vol. 7 (Harmondsworth, Penguin, 1977).

Friedan, Betty, *The Feminine Mystique* (New York, W. W. Norton, 1963).

Frow, John, *Marxism and Literary History* (Oxford, Blackwell, 1986).

Fuss, Diana, *Essentially Speaking: Feminism, Nature and Difference* (Routledge, 1989).

Gallop, Jane, *Feminism and Psychoanalysis: The Daughter's Seduction* (Macmillan, 1982).

—— *Reading Lacan* (Ithaca, NY, Cornell University Press, 1985).

Gilbert, Sandra M., and Susan Gubar, *The Madwoman in the Attic: The Woman Writer and the Nineteenth-Century Literary Imagination* (New Haven, Conn., Yale University Press, 1979).

—— and —— *No Man's Land: The Place of the Woman Writer in the Twentieth Century* (New Haven, Yale University Press), vol. 1: *The War of the Words* (1988), vol. 2: *Sexchanges* (1989).

—— and —— (eds), *Shakespeare's Sisters* (Bloomington, Indiana University Press, 1979).

Gonda, Caroline (ed.), *Tea and Leg-Irons: New Feminist Readings from Scotland* (Open Letters, 1992).

Greene, Gayle, and Coppélia Kahn (eds), *Making a Difference: Feminist Literary Criticism* (Methuen, 1985).

Grewal, Shabnam, Jackie Kay, Liliane Landor, Gail Lewis and Pratibha Parmar (eds), *Charting the Journey: Writing by Black and Third World Women* (Sheba Feminist Publishers, 1988).

Grosz, Elizabeth, *Sexual Subversions: Three French Feminists* (Sidney, Allen & Unwin, 1989).

—— *Jacques Lacan: A Feminist Introduction* (Routledge, 1990).

Hall, Catherine, *White, Male and Middle Class: Explorations in Feminism and History* (Cambridge, Polity, 1988).

Hanscombe, Gillian, and Virginia L. Smyers, *Writing for their Lives: The Modernist Women 1910–1940* (Women's Press, 1987).

Hartman, Geoffrey H., *Criticism in the Wilderness: A Study of Literature Today* (New Haven, Conn., Yale University Press, 1980).

Hartmann, Heidi, 'The Unhappy Marriage of Marxism and Feminism: Towards a More Progressive Union', in Lydia Sargent (ed.), *The Unhappy Marriage of Marxism and Feminism: A Debate on Class and Patriarchy* (Pluto, 1981).

Haug, Frigga (ed.), *Female Sexualization: A Collective Work of Memory*, tr. Erica Carter (Verso, 1987).

Hawkes, Terence, *Structuralism and Semiotics* (Methuen, 1977).

Heilbrun, Carolyn G., *Hamlet's Mother and Other Women: Feminist Essays on Literature* (Women's Press, 1991).

—— and Margaret R. Higonnet (eds), *The Representation of Women in Fiction* (Baltimore, Johns Hopkins University Press, 1981).

Herrmann, Claudine, *The Tongue Snatchers* [1976], tr. Nancy Kline (Lincoln, University of Nebraska Press, 1989).

Hirschkop, Ken, and David Shepherd (eds), *Bakhtin and Cultural Theory* (Manchester, Manchester University Press, 1989).

Hobby, Elaine, *Virtue of Necessity: English Women's Writing 1649–88* (Virago, 1988).

Howe, Elizabeth, *The First English Actresses: Women and Drama: 1660–1700* (Cambridge, Cambridge University Press, 1992).

Humm, Maggie, *Feminist Criticism: Women as Contemporary Critics* (Brighton, Harvester, 1986).

Irigaray, Luce, *The Speculum of the Other Woman* [1974], tr. Gillian C. Gill (Ithaca, NY, Cornell University Press, 1985).

—— *This Sex which is not One* [1977], tr. Catherine Porter with Carolyn Burke (Ithaca, NY, Cornell University Press, 1985).

Jacobus, Mary (ed.), *Women Writing and Writing about Women* (Croom Helm, 1979).

—— *Reading Women: Essays in Feminist Criticism* (Methuen, 1986).

Jardine, Alice, *Gynesis: Configurations of Woman and Modernity* (Ithaca, NY, Cornell University Press, 1985).

Jay, Karla, and Joanne Glasgow (eds), *Lesbian Texts and Contexts: Radical Revisions* (Only Woman Press, 1992).

Jefferson, Ann, and David Robey (eds), *Modern Literary Theory*, second edn (Batsford, 1986).

Jelinck, Estelle C. (ed.), *Women's Autobiography* (Bloomington, Indiana University Press, 1980).

Jouve, Nicole Ward, *White Woman Speaks with Forked Tongue: Criticism as Autobiography* (Routledge, 1991).

Kaplan, Cora, *Sea Changes: Culture and Feminism* (Verso, 1986).

Kennard, Jean E., *Victims of Convention* (Hamden, Conn., Archon, 1978).

King, Jeannette, *Jane Eyre* (Milton Keynes, Open University Press, 1986).

—— *Doris Lessing* (Edward Arnold, 1989).

Kristeva, Julia, *Revolution in Poetic Language* [1974], tr. Leon S. Roudiez (New York, Columbia University Press, 1984).

—— *Desire in Language: A Semiotic Approach to Literature and Art* [1977], ed. Leon S. Roudiez, tr. Thomas Gora, Alice Jardine and Leon S. Roudiez (Oxford, Blackwell, 1980).

—— *Powers of Horror: An Essay on Abjection* [1980], tr. Leon S. Roudiez (New York, Columbia University Press, 1982).

—— *Tales of Love* [1983], tr. Leon S. Roudiez (New York, Columbia University Press, 1987).

—— *The Kristeva Reader*, ed. Toril Moi (Oxford, Blackwell, 1986).

—— *Black Sun: Depression and Melancholia* [1987], tr. Leon S. Roudiez (New York, Columbia University Press, 1989).

—— *Strangers to Ourselves* [1988], tr. Leon S. Roudiez (Hemel Hempstead, Harvester Wheatsheaf, 1991).

Lacan, Jacques, *Ecrits: A Selection*, tr. Alan Sheridan (Travistock, 1980).

Larner, Christina, *Witchcraft and Religion: The Politics of Popular Belief* (Oxford, Blackwell, 1984).

Lauter, Paul, *Canons and Contexts* (Oxford, Oxford University Press, 1991).

LeClair, Tom, *The Art of Excess: Mastery in Contemporary American Fiction* (Urbana, University of Illinois Press, 1989).

Leighton, Angela, *Elizabeth Barrett Browning* (Brighton, Harvester, 1986).

Liddington, Jill, and Jill Norris, *One Hand Tied behind Us: The Rise of the Women's Suffrage Movement* (Virago, 1978).

Lovell, Terry (ed.), *British Feminist Thought: A Reader* (Oxford, Blackwell, 1990).

Macherey, Pierre, *A Theory of Literary Production,* tr. Geoffrey Wall (Routledge & Kegan Paul, 1978).

Marks, Elaine, and Isabelle de Courtivron (eds), *New French Feminisms: An*

Anthology (Brighton, Harvester, 1981).

Miles, Rosalind, *The Female Form: Women Writers and the Conquest of the Novel* (Routledge & Kegan Paul, 1987).

Mill, John Stuart, *The Subjection of Women* [1869] (Dent, 1982).

Miller, Jane, *Women Writing about Men* (Virago, 1986).

—— *Seductions: Studies in Reading and Culture* (Virago, 1990).

Millett, Kate, *Sexual Politics* [1969] (Virago, 1977).

Mills, Sara, Lynne Pearce, Sue Spaull and Elaine Millard, *Feminist Readings/Feminists Reading* (Hemel Hempstead, Harvester Wheatsheaf, 1989).

Minow-Pinkney, Makiko, *Virginia Woolf and the Problem of the Subject: Feminine Writing in the Major Novels* (Brighton, Harvester, 1987).

Mitchell, Juliet, *Psychoanalysis and Feminism* [1974] (Harmondsworth, Penguin, 1975).

Moers, Ellen, *Literary Women* [1976] (Women's Press, 1986).

Moi, Toril, *Sexual/Textual Politics: Feminist Literary Theory* (Methuen, 1985).

—— (ed.), *French Feminist Thought: A Reader* (Oxford, Blackwell, 1987).

Montefiore, Jan, *Feminism and Poetry: Language, Experience, Identity in Women's Writing* (Routledge & Kegan Paul, 1987).

Monteith, Moira (ed.), *Women's Writing: A Challenge to Theory* (Brighton, Harvester, 1986).

Morrison, Toni, *Playing in the Dark: Whiteness and the Literary Imagination* (Cambridge, Mass. Harvard University Press, 1992).

Moynahan, Julian, *The Deed of Life: The Novels and Tales of D. H. Lawrence* (Princeton, NJ, Princeton University Library, 1963).

Munt, Sally (ed.), *New Lesbian Criticism: Literary and Cultural Readings* (Hemel Hempstead, Harvester Wheatsheaf, 1992).

Nasta, Susheila (ed.), *Motherlands: Black Women's Writing from Africa, the Caribbean and South Asia* (Women's Press, 1991).

Newton, Judith, and Deborah Rosenfelt (eds), *Feminist Criticism and Social Change: Sex, Class and Race in Literature and Culture* (Methuen, 1985).

Nicholson, Linda, *Feminism/Postmodernism* (Routledge, 1990).

Norris, Christopher, *Derrida* (Fontana, 1987).

Olsen, Tillie, *Silences* (Virago, 1980).

Ostriker, Alicia, *Stealing the Language: The Emergence of Women's Poetry in America* (Women's Press, 1987).

Plimpton, George (ed.), *Women Writers at Work: The Paris Review Interviews*, intro. Margaret Atwood (Harmondsworth, Penguin, 1989).

Rich, Adrienne, *Of Woman Born: Motherhood as Experience and Institution* (Virago, 1977).

—— *On Lies, Secrets, Silence* (Virago, 1980).

Robinson, Lillian, *Sex, Class and Culture* (Bloomington, Indiana University Press, 1978).

Roe, Sue (ed.), *Women Reading Women's Writing* (Brighton, Harvester, 1987).

Rogers, Katherine, *The Troublesome Helpmate: A History of Misogyny in Literature* (Seattle, University of Washington Press, 1966).

Rose, Jacqueline, *Sexuality in the Field of Vision* (Verso, 1986).

—— *The Haunting of Sylvia Plath* (Virago, 1991).

Rule, Janet, *Lesbian Images* [1975] (Pluto, 1989).

Russ, Joanna, *How to Suppress Women's Writing* (Women's Press, 1984).

Said, Edward, *Orientalism* (Harmondsworth, Penguin, 1985).

Sargent, Lydia (ed.), *Women and Revolution: The Unhappy Marriage of Marxism and Feminism: A Debate on Class and Patriarchy* (Pluto, 1981).

Scott, Bonnie Kime (ed.), *The Gender of Modernism: A Critical Anthology* (Bloomington, Indiana University Press, 1990).

Selden, Raman, *A Reader's Guide to Contemporary Literary Theory* (Brighton, Harvester, 1985).

Shiach, Morag, *Hélène Cixous: A Politics of Writing* (Routledge, 1991).

Showalter, Elaine, *A Literature of their Own: British Women Novelists from Brontë to Lessing* [1977], revised edn (Virago, 1982).

—— *Sexual Anarchy: Gender and Culture at the Fin de Siècle* (Bloomsbury, 1991).

—— (ed.), *The New Feminist Criticism: Essays on Women, Literature and Theory* (Virago, 1986).

—— (ed.), *Speaking of Gender* (Routledge, 1989).

Snitow, Ann, Christine Stansell and Sharon Thompson (eds), *Powers of Desire: The Politics of Sexuality* (New York, New Feminist Library/Monthly Review Press, 1983).

Spacks, Patricia Meyer, *The Female Imagination: A Literary and Psychological Investigation of Women's Writing* (Allen & Unwin, 1976).

Spencer, Jane, *The Rise of the Woman Novelist: From Aphra Behn to Jane Austen* (Oxford, Blackwell, 1986).

Spivak, Gayatri Chakravorty, *In Other Worlds: Essays in Cultural Politics* (Routledge, 1988).

—— *The Post Colonial Critic: Interviews, Strategies, Dialogues* (Routledge, 1990).

Steedman, Carolyn, *Landscape for a Good Woman: A Story of Two Lives* (Virago, 1986).

Strachey, Ray, *The Cause: A Short History of the Women's Movement in Great Britain* [1928] (Virago, 1978).

Sturrock, John (ed.), *Structuralism and Since* (Oxford, Oxford University Press, 1979).

Taylor, Barbara, *Eve and the New Jerusalem: Socialism and Feminism in the Nineteenth Century* (Virago, 1983).

Taylor, Robert (tr. and ed.), *Aesthetics and Politics: Debates between Bloch, Lukács, Brecht, Benjamin, Adorno* (Verso, 1977).

Todd, Janet, *Women's Friendship in Literature* (New York, Columbia University Press, 1980).

—— *The Sign of Angellica: Women, Writing and Fiction, 1660–1800* (Virago, 1989).

Walder, Dennis (ed.), *Literature in the Modern World: Critical Essays and Documents* (Oxford, Oxford University Press with Open University, 1990).

Walker, Alice, *In Search of our Mothers' Gardens* (Women's Press, 1984).

Wall, Cheryl A. (ed.), *Changing our Own Words: Essays on Criticism, Theory, and Writing by Black Women* (Routledge, 1990).

Warhol, Robyn R., and Diane Price Herndl (eds), *Feminisms: An Anthology of Literary Theory and Criticism* (New Brunswick, NJ, Rutgers University Press, 1991).

Waugh, Patricia, *Practising Postmodernism Reading Modernism* (Edward Arnold, 1992).

—— (ed.), *Postmodernism: A Reader* (Edward Arnold, 1992).

Weedon, Chris, *Feminist Practice and Poststructuralist Theory* (Oxford, Blackwell, 1987).

Welty, Eudora, *The Eye of the Story: Selected Essays and Reviews* [1979] (Virago, 1987).

—— *One Writer's Beginnings* [1983] (Faber, 1985).

Widdowson, Peter (ed.), *Re-reading English* (Methuen, 1982).

Wilcox, Helen, Keith McWatters, Ann Thompson and Linda R. Williams (eds), *The Body and the Text: Hélène Cixous, Reading and Teaching* (Hemel Hempstead, Harvester, 1990).

Williams, Raymond, *Marxism and Literature* (Oxford, Oxford University Press, 1977).

Williamson, Judith, *Decoding Advertisements: Ideology and Meaning in Advertising* (Marion Boyars, 1978).

—— *Consuming Passions: The Dynamics of Popular Culture* (Marion Boyars, 1986).

Wittig, Monique, *The Straight Mind and Other Essays* (Hemel Hempstead, Harvester Wheatsheaf, 1992).

Wollstonecraft, Mary, *A Vindication of the Rights of Woman* [1792] (Dent, 1982).

Women in Publishing, *Reviewing the Reviews* (Journeyman, 1987).

Woolf, Virginia, *A Room of One's Own* [1929] (Harmondsworth, Penguin, 1945).

—— *Three Guineas* [1937] (Harmondsworth, Penguin, 1977).

—— *A Woman's Essays* (Harmondsworth, Penguin, 1991).

Wright, Elizabeth, *Psychoanalytic Criticism: Theory in Practice* (Methuen, 1984).

Yorke, Liz, *Impertinent Voices: Subversive Strategies in Contemporary Women's Poetry* (Routledge, 1991).

Index